Additional Praise for

Blueprint to a Billion

"The Blueprint not only gives me confidence that even mature industries can find growth, it provides a road map for all business leaders to follow."

—Mike Petrak, VP Marketing, Knight Ridder, Inc.

"Provides nonprofit leaders with exciting approaches to create a vibrant, growing organization. Utilizing the 7 Essentials approach, Thomson has identified practical guidelines and tools to achieve transformation and growth of an organization. This is a significant new resource for social sector leaders."

— Frances Hesselbein, Chairman, Leader to Leader Institute, formerly The Drucker Foundation

BLUEPRINT
TO A BILLION

BLUEPRINT TO A BILLION

7 ESSENTIALS TO ACHIEVE EXPONENTIAL GROWTH

David G. Thomson

WILEY

John Wiley & Sons, Inc.

Published by John Wiley & Sons, Inc., Hoboken, New Jersey.
Published simultaneously in Canada.

For general information on our other products and services or for technical support, please contact our Customer Care Department within the United States at (800) 762-2974, outside the United States at (317) 572-3993 or fax (317) 572-4002.

Wiley also publishes its books in a variety of electronic formats. Some content that appears in print may not be available in electronic books. For more information about Wiley products, visit our Web site at www.wiley.com.

Library of Congress Cataloging-in-Publication Data:

Thomson, David G.
  Blueprint to a billion : 7 essentials to achieve exponential growth / David G. Thomson.
      p. cm.
  Includes bibliographical references.
  ISBN-13: 978-0-471-74747-5 (cloth)
  ISBN-10: 0-471-74747-5 (cloth)
  1. Corporations—Growth.   2. Industrial management.   I. Title.
  HD2746.T56 2006
  658—dc22

                                                                          2005019111

Printed in the United States of America.

10 9 8 7 6 5

This book is dedicated to my family. I am especially thankful to my wife, Eileen, and our four children—Christine, Allison, Julie, and Kevin. I am blessed to have their love, which allowed me to take special family time to research and write this book. Also, I am very thankful for my parents' support and contribution.

Contents

Foreword

Blueprint to a Billion provides a roadmap for the future. This road-map can help leaders take their organizations to the top *and* it can help companies thrive in the face of incredible global competition.

The lifeblood of every person, company, and even the country's success is innovation and the creation of new opportunity. Many of the historically great companies in the United States are either gone or in trouble. The demise of many of America's leading companies has been amazing and dramatic. Who could have ever predicted that at this writing:

- AT&T, once the world's most powerful and valuable compa-ny, would be purchased by SBC at a value that was one-third what Procter & Gamble paid for Gillette, a company that is best known for making razor blades.
- United Airlines, formerly a global leader in air transporta-tion, would be in bankruptcy.
- Sears, the long-time king of retailing, would be purchased by Kmart, a company that itself just emerged from bankruptcy.
- General Motors, an icon of American industry, would be so financially weak that its bonds have been lowered to "junk" status.

AT&T, United Airlines, Sears, and General Motors are not the leaders of the future!

While the United States has had great economic success, partic-ularly in the latter part of the 20th century, its future is less certain unless companies and their managements focus on innovation. Society's hope for the future is the continued creation of vibrant, growing organizations that produce great new products and pro-vide exciting new jobs. *Blueprint to a Billion* describes how small companies have become big winners. More important, it provides practical guidelines that leaders—at all levels—can use to ensure that this keeps happening.

Nothing is more important to me than the success of my clients, students, and friends. I have had the privilege of knowing and working with David Thomson for many years. In the same way that it is incredibly difficult to turn a billion-dollar idea into a billion-dollar business, it is incredibly difficult to turn a great dream into a great book! David has spent three years analyzing what Blueprint Companies have done right. He has distilled this knowledge into practical guidelines that leaders can use to transform their own business. He has a wisdom that has been forged through years of real-world management experience, countless interviews, thousands of hours of analysis, and a passion and curiosity that drove him to make this project a reality.

Along with being a guide for business growth, the Blueprint provides tools that any leader can use to create a huge impact. As David notes, "The Blueprint is about how you can create exponential impact in your business, your organization, and your team."

David has done a wonderful job of illustrating what works and describing why it works. He has analyzed the winning companies and identified what they did right. He has done his job. The more important work remains for us, the readers, to do.

How can we use this knowledge to not just make an impact, but to make a *huge* impact? How can we lead massive value creation in our organizations or teams? How do we turn our great ideas into thriving organizations that are creating jobs and making the world a better place?

The real value of this book is not its interesting stories, thorough analysis, and great suggestions. The real value lies in what we do with what we learn.

Like a good architect, David has given us the Blueprint. We need to get to work and do the building, the building that can last.

MARSHALL GOLDSMITH

Marshall Goldsmith is a world-renowned executive educator and coach. The American Management Association recently named Goldsmith as one of 50 great thinkers and business leaders who have impacted the field of management over the past 50 years.

Preface

During the height of the 2000 boom, the rubber hit the road in a manner of speaking. At that time, I was being courted for a position as the CEO of a smaller-sized high-tech equipment firm. This was a turnaround situation. I assessed the company's potential in light of its still-committed investors and founders. Could this company be turned around or was it going down with all hands on deck? I could not find customers who were all that excited about its product. There was an empty sales funnel, no strong customer prospects, and a lack of cash (which would not materialize without customers or at least customer commitments). The "top-drawer" investors wanted a larger order from a premier customer before reinvesting.

Given the short runway, I found myself at odds with the investors over the potential of this company. We did not share the same perspective on the company or its future because we were looking at it from different frames of reference. They wanted a customer before infusing a limited investment into this company. I believed customers needed to buy from a company with committed investors who would ensure that the company was adequately funded. It was then that I realized that there was no common frame of reference for building a great company. Upon turning down the opportunity, the recruiter said I should have just taken the risk but I wanted more than luck to counter the odds. As a general manager and sales executive who has transformed teams and customer relationships, I wanted to base my actions on more than a gamble. As it turned out, the company soon went out of business.

What *is* the pattern of success for America's highest-growth companies? My CEO friends did not have any more of an idea than I did. They could tell me anecdotally about companies that failed or succeeded. But none of them had a completed business-building roadmap or a blueprint. Luck is not my kind of strategy. I wanted a blueprint—a blueprint to tell me if I am building a small building or a skyscraper of business. It is not what the walls are made of; the blueprint is about laying the foundation and structure for a truly great business, not another shaky, imperiled venture.

As I continued my search for what makes a company truly successful, I applied my line executive background from Nortel Networks and Hewlett-Packard as well as my consulting skills from McKinsey & Company. Despite this combination of intuitive and fact-based problem-solving skills, I began to feel that I was working around the problem, not through it. People talked a lot about their experiences, but I could find no fact-based pattern from which I could be prescriptive rather than descriptive.

As I focused on what makes a company successful—what drives a firm from an idea to a billion-dollar business—I considered the classic explanations: superior innovation, great management teams, and superior organizations. Yet none of these, or even the combination of all three, provided a quantifiable frame of reference for business building. For example:

- Understanding the natural evolution of organization life-cycles from infancy to maturity did not explain why some companies made it to a billion while others did not.
- Great management teams could fail to grow great companies. How many companies do you know with a brand-name CEO that did not succeed?
- The technical community often focuses on breakthrough technologies, yet many companies have died with such advanced technology still in the lab.

I came to the conclusion that no one had the answer to the killer question: What is the *quantifiable* success pattern for America's highest-growth companies? It was then that I decided to "primary research" the answer in clear and measurable terms.

What You Can Expect from This Book

This book identifies how America's highest-growth companies made it to the top—the seven common essentials of a unique set of 387 companies that went from an initial public offering since 1980 and achieved $1 billion in revenue. They are called the *Blueprint Companies*.

This book is about the success *patterns* that winning companies follow that produce the performance many admire and desire to emulate. These Blueprint Companies are known not only for their innovation, but also for their exponential revenue and returns—growth irrespective of economic or business climate.

This book provides a blueprint that is fact based and actionable. It contains fresh research that provides time-tested insights into success-based business building. Adoption and execution of one or more essentials will maximize your growth—both personally and corporately. Executing all 7 Essentials will enable your company to achieve exponential growth.

This book serves a broad audience and is written for management teams, large and small, general and functional, and in big corporations and stand-alone companies. *Blueprint to a Billion*™ can also serve investors, board members, educators, students, regulators, and legislators who are concerned with creating a successful environment for business growth. Anyone who wants to stimulate innovation and business growth should find the Blueprint Companies and how they achieved their success worth knowing. The leadership and management of international corporations that deal with high-growth American businesses will also find this book valuable, especially if they wish to benefit from the success pattern of U.S. Blueprint Companies.

The Study

Blueprint to a Billion presents the *first* quantitative dissection of America's most successful growth companies. This is the first work to display the common financial pattern of America's Blueprint Companies. While this book has a quantitative foundation, I have supplemented it with what I hope are insightful analysis and vibrant personal stories from many Blueprint Company leaders.

These insights come from a series of research projects that took place over three years. I collaborated with line executives, customers, investors, and consultants to problem solve for each of the essentials in order to make them quantifiable and actionable. The financial research was conducted using data from Standard & Poor's Compustat database along with customized financial models. Various databases were utilized to capture corporate histories such as Thomson/Gale's Business & Company Resource Center (BCRC). Finally, I conducted over 75 interviews to complement the research and strengthen each of the essentials. In total, the work has been vetted by over 1,000 executives and investors as I presented my early findings in numerous forums.

This research initially showed that over 90 percent of shareholder value is generated by financial performance regardless of a company's uniqueness or industry type. Exponential success is achieved by significant revenues and cost containment. Management teams earn the right to realize superior returns only if they generate superior revenue growth. Great companies were able to generate both revenue and cash flow growth simultaneously.

The "bottom line" is not about the *coolness* of the brand, the positioning of the business, or the pedigree of the CEO. Those can be important inputs; however, it is exponential revenue growth that makes a great company—so long as the management team ethically seizes the opportunity that it creates to achieve profitability, maintain positive cash flow, and produce high return on capital.

With this in mind, I decided to start my journey focusing on revenue and revenue growth.

From a global perspective, the business world is organized vertically by industry. The investment community specializes by industry. Management teams rarely manage outside of their industry. Comparative financial assessments are done by industry. We even plan our careers within an industry.

During my research, I decided to look for patterns across industries. Is there a common set of essentials that successful companies utilized across multiple industries?

To answer this question, the study's problem-solving approach had a number of parallel work streams (described in detail in Appendix D: Methodology):

1. *Blueprint Financial Pattern.* The overall financial pattern of the Blueprint Companies involved a multiyear study of revenue as well as financial and shareholder-return metrics. Of the 387 Blueprint Companies, I studied the financial pattern of the 250 companies with revenues of less than $170 million at the time of going public. This enabled a quantitative analysis using public data combined with real-market values. The ranking of these companies was determined using a market-value normalization methodology—that is, revenues were normalized to $1 billion and then indexed to 2004 market values using the NASDAQ index (because it spans 25 years). The "fall off" rate of Blueprint Companies was derived by identifying companies that made it to $1 billion revenue but fell back. Inevitably 20 percent of these companies will fall off trajectory post-$1 billion revenue and fall back below the $1 billion threshold.

2. *Identification of the 7 Essentials.* Next, I pored through hundreds of corporate histories across multiple sectors, setting up a template that would help identify what Blueprint Companies had in common as they hit their "lift-off" points and began their ascent to $1 billion revenue. Despite the diversity of companies and industries, I identified 7 Essentials that these companies had in common.

   Along with the BCRC, thousands of articles from such publications as *Fortune*, *BusinessWeek*, *Forbes*, industry journals, newspapers, and analyst reports were researched to complement initial findings.

   The identification of these essentials led to the third work stream:

3. *Defining the 7 Essentials.* Parallel work streams were established to determine each of the essentials. My team, comprised of line executives, investors, consultants, management-behavior experts, and statisticians worked through a disciplined problem-solving process to prove or disprove hypotheses relative to each essential. In most cases, interviews were conducted by two interviewees so that impor-

tant perspectives were recorded completely. Finally, interviews in this book were checked with all interviewees to ensure that their perspectives, as reported, are accurate and complete.

Applying This Book

This study identifies the success-based financial pattern and key essentials that you can apply to any business to improve its performance. The book is written around an approach that identifies the financial pattern to uncover the essentials and then discusses each essential in detail. In Chapter 9, the essentials are linked to show you how the Blueprint Companies created exponential growth.

Chapter One begins the journey with a Blueprint Thesis. Why a journey? Because the lessons will continue to unfold. The success pattern of these companies is one that should be identified and understood—but, by necessity, will evolve slightly. The journey tells us what business has been doing right for the last 25 years and foreshadows the pace business will need to maintain in the coming years in order to remain competitive.

DAVID G. THOMSON

Overland Park, Kansas
October 2005

Acknowledgments

It takes a special team of friends to create what I hope is an insightful book on the Blueprint journey. The support from this highly experienced team contributed much to this book's creation. On behalf of this team, which has become a "Blueprint Community," I hope you learn from this book and apply the knowledge to achieve the best company you can be associated with and become the best business person you can be.

I am indebted to those who were interviewed for this book. They opened their doors to share their experiences. I would especially like to thank Nancy Bailey, Chairman of Bailey & Associates; Roger Boeve, retired founder and CFO of Performance Foods; Mel Booth, retired President and COO of MedImmune; Tim Boyle, President and CEO of Columbia Sportswear; Dick Campbell, former CFO of Paine Webber; Terry Eger, former Vice President of Sales at Cisco; Brent Frei, founder and former CEO of Onyx Software; Jordon Glatt, President of Magla; George Kelly, Advisory Director of Morgan Stanley; Howard Lester, Chairman of Williams-Sonoma; Roger McNamee, Cofounder and General Partner of Elevation Partners; Robert Moone, Chairman and Chief Executive of State Auto Financial; Toby Redshaw, Vice President of IT Strategy and Architecture of Motorola; Joe Scarlett, Chairman of Tractor Supply; George Schaefer, President and CEO of Fifth Third Bancorp; Tom Siebel, Chairman of Siebel Systems; Tom Stemberg, Chairman Emeritus of Staples; and Jeff Weedman, Vice President of External Business Development at Procter & Gamble. Thank you for being such remarkable executives and sharing such practical insights with me. I would like to especially thank Roger NcNamee for his thoughtful coaching to take this work to the next level.

This work is so much better because of the problem-solving team members who helped strengthen the analysis that underpins this book. As I arrived at the problem-solving process, in which I was struggling to understand the unique characteristics of Blueprint Companies and the seven common essentials, I found help coming from many directions. Assistance came from the United States, Canada, and Europe. It came from consultants, investors, and line executives. The resulting team formed a very unique blend of fact-based and line-oriented problem-solving skills that helped to clarify and add depth to each one of the essentials. The investment was a three-year-long research project that represented a major undertaking of time, talent, and investment.

Throughout the making of *Blueprint to a Billion*, I have relied on a select group of friends who have helped me to integrate the book. Deirdre Campbell was my partner on the initial research. I thank Glenn Falcao, who served as executive vice president of an equipment company when it grew from $200 million to $31 billion market value at the height of the 2000 bubble. Glenn has been a real friend through this journey. As I started to shape the Marquee Customer and Alliances essentials, David Cox, former CIO for Nortel Networks, Bell Canada, and Motorola played a key role. Mike Unger led an equipment business from $10 million to $10 billion and applied his key learnings to the Essentials Scorecard. Mike applies the Blueprint today as he serves on the boards of such venture firms such as Kleiner Perkins, Celtic House, and the Business Development Corporation of Canada. Bart Stuck, of Signal Lake Ventures, was a mentor and pressure tested my thinking. Avery Lyford, former CEO of several venture-backed companies—and part of ramping both IBM PC and Intel Server businesses to over $1 billion in revenue—was also a thought partner. Mark Hatfield piloted a process for performing due diligence. I am also indebted to Marshall Goldsmith for his friendship and encouragement.

Mark Mitten and Eric Arnson—cofounders of ENVISION, a top brand strategy firm and former McKinsey & Company partners—are experts in growth strategies and the value of tangible and intangible benefits. They contributed greatly to these topics for

Chapters 2 and 3 as well as Appendix B. I also thank them for their passion for shaping the title of this book.

An extended team worked on specific chapters with me. I would like to thank Tim Sepp of Standard & Poor's for his hard work and stamina on the development of the financial models. As I wrote the Inside-Outside Leadership chapter (Chapter 7), Bob Sadler of Sadler Consulting and Peter Robertson of Human Insight kindly helped shape the research and apply the Human Insight tools that we used to examine Blueprint Company management teams. Andy Binns, now an executive coach for a large corporation in Europe, also helped structure and pressure test this chapter.

Many others added to this book in special ways. I would like to thank Beth Axelrod, Tom Ball, Bruce Branyan, Gerry Butters, Liz Byland, Jim Citrin, Jeff Edlund, Glenn Egan, Walt Farrell, Alan Fraser, Tammy Halevy, Hewitt Heiserman, Alan Lutz, Chris Mankle, Denny Matteucci, Mike Petrak, Will Prout, Keith Phillips, Barbara Reinhardt, Kevin Roberts, Joe Sinfield, Dan Stock, Mike Stout, Erik Vogel, Joe Walsh, Bryan Whelock, and Dora Vell.

My friends at McKinsey & Company supported me when I joined the firm as an experienced hire. Thank you Scott Arnold (now an alum), Dick Ashley, Greg Besio (now an alum), Gerhardt Bette, Peter Bisson, Steve Coley, Tarek Elmasry, Chip Hardt, John Livingston, Julian Mack, Marc Singer, Saf Yeboah-Amankwah, and Pat Oaklief for your intellectual and personal encouragement.

This book had a unique set of editors. Erik Calonius, with experience as a writer at *Fortune* and the *Wall Street Journal*, worked hard to ensure that each chapter was well thought out and clearly presented. As we finished the Blueprint Thesis, a very quantitative chapter, Erik was instrumental in shaping the 7 Essentials chapters into narratives that brought the frameworks to life. Together, we interviewed many of the executives represented in this book. Erik was quite thoughtful in asking clarifying questions on behalf of the reader, and is gifted with a fluid writing style. Jennifer Futernick, thank you for your extra special touch and feedback during the early stages of this manuscript and for encouraging me to address how we learn from best practices. Most of all, I am grateful for your support in refining the manuscript in its final stages. You are a wonderful and caring person to work with. To Pamela van Giessen, Editorial Director at John Wiley & Sons, appreciation for your championing of this book and guidance in shaping it into the best book it could be. Your deft touch and mentoring helped streamline both the storyline and format to make the book an easier read.

Thank you all. You are a great team.

D. G. T.

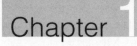

The Blueprint Thesis

A Different Approach to Growth

The odds are one in 50 that an idea becomes a business, one in 20 that a funded business sees an *initial public offering* (IPO) and, finally, one in 20 that a public company achieves $1 billion revenue.[1] The odds of turning an idea into a billion-dollar business, then, are one in 20,000! A long shot. Nevertheless, we chase this dream. We want to be among the few winners.

Why do so many want to take this chance . . . one in 20,000? Do we think we are better than most and can make it? What if we just took a small company public and built it to a $1 billion revenue? Then the odds are better . . . one in 400. Are there enough years in our lives to keep trying in order to learn or be lucky? How many times do we have to try to become a winner?

The Blueprint to a Billion Growth Pattern

In short, what does it take to become a billion-dollar company? I realized that the answer would not come from soft subjects such as organization or leadership theory, or from an examination of divisions or operating units in larger companies. It would come from a quantitative and fact-based analysis of America's fastest growing companies.

1

Furthermore, the analysis had to hinge on what is often over-looked: *revenue performance*. Every company can invest, even over-invest, to grow. However, not every company can create revenue growth. How many times have you heard a CEO announcing quarterly results stating that earnings did not meet expectations because of a revenue shortfall, yet expenditures met or exceeded budget?

My research began by looking for all of the American companies that grew to $1 billion revenue since going public after 1980. I identified 387 companies out of 7,454. These 387 U.S. companies will be referred to as the *Blueprint Companies*.

The Blueprint Companies have a simple but definable characteristic: They not only grew fast, they exhibited exponential revenue growth. Exponential is super-compounding. It describes companies that can double revenue every year, for example. Growth rates may slow as revenue approaches $1 billion, but these companies still grew at an exponential rate. The non-$1 billion companies had random, linear, or no growth (see Figure 1.1).

This book focuses on these 387 companies and that part of their

FIGURE 1.1

Revenue Growth: The Masses versus Blueprint Companies

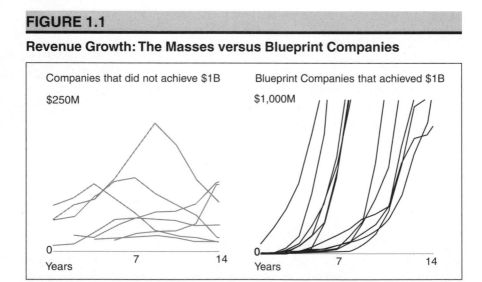

Source: Standard & Poor's Compustat, Blueprint analysis

growth up to the $1 billion revenue mark. The success pattern beyond this point is not explored in order to concentrate on this key benchmark.

When the Blueprint Companies were compared to the remaining 5,048 companies that went public since 1980 and are still active in 2005 (2,019 of these companies have since gone out of business), I was amazed at the impact such a few companies have achieved (see Figure 1.2).[2]

> Blueprint Companies represent 5 percent of American companies that went public since 1980 and account for 56 percent of employment in 2005 and 64 percent of market value!

The disproportionate success of the Blueprint Companies makes it apparent that they are the heart of America's innovation and growth. These companies are the best-in-class set from which this study draws from. This highly disproportionate ratio suggests that unless their different approach is utilized, the odds were—and are—higher for business teams to be part of the 95 percent than the

FIGURE 1.2

Blueprint Companies Are America's Growth Engine

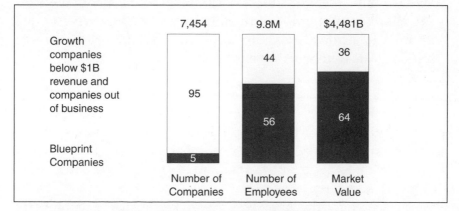

Source: Standard & Poor's Compustat, Blueprint analysis

5 percent. Do you think you can change your odds by understanding the success pattern of this select set of companies? I did.

No wonder Warren Buffett likes to invest in companies that he knows, companies he can relate to as a customer. Look around and you will find Blueprint Companies everywhere. Their products enhance our everyday lives. They are at the top of their markets. When was the last time you used Microsoft software; used the Internet (which rides on Cisco equipment); searched the Web using Google; sipped a Starbucks latte; shopped on eBay or Amazon.com; purchased products at Williams-Sonoma, Staples, or Home Depot; watched movies from Time Warner; took medicine made by Amgen, Genentech, or MedImmune; used financial services from Charles Schwab; or rode your Harley-Davidson motorcycle? Do you depend on Express Scripts, UnitedHealth Group, or HCA for your health plan?

How could a company selling coffee transform itself into an enterprise that is the 372nd largest company in the United States today?[3] Why could Charles Schwab create exponential revenue growth when others in the same industry, with the same opportunities and resources, could not? How could a little company that made motorcycles become one of the fastest growing firms in America?

> We may think that our situation is unique. And it is. But there is something in common that the minority saw about what to do in order to create a successful company that the rest of us are missing. The numbers prove it.

This book identifies the common essentials exhibited across Blueprint Companies in all industries, it is not about the lessons learned from one or even a few successful companies within one industry. Here we want to discover the roadmap to $1 billion revenue, not $1 billion market value.

The research for this book was driven by the desire to know the answers to the *what* questions such as, "What role did customers play in shaping an exponential growth company?" "What was the investment profile for creating exponential growth—overinvest to grow or become cash flow positive early and scale?" I wanted answers that could be applied to the top and bottom lines in order to achieve exponential growth.

Significant Insights about Blueprint Companies

By first looking at the financial patterns of Blueprint Companies and defining the actions required to create their financial impact, I found that it is possible to reverse engineer the behaviors and skills required. This eliminated the behaviors and actions that were not relevant. As a result, this revealed a set of significant insights that truly created impact.

The common revenue pattern across the Blueprint Companies is a unique pattern that only these kinds of companies demonstrate. Like a rocket, these companies need to be on the right flight trajectory and have the speed to break the pull of gravity—to escape being a mediocre, low-orbiting projectile.

Looking at the revenue curves, I identified three discernible patterns as shown in Figure 1.3.

The *exponential* revenue growth curves have three parts: (1) a variable runway; (2) an inflection point where revenue breaks out into an exponential trajectory; and (3) variable growth rates to $1 billion revenue. Regarding the variable runway, the companies on the left side of Figure 1.3 have a discernibly shorter runway than those on the right side. They have a common inflection point. In some cases, the companies on the left had a similar growth rate as the companies on the right—just the timing was different.

When researchers study business trends, they typically start their analysis at the company's founding year, or at the year of IPO. The Blueprint models are anchored at the *inflection point*—the point where the business demonstrates its breakout to exponential revenue growth. Why? The pattern for starting a company is different

FIGURE 1.3

Exponential Revenue Growth Patterns: Blueprint Company Examples

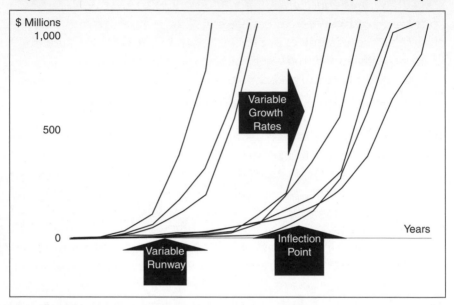

Source: Standard & Poor's Compustat, Blueprint analysis

from the pattern as it scales to $1 billion revenue. Second, the inflection point marks the moment when the business was fully formed as a system—when it had a pipeline of customers, a product or service that was being shipped, and an organization capable of the functions to sustain ongoing growth. Third, as mentioned above, I identified potential common patterns in the exponential growth rates after the inflection point, even though timing was different.

Utilizing this different approach to analyzing growth, I set out to discover the insights of Blueprint Companies.

Insight: Growth to $1 Billion Revenue Has Two Distinct Parts

The first significant counterintuitive insight was the timeframe and trajectory of Blueprint Company revenue growth (see Figure 1.4). By centering the revenue curves at the inflection point, also known as *year 0* in normalized time, I found that revenue growth has two distinct parts: the *time to the inflection point* was highly variable from the founding year to the inflection point, which was then followed by *three trajectories to $1 billion revenue* that centered on a four-, six-, or twelve-year trajectory. Since the nature of the curves had fairly consistent exponential revenue growth, this creates a unique opportunity to benchmark growth trajectories.

One might naturally assume that the time to the inflection point is correlated with the trajectory that the business follows to $1 billion revenue. Not true. For example, Google went from its founding to the inflection in two years and went up the front side of the four-year trajectory to become one of the fastest growing companies. In contrast, Cisco took seven years to get to the inflection

FIGURE 1.4

Growth Has Two Parts: Variable Time to Inflection and Three Trajectories to $1 Billion Revenue

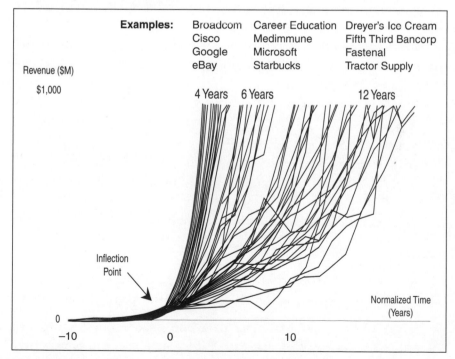

Source: Standard & Poor's Compustat, Blueprint analysis

point before going up the four-year trajectory. In an extreme example of a lengthy timeline to the inflection point, Fifth Third Bancorp had its beginnings in the middle of the 19th century. The company passed through the inflection point in the late 1980s to ascend on the back side of the 12-year trajectory to achieve $1 billion in 1994.

With this insight, I started to look at companies at the inflection point. My own business skills fit best with companies from the inflection point to $1 billion revenue versus ones coming from the garage to the inflection. This was a key understanding on the journey to find where my own quantitative skills, combined with 20 years of business experience, could best be utilized. So, where should you focus?

Insight: Blueprint Companies Can Grow in Any Sector

You might believe, as I did, that exponential growth occurs in high-innovation economic sectors such as Information Technology (IT). Given the meteoric rise of Google, eBay, Microsoft, and Cisco, it is not hard to understand why people believe that the most rapid growth in recent years has been in high-tech firms. But is this really the case?

Contrary to popular perceptions, Information Technology accounted for only 18 percent of the Blueprint Companies as shown in Figure 1.5. The Consumer Discretionary sector—that is, retails stores, Internet retail, and the like—actually outrank the tech sector. You know the names because you, your family, and your friends shop at them every day: Staples, Home Depot, AutoZone, Williams-Sonoma, and Best Buy to name a few. What did this mean? America has generated more growth companies in the service sector than many thought.

Insight: The Disproportionate Value of Blueprint Companies

The top 100 of the 387 Blueprint Companies accounted for half of the value created by this set. One billion dollars in revenue pro-

FIGURE 1.5

Frequency of Blueprint Companies: Percent of Blueprint Companies by Economic Sector

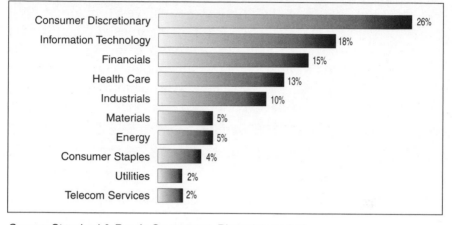

Source: Standard & Poor's Compustat, Blueprint analysis

vides management with the opportunity to create shareholder returns extraordinaire. Yet while some Blueprint Companies were highly prized by the market at a billion dollars, others were not.

To identify these companies, I determined the year they achieved $1 billion revenue. By normalizing their market caps to 2004 dollars, the Blueprint Companies were ranked resulting in the ranking of the top 100 shown in Figure 1.6. (Appendix A lists the top 100 Blueprint Companies.)

I was somewhat surprised by where companies ranked on the list as well as such a definitive curve of disproportionate market value created across Blueprint Companies. The very top companies were predominantly technology or biotechnology companies. Microsoft was the number-one Blueprint Company with a normalized market value of $42 billion, followed by Amgen, eBay, Veritas, and Google. At the tail of this chart, companies that achieved $1 billion revenue had market values of $300 million. The median, or the market value of the 193rd company, was $1.8 billion. A secondary insight was the varied mixture of companies by vintage; early

FIGURE 1.6

Disproportionate Value of Blueprint Companies

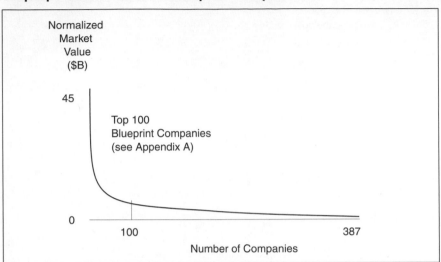

Source: Standard & Poor's Compustat, Blueprint analysis

1990s companies such as Cisco, as well as new companies such as eBay, had similar superior market values when normalized.

These Blueprint Companies show up as the most highly valued companies on our stock exchanges. If you look on the NASDAQ 100 Index, over 60 percent are Blueprint Companies.

The top 100 Blueprint Companies account for half the market value of all 387 Blueprint Companies—an unbelievable impact from such a few companies.

Why does the Information Technology sector have the cachet it does when it comes to investors? Because it has generated the most value for shareholders (see Figure 1.7). Consumer Discretionary fell in comparison to Information Technology. For a sector (consumer) with 50 percent more Blueprint Companies than Information Technology, you can only conclude that IT companies were valued significantly more than their counterparts in the Consumer sector.

Is there an interesting play for the future to bring technology to

---

FIGURE 1.7

The Market Value of Blueprint Companies ($B)

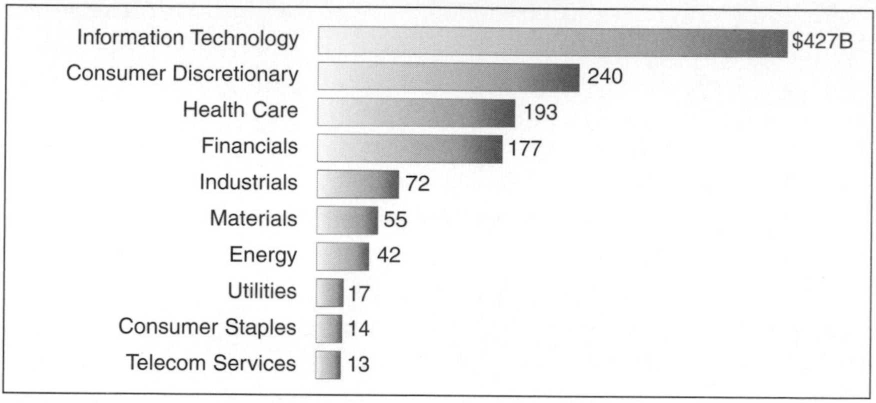

Information Technology	$427B
Consumer Discretionary	240
Health Care	193
Financials	177
Industrials	72
Materials	55
Energy	42
Utilities	17
Consumer Staples	14
Telecom Services	13

Source: Standard & Poor's Compustat, Blueprint analysis

the industries in the Consumer Discretionary sector? To get the best of both: high probability with higher market capitalization? Are you wondering what the smartest investors might have to say about this observation? (If you are looking for this answer, you will enjoy the interview with private equity investor Roger McNamee in Chapter 10.)

Insight: The 7 Essentials to Achieve Exponential Growth

During my tenure as a consultant at McKinsey & Company, I learned that business dynamics can identify the underlying inter-linked forces that lead to exponential growth. While it is impossible to model the particular business dynamics for each Blueprint Company, I could determine the dynamic essentials that seemed common to most of them. I call these the 7 *Essentials*. These are the essentials necessary to create exponential growth. Despite the diversity of companies and industries, I found these common essentials across the total set of companies and industries that I examined.

To prove that these seven common essentials are unique to Blueprint Companies, I compared companies in the same indus-

Despite the diversity of corporate histories in different economic sectors, the seven common essentials rose to the surface again and again. Five or more of these seven showed up in over 90 percent of the Blueprint Companies studied. These 7 Essentials are necessary to achieve and sustain exponential growth.

try—one set drawn from the Blueprint list, the other from a group of companies that had the same opportunities but had failed to grow at an exponential rate.

As I presented the Blueprint to CEO roundtables, investors, and management teams, they challenged me to simplify the insights. The insights could not to be too simple, however, for while they might be more easily understood, they might not be convincing. In actual fact, the 7 Essentials are aligned to create financial impact in what I call *The Essentials Triangle*™ framework (see Figure 1.8). The inbound side requires a *Big Idea* or value proposition. To create

FIGURE 1.8

The Essentials Triangle

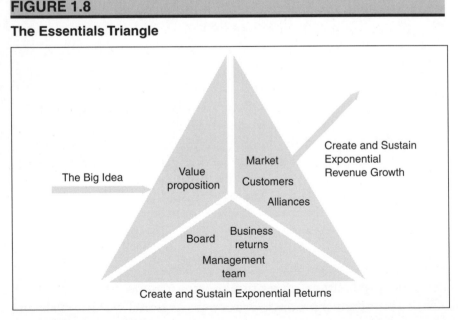

Source: Blueprint analysis

exponential revenue growth from the Big Idea, there are three essentials required. To capture the opportunity for exponential returns, there are three more essentials required. The framework for these essentials is The Essentials Triangle. Each side of this triangular framework aligns with a company's financial statement.

Blueprint Companies create a Big Idea that delivers breakthrough value for their customers. It is superior to competitors because the company fulfills an unmet need the best way. Not just at the beginning, but all the way to $1 billion revenue. Most companies accept the status quo of their industries. Not Blueprint innovators. They look for blockbuster ideas with quantum leap value propositions.

Blueprint Companies that create and sustain exponential revenue growth give the management team the option to create a business model of exponential returns. Attractive markets, customers, and alliances enable exponential revenue growth. Blueprint Companies use them all to achieve exponential revenue growth.

Blueprint Companies create a business model of exponential returns by managing expenses and investments to deliver positive return on investment (ROI) and cash flow early and consistently. For the technology companies, the role model for exponential returns, I found that cash flow, on average, was a constant percentage of revenue. Therefore, the absolute value of cash flow paralleled the exponential growth of revenue depending on the trajectory—four, six, or twelve years. Cash flow and return on investment are the primary drivers of market value (or shareholder value). To achieve these returns, the management *team* had to execute all seven essentials. No one leader could do them all.

The 7 Essentials of Blueprint Companies are described in the following sections.

1. Create and Sustain a Breakthrough Value Proposition

A value proposition states the benefits customers receive from using a company's products or services in terms that the customer understands.

The best Blueprint Companies not only have compelling value propositions, they have breakthrough value propositions. There are three kinds:

- *Shapers of a New World*, truly create a new market for their products and services.
- *Niche Shapers*, follow New World Shapers with products or services that redefine a specific market segment.
- *Category Killers*, optimize a market by attacking the existing incumbents with a better-faster-cheaper value offer.

A Shaper of a New World would be eBay, Microsoft, Amgen, or Genentech; a Niche Shaper would be Starbucks; and a Category Killer would be Home Depot or Staples that offer lower prices compared to specialized retailers. While I initially thought that the greatest number of Blueprint Companies would be Shapers of a New World, I found over 43 percent of top Blueprint Companies to be either Niche Shapers or Category Killers. This finding counters the notion that most great companies require new innovation waves or eras in order to grow.

2. Exploit a High Growth Market Segment

Opportunities exist in a lot of industries. Some industries have more opportunities than others. Fresh industries such as Biotechnology and Internet Retail spawned multiple Blueprint Companies in the 1990s. However, industries such as Specialty Stores generated the highest number of Blueprint Companies with 18 firms. This occurred because there were multiple market segments to address within this industry: office supplies, teenager fashion, and pet supplies to name a few. Right behind Specialty Stores was Property and Casualty Insurance with 15 companies. There was not one technology industry in the top five, which is astonishing. In contrast, there are numerous cases where a single company arises out of an industry to become the only player to achieve $1 billion in revenues—witness Harley-Davidson. When we interviewed the

CEOs in these top industries, we found a set of lessons that can be applied to companies in any industry. More important, we heard these CEOs indicate that their industries are not expected to be the leaders going forward in terms of generating the equivalent number of new Blueprint Companies. This means that there is an opportunity for other industries to become America's leaders.

3. Marquee Customers Shape the Revenue Powerhouse

Customers can be more than customers. The best of them can serve as an extension of your sales force—they become your most effective sales team! I call these *Marquee Customers*—that is, customers who shape the company by testing and deploying the product, recommending the company to their peers, and simply by providing exponential revenue growth on a per-customer basis. Think of these customers as one of a company's most important assets.

Marquee Customers often exist with consumer companies. For example, eBay's top customers are part of a feedback system that helps shape eBay's new services. These top customers are also a powerful word-of-mouth sales force to attract other customers.

The underlying driver for corporate exponential revenue growth is exponential revenue growth within each Marquee Customer. Maximizing customer lifecycle revenues is fundamental to achieving exponential revenue growth per customer.

4. Leverage Big Brother Alliances for Breaking into New Markets

The complement to Marquee Customers is a Big Brother–Little Brother alliance relationship. These alliances, in which a bigger company helps a smaller one, provide credibility to the Little Brother, give it market intelligence, and lead it to Marquee Customers. It is a two-way street. Big Brothers also need Little Brothers to help them remain on the cutting edge of innovation. During our interviews with the Big Brother Masters, we learned that understanding the win–win motivations between partners can take longer and is more important than their alliance agreement. Surprisingly, we found that Big Brothers find it as difficult finding the right Little Brother as Little Brothers have in trying to get access to the right Big Brother champion.

5. Become the Masters of Exponential Returns

A fairly common management behavior suggests that allocating more resources toward developing and introducing products will solve innovation problems.[4] This often leads to directing too much investment resulting in an overinvestment situation. The technology industries serve to illustrate what it takes to create the highest value per company. To achieve such high market values relative to companies in other industries, they were cash flow positive early and sustained this positive cash flow to $1 billion revenue. I found that shareholder value is maximized by three factors: high revenue and revenue growth, high return on investment, and sustained revenue growth. To maximize shareholder value, a return on invested capital that significantly exceeds the cost of capital is required. Delivering consistent performance across these three factors is the path to success. Blueprint Companies implemented a process for executing, measuring key financial and customer metrics as well as providing the incentive to their organization to achieve exponential returns.

Shareholder returns for being a top-performing Blueprint Company are more than compelling: Blueprint Companies on the four-year trajectory delivered an average of 87 percent returns to their shareholders while exceeding analysts' expectations 80 percent of the time!

6. The Management Team: Inside-Outside Leadership

One of the pivotal essentials that enables the other essentials to be simultaneously executed is a strategic leadership pairing in which one leader (or team) faces outward toward markets, customers, alliances, and the community with the other leader (or team) focusing inward so as to optimize operations. Contrary to the somewhat popular belief that one leader is "the" leader, this Inside-Outside leadership pair is highly prevalent among Blueprint Companies: Microsoft, eBay, Yahoo!, Tractor Supply to name just a few. The inside executive is typically the chief operating officer (COO); the external-facing executive is the chief executive officer (CEO). Together, they manage forward and innovate continuously, whether in product or marketing innovation. They make swift decisions—and quickly correct their mistakes. Most important, they have complete trust in and respect for one another. This pair works to execute all the essentials simultaneously.

Leadership characteristics that distinguished the Inside-Outside pairing include the consistent communication about the company's direction and priorities; consistent values, particularly during defining moments; problem-solving skills; and having a passion to address customers' unmet needs. They are hands-on leaders who care about the business first—not hands off and self-centered.

7. The Board: Comprised of Essentials Experts

Blueprint boards were not packed with investors, as one would think. Blueprint Companies recruited customers, alliance partners, and other Blueprint CEOs on the board and that makes a big difference. I call them *Essentials Experts* because their role is linked to the shaping and execution of one or more of the essentials. Because most investors have not scaled Blueprint Companies to $1 billion

> The bottom line is this: Board composition is a reflection of the execution of the essentials. It is important to balance management and investors board members with outside members who are CEOs, customers, alliance partners, and community members.

revenue, CEOs who happened to be CEOs from Blueprint Companies often were recruited to provide insight into exponential growth. In contrast, boards composed of investors and management tended to be associated with struggling companies.

Linking the Essentials

Do you have to do it all? You may be asking this question and so did many of my initial readers and thought partners. The answer is: yes. This research shows how the Blueprint Companies executed these essentials to average or above levels of performance when compared to their counterparts in the masses that did not make it to $1 billion. Blueprint Companies created explicit processes for executing and linking the 7 Essentials. The creation of these processes was driven from previous experiences, intuitive problem solving, or understanding what success required. Chapter 9 illustrates that what differentiates Blueprint from non-Blueprint Companies is the consistent execution of *all* essentials.

You may be thinking that the Blueprint Companies are just lucky and that is a fair question to be asking. MedImmune's story may be instructive.

MedImmune, Inc., one of the top 100 Blueprint Companies, was at a crossroads in late 1993 with critics pondering its future. The company had invested in the development of a drug, RespiGam, a polyclonal antibody that ultimately proved to be an important advance in preventing hospitalization of high-risk infants from a serious lower respiratory tract disease, Respiratory Syncytial Virus. Unfortunately, the path to success was bumpier than the company liked. Initially, the United States Food and Drug Administration (FDA) did not approve MedImmune's application to market the product. To answer the questions raised by the FDA, MedImmune's management team, led by CEO Dr. Wayne T. Hockmeyer, conducted an additional clinical trial costing millions of additional dollars and taking another year to complete. "The strategy that we pursued was 'bet the farm,'" Dr. Hockmeyer told

The Washington Post at the time.[5] He added that "employees were tense. They were single minded. They were focused. The entire organization hummed."

The company's perseverance with RespiGam paid off, as it did with its concurrent investment in the next-generation product, Synagis, which became the first monoclonal antibody approved by the FDA to prevent an infectious disease. Synagis was approved in the summer of 1998 and went on the market a few months later. A *Washington Post* article the following year called it "one of the most successful new products in the history of the biotech industry."[6] Now a $1-billion-a-year product with sales worldwide, Synagis has proven the *Post's* predictions to be right on. I asked Melvin D. Booth, MedImmune's president and chief operating officer from 1998 until 2004 (when MedImmune went from approximately $100 million to $1 billion in total revenues), about the role of luck:

> MedImmune focused on what I consider to be the top three essentials of great business building: making sure it always had the best team, focusing on delivering leading-edge innovation, and creating a new market for important, unmet medical needs. MedImmune's persistence and hard work, knowledge of the latest scientific advancements, and joint commitment to getting the products approved add proof that the company's ultimate success *was not based just on luck*. The luck MedImmune did have involved such things as being fortunate to have had FDA reviewers that understood the safety and efficacy data submitted for RespiGam and Synagis, which at the time were among the first biological products to be submitted to the agency.

How You Can Apply the Blueprint

You know you are on the right track in solving a problem when the solution that you identify can help solve multiple problems. In other words, you have identified the overarching problem and, in the process, you discover the other interrelated problems. This was one important problem-solving insight that I learned during my consulting career. If solutions for the central problem of exponential growth in business could be found, you could apply the *Blueprint to a Billion*™ approach to many associated problems such as:

- *Strategy.* You can use the Blueprint financial pattern, along with the 7 Essentials, to contribute to shaping the business strategy and strategic initiatives. The Blueprint Companies provide an invaluable set of financial and essentials benchmarks. They are a reference tool to guide your particular situation.
- *Leadership.* The 7 Essentials can help you identify the skills and roles of top-performing leaders, as well as the degree of cross-functional leadership required to become a great company. Also, they can serve as a guide for assessing management teams and roles to ensure that the team is managing all of the essentials for superior performance.
- *Teams.* For either functional or cross-functional teams, these findings can serve as a guide to align their performance or to provide invaluable business context for cross-functional teamwork.
- *Financial Performance.* The financial models explained in this book can serve as a valuable benchmark when planning for growth.
- *Picking the Up-and-Coming Blueprint Companies.* Viewing the highest growth companies through the lens of the Blueprint essentials helps in selecting the best investments (personal or corporate), choosing alliance partners, screening for new customers, supply-chain procurement (vendor selection), and even interviewing for a new employer.
- *Education.* This quantitative approach to business building can be a contribution to corporate and academic education.

The Timeless Blueprint

Over the past three years, as I have presented these Blueprint observations, people ask if I am using the most recent data—as though the pattern changes with this quarter's hot companies or hot sectors. The good news is that the pattern is consistent. With a statistically significant population, outcomes are more a question of frequency versus a unique outcome.

Think of this work as a search for the pattern of those companies that have gone before us. The enduring essentials, linked to financial performance, remain true for building great companies. Unlike a number of other business research efforts, this work is not static. The list of Blueprint Companies naturally evolves. That said, what I hope to prove is that these findings are part of a megatrend. Therefore, 10 years from now, the expectation should be to find a growing number of Blueprint Companies and to see that they executed these same 7 Essentials to achieve exponential growth.

What is new and exciting is that some of today's "hot-growth companies" fit the Blueprint pattern. For example, in the 2004 issue of *BusinessWeek*'s special report on "Hot Growth Companies," the winners identified for highest shareholder return were Blueprint Companies with their two-year returns shown in parentheses: Career Education (184 percent), International Game Technology (142 percent), and Apollo Group (135 percent).[7]

In fact, the United States has been generating Blueprint Companies in good economic times and bad. Looking at the pattern for this timeless consistency, I found that an average of 31 new Blueprint Companies per year has been generated in this country (see Figure 1.9). You may be thinking, as I did, that this average should be highly volatile. During the past five years the pattern has actually been quite consistent! Compared to the pre-2000 period, the United States continues to track with an average of 28 to 37 companies each year. Right in line with the 10-year average of 31.

The United States' challenge is not to sustain the run rate in the low 30s, but to better the 10-year average of 31 companies per year. *The options to address this challenge are that either more companies must be funded or the success rate of funded companies must be improved.*

As you immerse yourself in the coming chapters, keep one key point in mind. This book is not about one unique company, its innovation, time period, innovation era, or the financial returns

FIGURE 1.9

Rate of Blueprint Companies Achieving $1 Billion

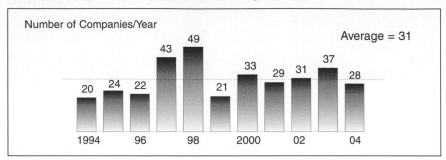

Source: Standard & Poor's Compustat, Blueprint analysis

achieved; it is about the common success-based pattern *shared by all*, independent of economic cycle. It is about how you can use the 7 Essentials to better your business, organization, or teams in order to produce exponential growth. It is about executing the 7 Essentials and linking them. It is about taking the actions that matter while avoiding pitfalls.

Can you imagine building a house without a blueprint? A blueprint serves as a common framework for teamwork, terminology, design, linking parts, and as a measure for progress. Whatever you are building, your execution will be enhanced if you employ a blueprint. Whether you aspire to achieve exponential growth or are experiencing it today, the application of the 7 Essentials, which are detailed in the following chapters, should help you achieve enhanced execution.

The book builds these 7 Essentials in a logical order, starting with the Big Idea in the Essentials Triangle framework, so that when you arrive at the Linking the Essentials chapter, Chapter 9, you will have the background and foundation to put it all together. As we transition from this Blueprint Thesis, you will find each essential described with frameworks augmented by illustrations, stories, and interviews by leaders who have created Blueprint Companies.

Create and Sustain a Breakthrough Value Proposition

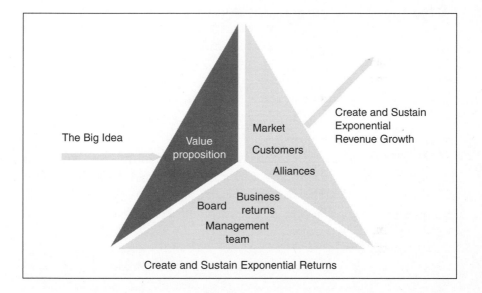

The Big Idea

Value proposition

Market
Customers
Alliances

Create and Sustain Exponential Revenue Growth

Board
Business returns
Management team

Create and Sustain Exponential Returns

Whether the industry is chemicals, clothes, technology, or financial services, Blueprint Companies have a big idea. Not just any big idea. Not just an idea about innovation. An idea with legs. A set of breakthrough capabilities that delivers high value to customers. These capabilities come in the form of breakthrough products (such as new drugs), breakthrough services such as Internet-based banking, or breakout levels of new value such as more frequent and lower cost airline flights.

23

These are value propositions, clear statements of the tangible benefits a customer gets from acquiring and using a product or service.

Looking across our 387 Blueprint Companies, three kinds of value propositions have been identified: Shaping a New World, with a really significant innovation that clearly offers a break-through set of benefits; Shaping a Market Niche, which delivers a unique product/service mix; and becoming a Category Killer, a company that offers breakthrough levels of value in comparison to the established providers.

Ever interview the founding team at a new company that declares it has the hottest innovation since the Wright Brothers? After probing you find that the company is only four months ahead of the big gorilla in the market. Not these Blueprint Companies. Their big idea is big enough to be far ahead of the pack. Realizing the full potential of this big idea becomes the mission of the company. Microsoft wanted to put a PC on every desktop. Tractor Supply aimed to provide legendary service and great products at everyday low prices.

As the book launches you into the first essential, keep in mind that understanding the platform for the value proposition is critical to how you execute the other essentials. The first turn on the Blueprint journey is the most critical.

Chapter 2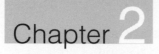

The Blueprint Value Proposition

Are you creating and sustaining a
breakthrough value proposition?

If you've been a serious investor, especially in high technology, then Roger McNamee is probably a cultural icon to you. That is because McNamee and a handful of other Silicon Valley venture capitalists have been extraordinarily good at spotting innovative Blueprint Companies—and making them into billion-dollar companies.

Roger not only managed the largest tech fund in America during the late 1980s (T. Rowe Price's Science and Technology fund), but later cofounded Integral Capital Partners, a partnership with the venerable Kleiner Perkins Caufield & Byers. He also founded Silver Lake Partners, the first private equity fund in the technology world. Among Roger's prescient picks have been Cerent (Cisco), Flextronics, Intuit, MCI, and Seagate Technology. Most recently, McNamee cofounded Elevation Partners, a newly formed private-equity firm that makes large-scale investments in market-leading media, entertainment, and consumer-related businesses.

As he was driving to a client meeting one afternoon, McNamee was on his cell phone, explaining how he developed a sixth sense for spotting breakthrough innovations. "At a time when nobody on Wall Street cared about technology, I developed relationships with executives, not based on being an investor, but on being an industry insider," McNamee told me. That meant that McNamee was able to infiltrate the trade shows and conferences that were being held nearly every week in Silicon Valley. "I didn't threaten anyone as long as I had something intelligent to say," he added. "My input was actually valued by the people with whom I interacted."

In return, Roger got an inside glimpse at what would soon be the most exciting industries in America. And what was he looking for? McNamee did not care about spreadsheets or even the incremental innovations. He was looking for the breakthrough innovations—the kind that would change people's lives.

"What I realized is that time is scarce," he explained. "So I started with this macroview that caused me to look in certain places—mobility, connectivity, and interactivity. They were really social themes. I was practicing real-time anthropology." Using those themes as a filter, McNamee focused in on companies that seemed poised to change the world. When Roger found them, that is where he put his money.

The Value Proposition

As we started our search for the secrets of Blueprint Company success, my team and I decided to start with the *value proposition*. A value proposition, after all, lies at the core of every company. It is the fundamental benefit that the customer obtains from doing business with the company. Some value propositions are strikingly clear ("on a hot summer day, *things go better with Coke*"). And some value propositions are downright disasters. (Dare we mention "New Coke"?)

As we sorted through the Blueprint Companies, we realized that every one of them had a compelling value proposition. All were founded on the delivery of a breakthrough set of customer benefits.

But as we examined the top 100, we realized that these firms not only had good value propositions, they had *breakthrough* value propositions—big ideas that went far beyond mere improvements to existing products and services.

These Blueprint Companies may not have reinvented the proverbial wheel, but they have actually come close, delivering breakthrough products and services better, faster, and cheaper than what existed previously. That is what we saw when we looked at the top Blueprint Companies—the same kind of eye-opening innovation that Roger McNamee has hit upon time and again.

The Elements of a Value Proposition

A breakthrough value proposition requires more than a breakthrough product. The product innovation has to be aligned with the needs of the outside world. When the product is good and the environment is ready—that's when a breakthrough innovation becomes a breakthrough value proposition.

Blueprint Companies create breakthrough value propositions by asking three critical questions:

1. What market segment are we addressing?
2. Who are our targeted customers?
3. What benefits are we delivering?

The answers, in turn, become actionable through the following equation:

$$\text{Value proposition} = \text{Addressed market segment} \times \text{Targeted customer} \times \text{Higher-order benefits}$$

Addressed Market Segment. Blueprint Companies can create new markets, redefine existing markets, or optimize mature markets. But in each case they are aligning their contribution to the unmet needs of the outside world. Genentech created a new market in biotech products, for instance; Starbucks refined an existing market; and JetBlue has invigorated a mature market. In each case, the innovation arrived at just the right time. (Imagine if JetBlue had tried its wings before airline deregulation.) Blueprint founders and CEOs sense that the time is right and then shape their product and services to fulfill the unmet need.

Targeted Customer. Many of us still harbor the romantic image of the mad scientist working alone in the lab developing amazing innovations. Blueprint Companies, however, are not founded on bright ideas or clever products alone. Blueprint founders and CEOs see *people* on the other side of their products, and that is who they design the products or services for. Michael Dell used to bring customers up to his dorm room at the University of Texas where he developed his latest computers and from there developed his company.[1] Tom Stemberg, the founder of Staples, interviewed small businesses and played purchasing agent to identify unmet needs. The point is that to make breakthrough innovations, Blueprint Companies put real faces on the market. Call it demographics, social profiles, needs clustering, or previous purchase behaviors, they know their customer.

Higher-Order Benefits. Blueprint Companies also recognize that there are two kinds of benefits: functional and emotional. For JetBlue, for instance, the functional benefits include on-time arrival and departure, nonstop flights, and a choice of flight times. The emotional benefits include enjoyment, comfort, and peace of mind (from minimal disruptions). Have you ever eagerly tried a new product, only to be disappointed in its functional shortcomings? Or found a product useful, but neither very exciting to use nor igniting your imagination? Blueprint Companies succeed in delivering both functional *and* emotional benefits.

Three Kinds of Blueprint Value Propositions

As we studied and restudied our results, these breakthrough value propositions fell into three categories. The top Blueprint Companies were either *Shapers of a New World*—companies that literally created a new way for the world to live or work. For example, Genentech created new drugs and Cisco created the routers for the Internet. Then there were *Niche Shapers*—companies that followed the *Shapers of the New World* by redefining the market to create a large market or product niche that filled an unmet need. Starbucks redefined the coffee experience as did Harley-Davidson with motorcycles.

Then come the *Category Killers*—companies that optimize a market by creating and disrupting the value proposition platforms of the established incumbents. Typically they attack price, commoditizing the product or service. Other times they attack by speeding delivery or by broadening the choice of products. Whatever the case, they are successful in stripping market share from the incumbent. The "big box" stores are particularly good at this: AutoZone for auto parts, Staples for office supplies, Best Buy for electronic goods, and Home Depot for hardware goods. When these Category Killers turn up, they attack with the right prices and just the right amount of quality.

Wave 1—Shapers of a New World: Creating a New Market

There are two kinds of Shapers of a New World: first there are *Shapers of a New Market* (who create a new market) and then there are *Gap Fillers*, who quickly follow to fill critical gaps in the new markets. Together, both have a huge impact on shaping a new way of life for their customers, at home and globally.

Among the top Blueprint companies, the top Shapers of a New Market are Amgen, eBay, Medtronic, Yahoo!, Cisco, and Genentech (see www.blueprinttoabillion.com for the list of top Blueprint Companies). Each shaped a new world in drugs, Internet retail, medical devices, search engines, and networking equipment.

Each of these companies developed its breakthrough innovations in different ways. Yet as we looked through the company histories, we found very similar stories. Genentech, for instance, which develops, manufacturers, and markets human pharmaceuticals derived from gene splicing (that is, recombinant DNA), was founded in 1976 by Robert Swanson, an MIT Sloan School graduate, and Herbert Boyer, a distinguished academic scientist. The two had already seen a few small companies try to fabricate new organisms from gene cells through a process called recombinant DNA or, more colloquially, "gene splicing." Boyer and Swanson decided to try to replicate a cell that had simple composition.

The first experiment with Somatostatin required seven months of research. Scientists on the project placed the hormone inside *E. coli bacteria*, found in the human intestine. The anticipated result was that the bacteria would produce useful proteins that duplicated Somatostatin, but that did not happen. Then a scientist working on the project hypothesized that proteins in the bacteria were attacking the hormone. In the next trial, the Somatostatin was protected, and the new cell was successfully produced. The good news was that Genentech's credibility was established. The bad news was that the product made no money.

Early in the summer of 1978, Genentech experienced its first breakthrough in recreating the insulin gene. To get to the next stage would require about $100 million and 1,000 human years of labor. Fortunately, by then Kleiner Perkins had looked Genentech over. It was a long shot (the investment today is called Kleiner Perkins "moon shot"), but the firm decided to take the bet. By 1982 the company had won approval from the Food and Drug Administration (FDA).

At the same time, Eli Lilly and Company, the world's largest and oldest manufacturer of synthetic insulin, commanded 75 percent of the U.S. insulin market. Swanson knew that Genentech stood little chance of competing with them. He informed Eli Lilly's directors of Genentech's accomplishments, hoping to attract their attention. He believed that the mere threat of a potentially better product would entice Eli Lilly to purchase licensing rights to the product, and he was correct. Eli Lilly bought the rights and marketed the product as Humulin. This maneuver provided ample capital for Genentech to continue its work. By 1987 the company was earning $5 million in licensing fees from Eli Lilly.

Swanson pursued a similar strategy with the company's next product, Alpha Interferon. Hoffmann–La Roche purchased the rights to Interferon and paid approximately $5 million in royalties to Genentech in 1987. Revenues from these agreements helped to underwrite the costs of new product development, which ran from $25 million to $50 million per product prior to FDA approval.

The first product independently marketed by Genentech, human growth hormone or Protropin, generated $43.6 million in sales in 1986. Demand for this hormone increased as the medical profession learned more about the drug's capabilities and diagnosed hormone inadequacy more frequently. Protropin enjoyed record-setting sales over the next six years, topping $155 million by 1991. At the end of 1991, Genentech's Protropin maintained an impressive 75 percent share of the human growth hormone market.[2]

After being buffeted by a wave of takeovers and mergers that shook the industry in the late 1980s, Genentech emerged in the 1990s as one of the most solid biotechnology companies in the world; one of the Fortune 500 for 2005.

The elements of the Genentech story are true for other Shapers of a New Market and sound astoundingly similar. That is, they fundamentally change people's lives for the better by:

- *Creating a breakthrough innovation that addresses a huge unmet need in a very unique way.* Drugs, pacemakers, Internet portals and search engines, and the Internet infrastructure are such examples.
- *Delivering a breakthrough value proposition that was sustainable, that had legs.* Being a Shaper of a New Market, their innovation often created a new era of product life cycles. Their original innovation rapidly broadened into an impressive broad

portfolio of products or services. For Cisco, it was the iteration of bandwidth, protocols, capacities, and capabilities that
propelled this company beyond its first offerings.
* *Becoming the de facto standard.* These companies embraced
  their new markets and excelled to such a degree that they
  became the standard by which others are measured.

Filling a Critical Gap

Quite often, Blueprint Companies arrive just in time to fill a critical
gap in the service or products, which leads them to become a
Shaper of a New World. By filling the gap, these Blueprint
Companies unlock new worlds of services and products.

Broadcom, the highest-growth semiconductor company on the
Blueprint list of companies, serves as a great example. Founded in
1991 by Henry Nicholas III and Henry Samueli, two PhDs,
Broadcom developed the integrated circuits that enabled high-
speed communications. By late 1990s, Broadcom had its computer
chips in about 80 percent of America's cable modems and TV-set
top boxes and had evolved its product from a series of chips to one
powerful piece of silicon technology.[3]

Broadcom filled a critical gap in new technologies and, in so
doing, created a new world in itself. No one knows this better than
George Kelly of Morgan Stanley who, having brought Cisco public, was doing the same for Broadcom. "How could Broadcom
come out of nowhere and grow so rapidly that they passed the
major players: Texas Instruments, Intel, Advanced Micro Devices,
and National Semiconductor?" he asked. "It's as if these guys are
just mind readers, or did they get help?" The answer, he said, is
that Broadcom worked with their customers to define the need (for
high-speed communications) then worked backward to fill it. As
Kelly put it, "The Broadcom team then asked their customers, 'If
we give you this, is this what you want to buy?' and Broadcom did
just that—they quickly gave their customers what they wanted."

Broadcom quickly expanded from its first customer, Scientific

Atlanta, to include major cable equipment companies such as General Instrument (now a division of Motorola), Cisco Systems, 3Com, and Samsung. These manufacturers provide much of the equipment that cable providers—Time Warner, Comcast, and others—needed to provide consumers with high-speed Internet and digital television services. Meanwhile, as the regional Bell companies expanded into broadband with DSL, Broadcom quickly turned to provide similar chips to fill their gaps. Large equipment providers to the regional Bell companies (such as Nortel Networks and Cisco) became significant customers. In each of these cases, Broadcom worked closely with their customers to customize their chips to address their customer's needs.[4]

As the market has evolved into more sophisticated communications requirements, Broadcom has led by filling continued critical gaps. George Kelly explains how this company filled those gaps so well:

> First, they defined the company as being in the networking silicon business. The leadership team then asked where were the extremely large markets where we can apply our technologies? The team looked for high-volume applications where Broadcom could displace an incumbent's technology. They then took a fresh look at the products and at the suppliers in each of those markets. To illustrate this approach, they studied the tuner, which is a common component in VCRs and TVs. The team identified a better systems-on-a-chip solution using Broadcom's technologies that would upset the applecart because Broadcom could offer a significantly lower cost alternative. This common product line enabled Broadcom to quickly address an available market of 100 million tuners.

For example, as the market evolved for the high-definition television, Broadcom set a new performance standard in 2004 with a digital television receiver chip. In 2004, Broadcom also introduced the first systems-on-a-chip solution for Bluetooth wireless key-

boards and applications for personal computers in order to lead
demand for wireless peripherals.[5]

Wave 2—Niche Shapers: Redefine the Market

Many companies have ascended to $1 billion by finding an unmet
need and carving out a market niche. In our Blueprint list, the top
Niche Shapers are Veritas, Siebel Systems, Coach Inc., and Apollo
Group. However, if you want to find an easy-to-identify market
niche filler, go to the intersection of virtually any trendy urban or
suburban shopping district and look around. What do you see?
Probably a Starbucks, the Blueprint firm with some 8,500 coffee
shops and kiosks in the United States, Canada, the United
Kingdom, and elsewhere overseas.

In 1982, when there were just five Starbucks shops in the world,
Howard Schultz joined the company. Wandering the piazzas of
Milan the following year in search of inspiration, Schultz was captivated not only by Italy's coffee, but by the *culture* of coffee. (Milan
alone had about 1,700 espresso bars.) It gradually dawned on
Schultz that for Italians, coffeehouses are not just about coffee; they
are the *third* place to be (following home and work). Schultz
returned with this idea hotly "brewing"—and was promptly reject-
ed by his bosses at Starbucks.

In the spring of 1986, Schultz opened Starbucks' first coffee bar
in the tallest building just to the west of downtown Chicago.
Faithful to its inspiration, the bar had a stately espresso machine as
its centerpiece. At that time, Starbucks was selling coffee for 80 or
90 cents, while the competition was selling coffee in Styrofoam
cups for 40 cents. From this point on, Starbucks started changing—
everything from coffee drinkers' tastes to their customer experience to the language they used.[6] Schultz believed then that the
quality of Starbucks coffee would one day "alter how everyday
Americans conduct their lives." To achieve this cultural transformation, Schultz needed to convert an entire customer base that
grew up consuming tinned coffee.

What is the Starbucks value proposition? The number-one factor is having an appealing product. To Starbucks it is more than coffee. People choose to come to Starbucks for three reasons: the coffee, the people, and the experience in the Starbucks stores. Starbucks places the highest priority on the quality of their coffee. It is fanatical about buying the highest quality Arabica coffees in the world and roasting them to the desired flavor characteristics for each variety. Because 98 percent of coffee is water, every store has a special water filtration system. Behind the scenes, "Partners," as Starbucks calls its employees, go through extensive training to ensure that they will make the best coffee. Starbucks has a saying, "We're not in the coffee business serving people; we are in the people business serving coffee." Partners in each store pride themselves at passing on to customers their knowledge and passion about Starbucks. They greet customers and exchange a few nice words with them, and custom-make a drink exactly to the customer's taste so they are eager to come back. Their goal is to take the experience to a higher level so customers are treated positively and they feel special. As time has passed, the Starbucks stores are evolving into a "third place" after home and work. The stores are offering a deeper resonance and are offering benefits as seductive as the coffee itself: a taste of romance, an affordable luxury, an oasis, casual social interaction, and an extension of work and home.[7]

Just as Roger McNamee recognized that people did not have enough free time and for that reason would desire mobility and networking using the latest high technology, so Schultz realized that we Americans did not have a comfortable place to sit and drink our lattes. That simple but big idea has created one of America's largest corporations.

Newfield Finds a Niche

Niches, however, are not always people centric. In the case of Newfield Exploration, a new Blueprint Company that exceeded $1 billion revenue in 2003, it was the unique combination of technology, people, and strong financial management that shaped this oil and gas exploration niche. It was the courage to *focus* these assets when others used a broader approach that catapulted it to Blueprint Status.

In the 1980s, Joe Foster led Tenneco in becoming one of the most successful exploration firms in the Gulf of Mexico. In 1988, when Tenneco shed its oil properties, Foster started Newfield Exploration. It was a shoestring operation, with $9 million in seed funding and 26 employees. What was worse, though, was Newfield's business plan. Foster planned to concentrate on a 700-block area off the Louisiana coast; a piece of undersea real estate that other oil companies had pawed over for years and finally left, figuring the place was dry. While the majors had moved on to deeper waters, this area off of the Louisiana coast was not really "dry"; the major oil companies just considered the target sizes were too small and not worth their attention. The Gulf of Mexico was considered a maturing hydrocarbon province.

For the next few years, as the big oil companies gladly sold Joe Foster their drilling rights along the coastline at bargain prices, Foster began to roll out his secret weapon—that is, three-dimensional seismic mapping combined with a highly talented team of geologists. First Foster focused all of his 26 geologists in the shallow waters of the Gulf of Mexico. Through this *courage of focus*, Newfield had more geologists in this area than the majors. With over a $100 million investment in three-dimensional seismic technologies, Newfield's talented team had the best tools and best data from which to search for oil and gas. From this point, the main story is about proprietary techniques and talent to interpret the data; looking for bright spot anomalies and "tweaking" the data. Having a geographic focus enabled the team to also build a subsurface story by looking at the many well logs from wells Newfield had drilled.

By the end of 2003, Newfield was operating about 150 production platforms and producing about one half a billion cubic feet equivalent a day of natural gas from its Gulf of Mexico holdings.[8]

Then, Newfield moved onshore into Louisiana, with holdings in the Rayne, Live Oak, and Bayou Sale fields and 125 square miles of 3D data in Terrebonne Parish.[9] Newfield moved into onshore regions beginning in 1995. "Southern Louisiana represented our first onshore entry; the geology is very similar," Foster said. "We recognized the maturity of the Gulf of Mexico and knew that our asset base needed diversification to ensure profitable growth."

Newfield experienced a record-breaking year in 2003 when it surpassed the $1 billion revenue milestone with a record net income of $199 million. From the shallow waters of the Gulf of Mexico, the company migrated to onshore regions like South Texas, the Mid-Continent, and, most recently, the Rocky Mountains. Today, Newfield is larger in terms of reserves and production in the Gulf of Mexico than it was in 2003—and the deep water has been added as a growing focus area. To expand internationally, the company took steps to transfer the knowledge it gained to another part of the world: In March 2005, the company announced its first well in the North Sea.[10]

"An independent can't compete in the Gulf without technology," Foster told the *Oil Daily* in 1996. It took him a few years to prove himself in that respect, but the niche he finally carved out made Newfield the most successful independent Exploration and Production Company in the country.

Serving an Unmet Need: The Need to Offer an Alternative

Another type of market niche is one that offers an alternative to the incumbent. Remember the car rental wars of the 1990s? Hertz was number one and Avis was number two—and Avis tried harder. These *Second-but-Better* Blueprint Companies are the gutsy companies that offer a better than number-one alternative. Although these value propositions abound, there are just two among the top Blueprint Companies—Google and Juniper Networks. What makes them special is their ability to leapfrog over the number-one incumbent, positioning themselves with superior benefits. Blueprint

Companies strive to offer customers a better alternative, thereby taking market share.

That is what we see in the competition between Yahoo! and Google. Yahoo! is the clear number one—but Google arguably is Second-but-Better. Google started its directory to be different than most others in two significant ways. First, directory search results are ranked according to Google's proprietary PageRank relevance system. Second, Google uses the technology that powers its regular Web search to search over all the content of sites within a category, not just the titles and descriptions.[11] "The perfect search engine," says Google cofounder Larry Page, "would understand exactly what you mean and give back exactly what you want." While that is a far-reaching vision, Google's goal is to provide a much higher level of service to those who seek information whether they are at their desk or on wireless.

Google might have posed an imminent threat to Yahoo!, but a critical milestone was achieved in May 2000 when Google became Yahoo!'s official default search engine.[12] In other words, searches that Yahoo! could not process would be passed to Google. Since, then, Google's minimalist design and consistently relevant results, better than even Microsoft's MSN cluttered site, is attracting legions of users. Google has unlocked the secret of online advertising; its automated system notes a user's search request and then delivers discrete matching ads alongside the results.[13] Google is leaping ahead with innovations that span a broad portfolio of Google Services and Google Tools.

Google's revenues are generated from the sale of advertising displayed on Google and other sites across the Web. Google only displays ads based on being relevant to the results page being shown. Google has found that relevant text ads are much more effective than pop-up ads and ads that appear randomly. Thousands of advertisers use Google's AdWords program to promote their products. Google does not sell a better PageRank to its partners so users *trust* Google's objectivity.[14]

Another top Second-but-Better is Juniper Networks. While Juniper currently is dwarfed by Cisco ($1.3 billion revenue to Cisco's $22 billion), Juniper has been trying to show the telecom carriers that it is second—but better with its high-end routers. Juniper is gaining market share (23 percent versus Cisco's dominant 65 percent) and certainly impressing the stock markets: Of the eight computer networking companies to go public in 1999, only three have produced positive returns for shareholders. Juniper's stock has enjoyed a 326 percent split adjusted gain since its initial pricing, despite the downdraft of 2000.[15] Keep an eye on Juniper if the high growth market for routers returns and Juniper successfully diversifies into the enterprise segment. Also expect the typical Second-but-Better competition to continue to intensify between Cisco (number one) and Juniper (number two).

Redefining the market in the context of an established market can be achieved by fulfilling an unmet need with a highly differentiated service or product. To offer a differentiated value proposition, the company has to offer higher-order benefits such as superior capabilities or emotional benefits not found with adjacent market peers.

Wave 3—Category Killers: Optimize the Market

Just when a company has reshaped the world and is enjoying the fruits of its genius, more competitors arrive at the gate. These are the companies that take a market idea and optimize it—generally by cutting prices and/or improving quality. It is a proven strategy; Wal-Mart did it with everyday low prices and Southwest Airlines did it for air travel. They are known as Category Killers.

Top Blueprint Companies that optimized their markets are Clear Channel Communications, Office Depot, and AutoZone. This proves that entering a market late does not prevent great business-building success. How does a Category Killer spot a new market? Tom Stemberg, Founder and Chairman Emeritus of Staples explained it this way to us: "You identify a market that is growing and one with adequate margin structure built in so, with a more efficient value chain, you have a cost and price advantage. Finally, find a market where customers are underserved."

While the New World and Niche Shapers are focused on innovation and marketing excellence, the common value proposition around Category Killers is value. Price, of course, is the biggest weapon that the Category Killers carry. Behind price are higher performance, more convenient location, one-stop shopping, and better service. With these benefits, they can typically capture 10 percent to 20 percent of the incumbent's market share.

The past decades might be considered the era of the Category Killers. This "shift to value" had its roots in the 1970s and 1980s when Japanese automakers and consumer electronics manufacturers thrived by selling cheaper and initially inferior products that eventually became more reliable than those of the competition—and remained cheaper.[16] As value-driven companies in a growing number of industries move from competing solely on price to catching up on attributes such as quality, service, and convenience, many traditional players rightly feel threatened.

Two strengths underlie the growing power of value shapers in consumer markets. The first is an impressive cost advantage rooted both in industry-specific sources and in relentless execution. In the retail industry, Blueprint Companies such as Staples, Auto-Zone, Home Depot, Tractor Supply, and Best Buy combined excellence in distribution, better purchasing, deep vendor relationships, and a broad inventory so customers have a "one-stop shop." The second strength is a shift in consumer perceptions of the quality they offer. The gap, both real and perceived, is closing. For example, Tractor Supply focuses an inordinate amount of energy on training so their customer service is as good as it can be. Category Killers are attracting customers with a combination of low prices and "good enough" quality.[17]

The Category Killer's second strength is the ability to anticipate a shift in consumer perceptions of the quality customers will find acceptable. "PETsMART didn't define its market as the pet food market," highlighted Tom Stemberg, who also serves as a PETsMART board member. "They defined it through the lens of their customers. They are in pet grooming, pet care, and pet hotels. When it comes to service, convenience, and the buying experience, the gap between value players and their competitors, both real and imagined, has narrowed."

The JetBlue Attack

For the six major airlines that predate deregulation days— American, United, Delta, Continental, Northwest, and US Airways—a terrifying prospect is a low-cost airline attacker that actually offers better service. In the past two decades, that night- mare has come true, thanks to Southwest Airlines and other low- cost carriers. But if beating up the incumbents was fun before, no one is doing it better today than JetBlue Airways Corporation.

JetBlue was launched by David Neeleman "to bring humanity back to air travel." And unlike the early, on-a-shoestring launch of Southwest Airlines, JetBlue arrived on the scene with a huge amount of capital, brand new planes, satellite television, Web- based reservations, and expert personnel in key positions.[18] In par- ticular, JetBlue challenged American and United with increasingly frequent flights from JFK to the West Coast; since it arrived in 2000, those fares have dropped around 30 percent.[19]

Like a lot of incumbents, the established airlines have fought back vigorously. They do have the upper hand in the coast-to-coast flights, and they own most of the landing slots at numerous big city airports. Their hubs have been called fortresses, and they protect those properties as well. But the momentum is with the airlines that have sprung up after deregulation. The managers Neeleman assembled to build JetBlue were drawn from the pioneers in bring- ing trouble to the established airlines—Southwest and Virgin Atlantic. Like cost-obsessed Southwest, JetBlue started with a sin- gle type of plane, treated employees well, and stressed quick- turnaround, point-to-point service. And like Virgin, JetBlue used "buzz and hip" marketing to present the flying experience as much more than simply getting from Point A to Point B.[20]

Other factors are figuring in the formula. As JetBlue has just passed the $1 billion revenue milestone in 2005, it is becoming known for being ranked number one in customer satisfaction. Southwest is ranked second, followed by Delta Air Lines. Customers praised the airline for such things as ease of making a reservation, courtesy, and presentation.[21]

Home Depot Brings the Big Box to Hardware

By 1980, as Lowe's approached $1 billion revenue, the burgeoning do-it-yourself market began to change the face of the construction industry due to the rising cost of buying a home or having one remodeled.

Along came Home Depot in 1978. A team of out-of-work executives from Handy Dan realized that the do-it-yourself customer made up more than 60 percent of the building supply industry's sales volume. The identified unmet need was that the customer did not have the technical knowledge or expertise to accomplish most home repair improvement projects.

The Home Depot team set about to address this market and unmet need by becoming a Category Killer like Wal-Mart. They made sure all Home Depot stores were large enough to stock at least 25,000 different items versus a typical competitor with 10,000 items. To solve the skill gap of their customers, they trained the sales staff of each store to remove much of the mystery attached to home improvement projects.[22] Home Depot targeted urbanites with their larger warehouse-type "superstore" approach, which features stores averaging on the high side of 60,000 square feet, versus Lowe's 15,000-foot size.[23]

"What makes Home Depot so formidable isn't size alone," noted Asma Usmani, a hardware industry analyst with the St. Louis investment firm Edward Jones & Co. "I definitely think distribution plays a large part in Home Depot's success, along with their customer service. They're renowned for their service. Second is their product assortment and third is fair pricing. They're very competitive with their pricing; those three items alone indicate what attracts customers and why their customers are so loyal,"[24]

By 1989, Home Depot surpassed Lowe's in sales to become the largest home repair chain in the United States. Lowe's and Home Depot continue to do battle today.

> Value players such as JetBlue, Home Depot, and Staples are offering the powerful combination of low prices and high quality and are capturing the hearts and wallets of consumers in the United States.

The Pattern Continues Today

New World Shapers are always springing from the shadows to delight and amaze us. Niche Shapers follow. Then come the Category Killers to drive everything to that low, low Wal-Mart-like price. If this sequence of events has you humming "The Circle of Life" (the Elton John song from Disney's *The Lion King*), then you have got the picture. But the unfolding of this evolution is never predictable.

Consider exponentially growing companies from the *Business-Week* and *Fortune* lists of high growth companies: PetMed Express, Sigmatel, and Bradley Pharmaceuticals.

PetMed Express, which was the number-one company on *BusinessWeek*'s top 100 Hot Growth Companies in 2004, recently achieved $87 million revenue with a three-year revenue growth of 102 percent.[25] PetMed's annual report stated that it is "rapidly changing the way America buys pet medications . . . To accomplish this, we have invested in state-of-the-art information systems and infrastructure along with trained customer service agents . . ." Does this sound like the original sales pitch of Amazon.com, only with pet supplies rather than books?

If you listen to music, you should appreciate SigmaTel. Just the way most end user customers were not aware that Broadcom chips were enabling their access to the Internet, you might not know you are using SigmaTel's integrated audio chips in your Apple iPod. Most of the world's millions of MP3 music players rely on SigmaTel's single-chip solution to import music, decode digital audio formats, conserve battery power, control the display, and communicate with either a flash memory chip or a tiny hard disk drive.

If you own an Apple iPod, SigmaTel is inside. About 95 percent of SigmaTel's $195 million revenue comes from its high-performance audio chips.[26] Today, SigmaTel is following a similar strategy to Broadcom by providing chips that are akin to "systems on a chip." While Broadcom was on the four-year trajectory, SigmaTel is paralleling Broadcom's ascent on the six-year trajectory. *Fortune* ranked this company as one of 25 breakout companies to watch in 2005.[27]

A *Shaper of a Market Niche* is being executed by Bradley Pharmaceuticals, number 10 on *Fortune*'s Fastest Growing Companies for 2004. Bradley markets niche dermatology and gastrointestinal medications for common ailments like acne, and Bradley has carved out a strategy by acquiring prescription brands that lack blockbuster promise from leaders like Pfizer. The company outexecutes the "big guys" by repackaging and outselling, creating value through superior marketing. At $91 million revenue, Bradley's sales growth over the past three years is accelerating.[28]

And that's the way it goes: From Shaping a new World, to Niche Shaping, to Category Killing. When a company wins in one wave, it cannot rest while the next wave of competitors appears on the horizon.

Where's the Next Frontier?

The business press is constantly looking for the next wave of innovation, and so are investors (as though a disproportionate amount

of value is created only in the innovation). But when we catego-
rized the top Blueprint Companies, we were surprised to find that
only 57 percent of the companies are Shapers of a New World (see
Figure 2.1).

Another interesting finding: Niche Shapers companies filling a
market niche or companies playing the role of the Category Killers
accounted for 49 percent of the market value created by top
Blueprint Companies. These value proposition platforms were not
dependent on "catching the next innovation wave." Finally, it was
a big surprise that the average market value per company for
Shapers of a New World was not significantly higher than those
companies in the other categories.

> Companies do not have to be Shapers of a New World in order
> to create high market value. Our study showed that 43 percent
> of the top Blueprint Companies were either Niche Shapers or
> Category Killers. Therefore, great growth companies can be cre-
> ated in existing markets.

FIGURE 2.1

Value Proposition Platforms of Top Blueprint Companies

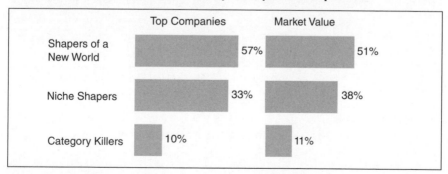

Source: Standard & Poor's Compustat, Blueprint analysis

Implications Going Forward—An Overview

At the beginning of this chapter, we mentioned that companies need to be explicit about their value proposition. Why? The execution of the essentials depends on this choice. For example, if a company is defining a new market, it must focus on securing leading customers early who can help them *prove-in* their breakthrough innovation. On the other hand, if a company is shaping a market niche, alliances are critically important. Category Killers are highly focused on out executing or optimizing the market with better value, lower prices being the primary offer. Therefore, Category Killers are typically focused on supply chain innovation in order to deliver better value.

Watch Out for Pitfalls

George Kelly has seen a lot of companies IPO—and many fail. George Kelly is an Advisory Director at Morgan Stanley. During most of his 20 years there he was a Senior Securities Analyst following the communications equipment industry. He was instrumental in bringing many Blueprint Companies public, including Cisco and Broadcom. What conditions spell doom for a company, we asked? He suggests three:

1. **Swarming**. By this he means too many companies swarming around an opportunity for anyone to succeed. Take the 802.11 Wireless Local Area Network chip market, he says, noting that some 65 companies were in that market, essentially doing the same thing. "Virtually all the companies have gone by the wayside and the people who dominate it now, Texas Instrument and Intel, scale for the lowest cost."

2. **A changing market structure that affects gross margins.** The Chinese have been hugely present in the networking industry. Take just one example, Huawei Technologies, the leading Chinese company in this industry. In Europe, the

Chinese have gotten their first carrier customers in 3G wireless systems—when many analysts thought it would take years. Kelly suggests, "Huawei hasn't penetrated North America yet, but in a few years it will be a considerable force due to pricing structures that are extremely competitive with today's market leaders."

3. **Customer consolidation.** When customers consolidate, leverage transfers to the customer. "In previous years the telecom equipment market was a wonderful market with a diverse set of communications service providers," said Kelly. "Today, a lot has changed as the industry has rapidly consolidated down to a few large telecom carriers. Now look at the margins of what's happened to this industry as the customers have consolidated."

Creating Breakthrough Customer Benefits

Blueprint Companies deliver more than functional benefits. They deliver intangible benefits; benefits with high emotional value. Are you thinking such benefits are mushy?

Actually, there are benefit frameworks through which we can examine these breakthrough value propositions. This approach can enable you to quantify the relationship and value of functional and emotional benefits (see Appendix B). It is based on the principle that offering customers higher-order emotional benefits creates strong customer loyalty. The higher a company goes from functional to emotional benefits, the greater the value and better the margins.

Simply put: "what a company offers" (the product or service benefits) is assessed by users for "what it does for me and my company" (functional benefits) and, importantly, "how do I and my company feel about it?" (emotional benefits). Providing emotional or intangible benefits results in customers giving "permission" to providers (permission benefits) as they endorse the broadening functional and emotional benefits.

To gain customer permission, think of this as building a house. The attributes are the foundation, the functional benefits serve as the frame, and the emotional benefits act as the roof. Customers want to live in your company's whole house, but only if it is built correctly. When a customer wants to live in the whole house, you have permission to add and extend to that house. Using a blueprint can help you build the right kind of house!

Home furnishings retailer Pottery Barn, part of Williams-Sonoma, has created stylish but affordable designs that have gained strong consumer acceptance. As their loyal, young adult target has aged and had children, Pottery Barn has extended this "relationship" by offering a separate children's outlet (Pottery Barn Kids) as well as teen furnishings line (PB Teen). They have leveraged their customers' permission by helping address home furnishing needs across life-stage milestones.

Consider our market Niche Shaper example, Starbucks. Starbucks is a powerful global brand not just because it serves coffee and customers like the taste, but also because the store experience conveys an image of a third place to home and work, a personally rewarding experience, and a place for peace of mind (see Appendix B for further elaboration).

The Power of Permission: The Google Example

Bill Gates is worried about Google. Today, Google is not just a hugely successful search engine; it has morphed into a software company that is emerging as a threat to Microsoft's dominance. Because Google does not sell its search products (it makes it money from its search results), it has combined software innovation with a brand new Internet model. "Unless Microsoft can deliver search that is plainly better, most users won't switch," says Piper Jaffray analyst Safa Rashtchy. Rashtchy adds, "Google is a huge brand. From where I sit, it is their game to lose."[29]

Google took the search function along with a suite of tools and transformed it into something that was competitively distinctive, thereby increasing its perceived value. By providing simple search capabilities that are fast, user friendly, accurate, and thorough, Google has established a bond of trust with consumers that acts as a foundation for permission to expand. Now Google can locate any program, document, photo, music file, or e-mail on a computer. It can provide search independent of device: PC, PDA, or Blackberry. This has created an intangible set of benefits for users that is allowing Google to move at a blinding speed with permission from their customers.[30]

Chapter Summary

Key Points

- Blueprint Companies create exponential growth by delivering a *breakthrough* value proposition. A value proposition is the fundamental benefit that the customer obtains from doing business with the company. Value propositions have three components: market served, targeted customer, and customer benefits.
- Determining the value proposition is critical, as this essential serves to set the context and direction for the other essentials.
- Value propositions are grouped in market platform waves: Wave 1 being the *Shapers of a New World*, Wave 2 being the *Niche Shapers,* and Wave 3 being the *Category Killers*.
  - *Shapers of a New World*, which truly create a new market for their products and services.
  - *Niche Shapers*, which follow New World Shapers with products or services that redefine a specific market segment.
  - *Category Killers*, which optimize a market by attacking the existing incumbents with a better-faster-cheaper value offer.

- Breakthrough benefits are achieved by delivering on functional, emotional, and permission benefits. Moving up the benefits hierarchy to deliver intangible benefits increases value, customer loyalty, and margins.
- Starbucks realizes higher margins by delivering emotional benefits and permission benefits.
- There are multiple examples that demonstrate that this pattern continues today; PetMed Express, SigmaTel, and Bradley Pharmaceuticals are just three.

Unexpected Findings
- Companies filling a market niche or playing the role of Category Killers accounted for 49 percent of the market value created by top Blueprint Companies. These value proposition platforms were not dependent on "catching the next innovation wave."
- The average market value per company for Shapers of a New World is not significantly higher than the other categories. This suggests that companies do not need to be first to market in order to create high market value.
- The impact of providing higher-order benefits, such as emotional benefits, improves gross margins, increases demand, and creates barriers to entry. Blueprint Companies (that is, Starbucks, eBay, Siebel Systems, Cisco, Staples) tended to be masters at benefit development.
- Google is an example of a company that capitalizes on the power of permission—the highest-order benefit because it provides a unique opportunity to add new products and have them rapidly accepted by customers.

CREATE AND SUSTAIN EXPONENTIAL REVENUE GROWTH

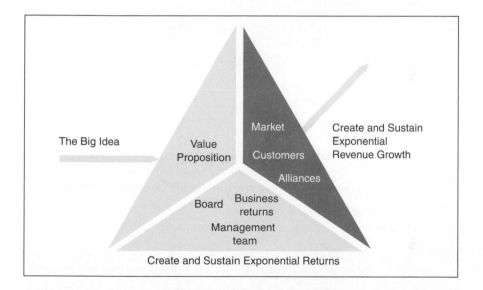

Exponential revenue growth is the distinguishing characteristic of Blueprint Companies. Creating and sustaining exponential revenue growth are often the hardest part of building a business. It's not so difficult to find great teams who knew how to spend and investors who knew how to invest. Developing markets, customers, and alliance partners, however, is the much more challenging part. When we examined the Blueprint Companies to find the common essentials of revenue-building, we identified three.

Blueprint Companies exploit a high-growth market segment. These market segments exist in mature and new industries. As we

51

have seen, almost as a subtheme throughout the research for this book, the law of disproportionate effects is again true with markets. Over two-thirds of the Blueprint Companies are in one-third of the industries. The top three industries are Specialty Stores, Property and Casualty Insurance, and Health Care Facilities. Contrary to popular perceptions, technology industries do not generate the highest number of Blueprint Companies. As we find in Chapter 3, important lessons can be learned about why certain service industries generated the highest number of Blueprint Companies.

To achieve their exponential revenue growth, Blueprint Companies have built a deep relationship with a special set of their best customers, called here *Marquee Customers*. Marquee Customers are generally big, prestigious, smart firms that literally uplift the revenue of the up-and-coming Blueprint Company. They help the young company define its product, define its value proposition, and then, when the bond is made, help them generate exponential revenue growth by buying their products and services in a big way. They are more than important customers. They serve as an extension of the Blueprint Company's sales force by *selling* to their peers.

As we studied the Blueprint Companies, we saw that their exponential revenue growth *per Marquee Customer* is the underlying driver for exponential revenue growth. A company cannot win enough new customers every year to create exponential revenue growth, as we learn in Chapter 4. This kind of growth has to start with current customers. Therefore, it starts with maximizing per-customer revenues across a relationship lifecycle, starting early and continuing over the long term.

When Blueprint Companies were small, they needed help to break into a new market and gain credibility with their Marquee Customers. While alliances are difficult to execute, many of these companies executed alliances early and leveraged them as they scaled to $1 billion revenue. This kind of asymmetric alliance relationships we call *Big–Little Brother alliances*—our topic in Chapter 5—and innovation industries, in particular, executed this essential.

Chapter 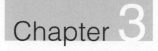 3

Exploit a High-Growth Market Segment

■■■■■■

Are we at the right place?

If you are looking for the product lines that create the greatest number of Blueprint Companies, do not expect to find routers, wires, high-speed chips, modems, and hard drives among the mix. Rather, the components you would likely find have names like Olivier, Absolu, and Duraclear. Not to mention Ruffoni, Krups, and Jardin Potager.

What kind of high-tech machines are these? They are not, as it turns out. These are just some of the cooking and houseware brands that live under the mighty roof of Williams-Sonoma, the $2.7 billion sales retail powerhouse—and the number 204 Blueprint Company.

But why would glassware and pots and pans be more representative of a Blueprint Company than the components of the high-tech communications revolution?

Well it came as a surprise to us as well. When we added up the total number of Blueprint Companies by industry, the Specialty Retail Store industry was far away number one, with 18 companies. Second was Property & Casualty Insurance, with 15 companies. Absent from the top of the list was Telecommunications Services—the Internet! In other words, cyberspace, for all its hype over the last 10 years, has not produced nearly as many Blueprint Companies as one would think (see Table 3.1).

TABLE 3.1

Top Blueprint Industries

Industry	Number of Blueprint Companies
Specialty Stores	18
Property & Casualty Insurance	15
Health Care Facilities	11
Data Processing & Outsourced Services	10
Health Care Services	10
Regional Banks	10
Apparel Retail	9
Real Estate Investment Trusts	9

Source: Standard & Poor's Compustat, Blueprint analysis

We believed there had to be important lessons to be learned about why so many Blueprint Companies grew in these somewhat unexpected industries: market structures, common success patterns, and cross-industry application of skills to name a few. To identify these lessons, we needed to interview the Blueprint leaders of each of these top industries.

Service industries in the United States have exhibited a track record for repeated Blueprint Company growth.

America's #1 Blueprint Industry: Specialty Retail Stores

As we look at the companies fueling America's growth, we find that Specialty Stores take the honors as number one. What are specialty stores? They are omnipresent retail chains that sell anything from tire jacks and sparkplugs in one case, office supplies in another, or kitchenware in a third. There has been a revolutionary proliferation of these retailers in the last decade, and, as we will explain, it is not only due to smart marketing and an inflow of consumer dollars. It is also part of a technological revolution in computers, product scanning, satellite-sent data, and real-time tracking of inventory that has made massive retailing possible.

By year-end 2004, U.S. publicly traded Specialty Stores accounted for $187 billion revenues. They were in the top 15 percent of industries for size.[1] The top four Blueprint Company gorillas in specialty retail are AutoZone, AutoNation, Office Depot, and Staples.

By examining the list of top Blueprint Companies in this industry, it is apparent that they typify two groupings of value-proposition platforms: the Niche Shaper and the Category Killer. The top six companies in this industry are Category Killers: automobile dealers and parts, office supplies, home furnishings, and pet care as shown in Table 3.2.

Autos and Auto Parts

Why are autos and auto parts a hot market segment? Because the United States is the world's largest retail auto market in annual sales of new vehicles. Moreover, the mid-1990s were a period of transformation for the retail suppliers of automotive parts and the retailers of used cars.

Gone are the days of the independent auto parts stores that generated sufficient revenue to be included in the upper echelon of their field; the enormous inventory of parts required by American consumers for their foreign and American cars is too huge for independent stores to keep up. On a broad level, the fortunes of the auto supply industry are driven by economic factors that determine consumer propensity to buy new or used cars. Beyond the primary demand for parts, cars have become more complex. Consumers redirected their automotive maintenance to garage mechanics, thereby leading the retailers to enter into the services business. Today AutoZone is the largest automotive parts retailer along with another Blueprint Company, O'Reilly Automotive. They are among the top Specialty Store Blueprint Companies.

As in automotive parts, automotive retailing throughout the world underwent a rapid transformation in the 1990s. The widely

TABLE 3.2

Top Blueprint Specialty Stores

Rank	Company	State	Year at $1B Revenue
42	AutoZone Inc.	Tennessee	1992
59	AutoNation Inc.	Florida	1996
92	Office Depot Inc.	Florida	1991
98	Bed Bath & Beyond Inc.	New Jersey	1997
129	PETsMART Inc.	Arizona	1995
149	Staples Inc.	Massachusetts	1993
165	Pier 1 Imports Inc.	Texas	1997
187	O'Reilly Automotive Inc.	Missouri	2001
193	Tiffany & Co.	New York	1997
204	Williams-Sonoma Inc.	California	1998
230	Linens 'N Things Inc.	New Jersey	1998
282	Tractor Supply Co.	Tennessee	2002
305	Claire's Stores Inc.	Florida	2000
345	Guitar Center Inc.	California	2002
362	Michaels Stores Inc.	Texas	1995
368	Regis Corp./MN.	Minnesota	2000
384	Hollywood Entertainment Corp.	Oregon	1999
386	TBC Corp.	Florida	2001

Source: Standard & Poor's Compustat, Blueprint analysis

fragmented retail structure gave way to larger consolidated dealer-ships. While demand for cars was relatively flat, most of the attention was on the rise of the superstore chains that assembled an extensive line of new and used cars in a customer-friendly environment. The superstore chains, such as AutoNation, are focused on mass merchandising as a category-killer concept.

Office Supplies

The big giants of specialty stores are not just in the automotive industry; they are also in office supplies. Two of the biggest players are super-retailers: Staples and Office Depot.

When we caught up with Tom Stemberg, Founder and Chairman Emeritus of Staples, he explained that he and his founding partner came out of the supermarket business. It just made sense to them to have shopping carts and wide aisles, and lots of "produce" to choose from. The real epiphany, he says, was realizing that people who wanted to stock their offices had to go to several stores— a stationery store for paper, a computer store for hardware and software, a wholesale club for supplies, an office-products store for office equipment, even a grocery store to buy paper towels and coffee. Why not put these products in one place?

As in the other category-killer success stories, the Staples founding team understood the size of the opportunity before them and the potential demand of a big market driven by a huge unmet need. They also understood that they competed against established companies, either by virtue of concept or execution, and that they could destroy them. Generally speaking, the founders of this business had a keen sense of supply chain management.

"We spent a lot of time" Stemberg said about learning unmet needs, "doing underground work to understand early on that the market wasn't served—talking to small business customers and playing purchasing agent, for example. It was clear to us there was a huge opportunity."

The Staples value proposition was a full selection not by what the channels sold, but what the customer used. "We put that under one roof and at about half the price," he noted.

Technology then and now has facilitated continued growth and productivity, which has allowed these retailers to share reduced costs with customers in the form of lower prices. It also allowed Staples to change its value proposition by making the experience easy—choosing products, checkout, and so on—and providing better service. Staples was the first to let customers order over the Internet while in the store (and have it delivered to their home or to the store). As Stemberg said emphatically, "There would be no superstore without technology."

Staples benefited from the technology revolution in other ways. "As PCs came into the market place with printers and as prices became much more accessible below $1,000, it was not about sell-ing technology; more importantly it was about [selling] the con-sumables the technology consumed," Stemberg explained. "We experienced a geometric growth in consumables—paper, ink jet cartridges, disks, to name a few."

In the future, Stemberg predicts that there will be fewer Cate-gory Killers than there have been in the past. After all, there are far fewer inefficient categories left. Some services are still being (or will be) inefficiently run, however, and these will provide niche opportunities.

Stemberg believes that Staples will be an even larger Blueprint Company 10 years from now. Yes, big-box retailers have not been very successful in transplanting themselves overseas. Staples, however, with a global perspective and shrewd businesspeople, may break the mold. "Besides," he said, "places like China will bring prices down even further, and that will only give Staples more bargains to offer the customer."

Cocooning at Home: In Search of Unique Value

Not all Blueprint Companies are superstore chains with lower prices with lower costs. Some base their value proposition on high prices in order to achieve higher margins.

The home furnishings market is as varied as the goods that it sells, and that means everything from kitchenware to linens and lamps. While discount and department stores stock a variety of items at lower prices, specialty retailers target upscale customers who want quality merchandise that is unusual, distinctive, and found nowhere else.

One such company, Williams-Sonoma, which includes Pottery Barn, Pottery Barn Kids, West Elm, and Hold Everything, has become synonymous with home furnishings. As Howard Lester, Chairman of Williams-Sonoma, recounted some American busi-ness history, setting the scene for his own business:

> In order to understand the specialty retail industry, you need
> to look back in time. In the '40s and '50s we built the freeway

system in America, which led to shopping center development. Developers had an idea to get big department stores as anchor tenants and leave space in the middle for specialized stores. As department stores grew nationally, along with the real estate industry, they started to dilute their brand. Over time, the specialty retailers started picking up categories from the department stores. And that provided a huge opportunity to create businesses in niches—shoes, clothes, and home goods, to name a few.

When Lester started looking for such a niche opportunity in 1978, he noticed the absence of a national kitchenware retailer. "There were 7,000 little cookware shops," Lester recalled. "Williams-Sonoma defined lifestyle stores that were aspirational. We wanted to be placed in malls by the couture stores—not the food court; to be associated with the great brands for the well-to-do customer that lived the aspirational lifestyle. In that I saw an opportunity to be a national brand."

Lester knew his company had to move quickly. He felt that if it could build 50 stores in the right locations, no one could catch Williams-Sonoma. Later, as part of Williams-Sonoma's growth strategy, it acquired Pottery Barn from the Gap. True to form, the Williams-Sonoma team redefined the Pottery Barn market niche. At the time, Pottery Barn was serving first-time urban apartment dwellers. "We totally redefined Pottery Barn," Lester explained, "first with a catalog and then with a design store. Everything in the store had a similar look versus a different selection of goods that didn't go together. We tried to offer one standard of quality to capture the imagination of the younger midmarket customer who wants to be tasteful. We were the first to bring fashion to the home, and it was that environment that was fresh and new and the availability of the real estate in the malls that helped us to grow."

Lester believes that the future niche segment of the specialty retail industry will not see the growth rate it enjoyed in the 1960s and 1970s. The megatrend that started in the 1950s and boomed through the 1970s and 1980s is slowing. Part of the reason is that the price of entry is much greater today. "In the early days, retailers could shop the world for the right combination of imported products," he highlighted. "But when the Category Killers arrived, you couldn't sell commodity goods any longer." To differentiate themselves, Williams-Sonoma and other niche players had to design and control the distribution of their own merchandise. This allowed them to price the goods to market. Lester shared how Pottery Barn controls its supply chain. "For example," he said, "at Pottery Barn we design everything. We get more quality because we cut out the middleman. Furthermore, two-thirds of our manufacturing is offshore. It's not so much about cost savings; it's about the best place to get the products made. When we need a certain kind of quality, we go to Europe. On the other hand, we do our cookware domestically."

Just as with the Category Killers, technology plays an important role in the distribution and supply chain of the Niche housewares players. "If you can operate with 20 percent less inventory or 60 days less manufacturing time, that is huge leverage," admitted Lester.

While the Category Killers have yet to make their mark overseas, Lester believes that specialty retailers have great opportunities internationally. "There are two huge shopping centers being built in London that are developing American-style leases," he explains. "American REITs [real estate investment trusts] will look abroad and will bring American-style leasing to these malls along with American retailers as tenants." Of course, international markets have their own risks. Lester believes we have a lot to learn about the demographics because these countries don't enjoy the broad middle class that we have in America.

The #2 Blueprint Industry: Property & Casualty Insurance

The United States has the largest and most advanced insurance industry in the world. Fire, marine, and casualty insurance companies account for an estimated one-third of the insurance industry's premiums. The Property & Casualty industry revenues in 2004 totaled $271 billion, which positioned this industry in the top 10 of 130 industries in terms of size.[2] Relative to the Blueprint industry list, Property & Casualty is ranked as the number-two Blueprint industry with 15 Blueprint Companies (see Table 3.3).

Despite the opportunities for global expansion, the industry found the 1990s to be plagued by a decrease in demand and a series of catastrophic events such as hurricanes and earthquakes that undermined growth and profits. Already struggling, the industry incurred extraordinary expenses from the September 11 terrorist attacks.

Two important keys to success in this industry during the 1990s were increased sophistication of sales approaches along with

TABLE 3.3

Top Blueprint Property & Casualty Companies

Rank	Company	State	Year at $1B Revenue
32	Cincinnati Financial Corp.	Ohio	1990
47	AMBAC Financial GP	New York	2003
53	MBIA Inc.	New York	2000
83	21st Century Insurance Group	California	1992
104	Mercury General Corp.	California	1997
106	Erie Indemnity Co.	Pennsylvania	2002
168	Berkley (WR) Corp.	Connecticut	1995
176	Old Republic International Corp.	Illinois	1986
266	Markel Corp.	Virginia	2000
277	State Auto Financial Corp.	Ohio	2003
292	First American Corp./CA	California	1992
311	Commerce Group Inc./MA	Massachusetts	2000
328	Fidelity National Financial Inc.	Florida	1998
350	Selective Insurance Group Inc.	New Jersey	2000
357	LandAmerica Financial Group	Virginia	1998

Source: Standard & Poor's Compustat, Blueprint analysis

corporate-wide focus on the customer. Insurance companies also realized significant cost reductions and improved customer service through automation technologies, which improved customer service, reduced errors, improved delivery time, and reduced human intervention. This was built on new computing systems, software engineering tools, multimedia training tools, and satellite-based delivery systems.

Based in Columbus, Ohio, State Auto Financial (STFC) is a leading provider of personal and commercial insurance products across 28 states. It is also a Blueprint Company having achieved over $1 billion revenue in 2003. State Auto's financial performance was recently recognized by A. M. Best Company, the industry's foremost authority on insurers' financial strength and stability. State Auto Mutual (parent of STFC) is one of only 15 insurance companies in the United States that has earned Best's highest rating of A+ (Superior) every year since the rating system began in 1954. As a result, we sought out Robert Moone, Chairman and Chief Executive, for his perspectives about why his industry is the number-two Blueprint industry.

Moone's belief is that a lot of the success stories in the insurance field resulted from an implosion of the industry; that is, a tremendous amount of consolidation. While the industry is easy to get into, the tough part of the business is to grow and be profitable simultaneously.

Given his 40 years in the industry, Moone can articulate the very cyclical and quite predictable pattern of the insurance industry:

> Using the metaphor of a clock face, we can see that, today, the industry has come full cycle, to "high noon," as companies are making great returns on their investment income and underwriting operations. However, we have been in this situation before. Since there are so many insurance companies [about 3,500] and competition is intense, some management teams will decide that their best strategy is to grow by being irrationally aggressive on price and terms and conditions. This inevitably leads to a market that is intensively com-

petitive and, in my opinion, ultimately not beneficial to any constituency.

As the hour hand turns toward six o'clock the industry profit deteriorates quickly. This happened in the late '90s when the industry hemorrhaged red ink. At some point, companies realize that this approach is not sustainable and the industry once again turns toward the fundamentals of good business. I suspect that most industries have a pricing cycle, but the intensity of these variations in the insurance sector is nearly unique. An example of this happened in 2001, when many companies facing huge underwriting losses were forced to increase prices in the commercial segment by as high as 35 percent or more. Simultaneously, certain lines or classes of business were being abandoned. This is not a positive model for the industry or the insuring public.

What makes State Auto different through these cycles? Moone sees that its approach never changes:

No constituency is well served by an insurance company flirting with insolvency. For State Auto, we have three basic principles, like a three-legged stool. I actually have one in my office! These three principles are making money from underwriting operations, achieving revenue growth, and being a low cost provider.

As Moone headed for an employee meeting, he expanded on what he meant by the three legs:

1. *Make money from operations.* We sell insurance products at a price level and with terms and conditions that we believe will cover the cost of claims and expenses, all the while providing a profit margin for shareholders. To achieve this goal, we have a very good actuarial team that looks at trends and determines the price levels we'll need going forward. Also, every second week we meet as a senior management committee to look at pricing for every line of insurance [15 lines

per state across 26 states] to satisfy ourselves that pricing is correct for every line in every state.

2. *Become a low cost provider.* We have to be very efficient in the way we deliver our product. We are currently among the lowest cost providers as measured by expense ratios, but aim to improve that ratio even more. How we do that is the utilization of technology. The days of agents submitting paper applications and the company entering that data into the issuance system are gone. The redundancy and opportunity for errors of the old model does not promote the efficiency we demand and that our customers deserve. We have become a recognized leader in Information Technology and how its applications translate into better relationships with the agents. We are even considering the possibility of delivering policy information to our policyholder customers electronically. That is just one more logical step in introducing Internet technology to reduce costs.

Another way we avoid costs is to not become bloated with management. We strive to have only five layers of management from the CEO to entry-level positions. We are proud that today we actually have six fewer employees than we had five years ago even though revenues have almost doubled and this was accomplished without violating our legacy of having no employee layoffs.

3. *Achieve revenue growth.* We grow two ways, organically and through mergers and acquisitions. We have a single distribution system: the "independent-agency system." As a consequence we have a bifurcated customer in the form of the policy holder and the insurance agent. We have added to the number of agencies, now 3,200 agencies with 22,000 agents representing us today. We've also increased the number of operating states up from 17 at the time of the IPO in 1991, to 28 by the first quarter of 2006.

We do not operate in a vacuum, so when a market becomes soft we will decrease our prices but never down to the point of knowingly selling at a loss. As a consequence, we don't have to have wild fluctuations in pricing. During soft-market cycles, we are willing to have modest growth since we realize that other companies can't sustain both low prices and loose underwriting standards. Thus, the market cycle will ultimately return to a period of greater emphasis on profit, which favors our strategy of strength, stability, and consistency.

Robert Moone explained that State Auto's personal-lines target market is the "Prime of Life" policy holder—that is, those drivers and homeowners age 45 or over. That segment currently represents over 40 percent of STFC policy holders. The company strives to develop family accounts with multiple policies and, in fact, has found that customer loyalty increases exponentially with the number of policies.

The other way the company is growing is to diversify from a predominantly personal lines position to one of greater balance with commercial lines. They are targeting commercial lines products for small/medium businesses such as property, general liability, workers compensation, and theft. As the industry consolidates, State Auto has made four acquisitions for $400 million of premium in order to expand and gain market share in additional states.

In the future, Moone sees the amount of consolidation in his industry increasing. One driver of this trend is technology. "In order to survive and compete in this industry, regardless of scale, companies need to have the latest technology required to maintain their businesses," he observed. "Thus it is likely that some smaller companies will need to find partners to spread these technology costs over a bigger base."

Regarding State Auto's growth as a Blueprint Company, the baby-boomer generation continues to play a big part. "In America, every seven seconds someone turns 50. While we have penetrated the baby boomer market, we have lots of opportunity for new customers, as does everyone else," said Moone.

Another Top Blueprint Industry: Regional Banks

Regional banks comprise another fast-growing Blueprint group. While there are many regional bank success stories over the last 20 years, none is more satisfying than Fifth Third Bancorp, which is not only a Blueprint Company, but also the highest market cap regional bank in our group (see Table 3.4).

If you ask George Schaefer, Fifth Third Bancorp's CEO, the reasons for the bank's success, he will politely acknowledge the work of his predecessor, Clement Buenger, who took the helm in 1981. "Buenger," explained Schaefer, "had a background in life insurance sales and brought a salesperson's ethic to Fifth Third. That meant that Buenger expected the company's employees to get out on the streets and *sell*. Buenger himself worked 10- to 12-hour days and expected his managers to do the same. He even made cold calls on prospective clients. Buenger also brought uncompromisingly high standards to Fifth Third: Shaky loans—the kind that brought down much of the industry during the S&L Crisis of the late 1980s—were not permitted."

TABLE 3.4

Top Blueprint Regional Banks

Rank	Company	State	Year at $1B Revenue
33	Fifth Third Bancorp	Ohio	1994
58	Synovus Financial	Georgia	1996
84	Commerce Bancorp	New Jersey	2002
121	North Fork Bancorporation	New York	2000
127	BB&T Corp	North Carolina	1995
162	Hibernia Corp	Louisiana	1998
175	UnionBancal Corp	California	1989
181	TCF Financial Corp	Minnesota	1998
306	BankNorth Group Inc	Maine	1999
316	Westcorp	California	2001

Source: Standard & Poor's Compustat, Blueprint analysis

In the early 1990s, the combination of a fired-up sales force, high standards, and Ohio's relatively open banking laws made Fifth Third Bank grow fast. Little wonder that in 1991 *Fortune* called Buenger "one of the best acts in the business."[3]

Schaefer revealed how Fifth Third created organic growth from its acquisitions. "A substantial amount of our growth has come since 1980, when we began expansion through both acquisition and organic growth utilizing our four lines of business. These lines are:

- *Retail business.* Fifth Third takes deposits, makes loans, and issues credit cards.
- *Commercial and corporate lines of business.* Main businesses are lending, cash and treasury management, and international services for middle market companies.
- *Investment advisory business.* Fifth Third has a team of money managers who handle $35 billion in assets.
- *Transaction processing business.* Fifth Third is a huge merchant acquirer, currently the fourth largest processor of credit card transactions in the United States. And Fifth Third leverages its own infrastructure and expertise to run ATM networks for 1,500 other banks. All in all, the company manages 12 billion electronic transactions annually. This last business is one that really sets Fifth Third apart from almost all other regional banks."

Staying close to the customer is critical. "If you bank with us in Louisville, Kentucky, you'd think the decisions are made locally, and the local president is the bank president," said Schaefer, "and you'd be right. Everyone in Louisville reports to the local president, so we really are a community bank. That way everyone is connected to the local customers and community. We have a local board for each of the banks." To make this happen, Schaefer described Fifth Third Bancorp's approach. "We copied what had originally been the Banc One concept of having separate banks in each market with their own financial metrics. Today we have 17 banks. While they may be measured separately, they all use the same back office operations."

A distributed corporate structure, with a common back office, can be a powerful enabler for customer focus. Along with the right metrics and aligned incentives, Fifth Third Bancorp illustrates the impact of a customer-centric corporate structure.

And the future? Schaefer sees that while the banking industry will be tougher in the next 10 years, due to heightened regulatory demands, Fifth Third will benefit from the great consolidation that is expected in the business. "You would be amazed at the cash still in use today," he said. "To earn the right to handle an individual's total financial needs, the basic approach *of taking care of the customer* is still the best. When you sit with the customer, they tell you what they want. What they want is pretty basic: a good positive relationship, a good positive experience, and their phone calls returned."

The Big Picture: Lessons from America's Top Markets

Powerful lessons can be derived from what top leaders have shared with us about why certain industries form the backbone of the Blueprint Company set:

1. *Most of the Blueprint Companies are growing in mature markets, not newer industries such as Internet retail.* This may seem counterintuitive, and it is. These mature industries represent huge markets: automotive, office supplies, home furnishings, financial services, and insurance. For the focus of this chapter, we chose not to detail other top industry groups such as health care and real estate but the market profile is similar.

   Do not assume that just because these markets are large and mature there is no room to grow a Blueprint Company. We did not see that behavior in the past nor are we seeing it today. Within the $187 billion Specialty Store industry, in 2004, there are 26 growth companies between $60 million and $1 billion revenues. Similarly in the $281 billion Property & Casualty Insurance industry, there are 39 companies, some of which have the potential to grow to $1 billion revenue.[4] The most successful Blueprint Companies focused their efforts on recognizing an ownable market space by discovering a desirable target and distinctly addressing unmet needs.

The Category Killer superstore chains became a segment unto themselves. Even the superstores focused on large market segments. In Staples' case, it focused on small and medium businesses. It located its stores in places convenient for businesses to access and carried a full product line to offer customers one-stop shopping along with significant savings, compared to shopping at multiple specialty supply stores.

In contrast, the home furnishing market enabled a number of companies to achieve $1 billion revenue by specializing in upscale customers with highly differentiated products. Witness Williams-Sonoma, a good example of a company drilling deep into an existing market that others serve more broadly. Williams-Sonoma's upscale value proposition and customer experience allows it to command a premium price and generate customer loyalty.

Tom Stemberg, Chairman Emeritus of Staples, is now with Highland Capital Partners. He summed up the concept of identifying markets quite well: "Very few things replace great markets that are growing with an adequate margin structure. Therefore, with a more efficient value chain, you can generate higher margins. All things being equal, a big market with unmet needs is priority one." This line of thinking seems almost too simple when you compare it to how the Shapers of a New World look at market opportunities. But it is just as powerful a business-building screen.

2. *Top Blueprint Companies used best management practices and technologies to stay close to their customers.* Even large insurance companies used the latest in market research and product innovation to develop niche-oriented products for

specific market segments. You might think these marketing techniques were reserved just for high-end retailers. One of State Auto's differential advantages to their agencies and agents was their leadership in deploying automated systems.

A distinguishing characteristic of these service companies was a business model that could scale with increased locations so that the company could be physically close to customers. Whether regional banks bought up smaller ones and added intangible value to achieve returns or retail stores expanded locations, being physically close to the customer was a hallmark of these companies. Even though resources are physically close, there is an "aggressive sales" culture that cuts across these service companies. Surprisingly, the sales culture of these Blueprint Companies was imported from other industries. For example, Staples and Fifth Third Bancorp imported their sales culture, through their leaders, from the insurance industry.

3. *Exponential revenue growth requires multiple product lines or service offerings.* Williams-Sonoma is a classic example of a company that leveraged multiple brands and shopping channels to address customers. Not satisfied to rest on its laurels, Williams-Sonoma extended the core brand into furniture and created a home furnishings portfolio to propel growth that includes Pottery Barn, Pottery Barn for Kids, West Elm, and Hold Everything. The different brands allow better marketplace coverage from a pricing and market coverage perspective (for example, home furnishings at Williams-Sonoma are premium price while they are more affordable at Pottery Barn), a style standpoint (Pottery Barn's comfortable décor is in sharp contrast to the minimalist stylings of West Elm), and drilling deep into a vertical space (storage is but one of many needs Pottery Barn addresses while it is the sole focus for Hold Everything).

For AutoZone, it was about providing not only replacement parts but upgrades, as well. As cars became more com-

> Blueprint Companies determined product line extensions by identifying unmet needs associated adjacent to their core value proposition.

plex, these retailers moved with customer needs and offered services to install the parts that they had just acquired. For PETsMART, it was about new services offerings beyond pet supplies such as Grooming Salon and PETsHOTEL.

4. *Partnering with suppliers to lower cost for product delivery, but also product differentiation.* In the 1980s, manufacturing was reengineering itself with just-in-time processes; large superstores did likewise in the 1990s. As stores became technologically advanced, they drove prices down, not just by higher volumes, but by becoming technically savvy with their suppliers. In late 2003, AutoZone, and other superchains in other industries aimed to link their suppliers electronically, eliminating paper and documents. It also pushed heavily into radio frequency identification tags (RFID) for inventory tracking.[5] Large superstores utilized the latest management and technology innovations in order to keep costs and prices down. This was core to AutoZone's value proposition— everyday low prices with a current inventory of a broad range of products.

As Joe Scarlett, CEO of Tractor Supply, shared with us regarding supplier partnering: "We like to serve as the test kitchen for our suppliers. We partner with our suppliers to offer our customers differentiated products that better fit with their lifestyle and offer unique quality and benefits from the superstores. We listen to our customers."

5. *Import the talents and lessons from adjacent industries.* We have heard two compelling stories of culture transfer during our interviews that seem counterintuitive (because many believe their situation is unique). First, Fifth Third Bancorp applied

the aggressive sales culture from the insurance industry to a more conservative banking culture. The resulting culture led to top revenue growth with a highly conservative cost culture. Not what you would expect of an aggressive sales culture. Second, Staples applied the principles of the super-market industry to their situation.

If Services Are Where the Cash Is, Where's the Flash?

There is a lot of innovation underlying America's services industries and Blueprint Companies. But America is known for shaping a new world—biotechnology, specialty chemicals, pharmaceuticals, Internet retail, software, and semiconductors to name a few. Where are they and how many are they?

As we built our Blueprint list, we found upwards of 10 percent of our 387 companies (or over 60) in these cutting-edge industries.

A Lot of Sizzle

And what about the vaunted members of the Internet group of companies? Priceline.com, eBay, and Amazon.com are certainly well-known names, and grace more than their share of magazine covers but, as a group, the Internet-retail industry only accounts for these three Blueprint Companies.

Easy Rider

Do you ever feel you are traveling to the beat of a different drummer? A total of 25 industries had only one Blueprint Company. They include aerospace and defense, retail drugstores and metal and glass container industries. Meanwhile 26 industries, ranging from environmental services to commercial printing to home entertainment software, had two.

In the motorcycles manufacturers industry, Harley-Davidson is the sole Blueprint Company.

These "lone" examples (just one or two in each industry) show that if you have a distinctive value proposition, you can ride alone.

■■■■■■

Chapter Summary

Key Points
- While Blueprint Companies developed across all economic sectors, Consumer Discretionary and Information Technology (IT) were the dominant sectors for the number of Blueprint Companies created.
- Blueprint Companies can be created across any industry. That being said, the odds are disproportionate. Retail Specialty Stores, for example, has a history of the highest number of Blueprint Companies because the market is large and highly segmented. Motorcycle manufacturing, on the other hand, does not support this type of market structure.
  - Two-thirds of industries accounted for one third of Blueprint Companies created.
  - One-third of industries accounted for two-thirds of Blueprint Companies created.
- America's largest markets, which are highly segmented, are prime industries for the growth of a high number of Blueprint Companies.
- The most successful companies exhibited a process and culture for staying close to their customers. They clearly understood their customers' unmet needs. They priced to value.
- Partnering with suppliers not only lowers the cost for products and services, it can be a source for product differentiation.
- Exponential revenue growth requires a broader product line that addresses multiple market segments. This can be achieved organically or through acquisitions. Williams-Sonoma's acquisition of Pottery Barn is a good example of a

company's applying its market approach to create a new level of customer value.

Unexpected Findings

- Consumer Discretionary sectors actually outranked the tech sector in creating a larger number of Blueprint Companies.
- Of the top 10 industries that accounted for the greatest number of Blueprint Companies, the technology sector was absent.
- Cultures and lessons from other industries can have great impact on companies in adjacent industries. Importing the sales culture from the insurance industry into the banking industry, or the supermarket approach into Category Killers for office supplies, are just two examples from our interviews.

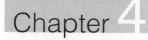

Chapter 4

Marquee Customers Shape the Revenue Powerhouse

■■■■■■

*Do you sell **to** customers or do customers sell **for** you?*

In the late 1980s, Terry Eger, Vice President of Sales at Cisco, was facing a salesperson's greatest nightmare: He was selling a product—routers—that none of his customers had ever seen, wanted, or could even comprehend. "I tried to explain that a router was like a telephone switch that could handle different languages—only this could handle different computer languages," he said. "But it was still tough going."

Fortunately, Cisco had a captive customer application: HP 3000 and 9000 servers could only interconnect with its product. Because of this one application, Cisco got a contract with Boeing. That soon led to other accounts. Eventually, Cisco landed Motorola, with a router that interconnected IBM Local Area Networks (LANs).

This was just the beginning. From there, Cisco landed its first really big customer, Solomon Brothers. The relationship actually began one Friday when a Solomon Brothers representative told Eger that Solomon had decided to go with Cisco's chief competitor. Solomon Brothers preferred Vitalink, Eger was told, because Vitalink had a relationship with Digital Equipment that promised, in the event of a breakdown, four-hour service. "Well how long can you afford to be down?" asked Eger. "Ten minutes," the Solomon representative replied. Eger responded that he could do better than that if he could just have until Monday to prove it.

That weekend, Cisco's engineers went to work. By Sunday night they had tested Cisco's system enough to know that the connection might go down for 26 seconds, under the worst of circumstances, but it would never fail completely. At the meeting on Monday, Eger arrived with Cisco's VP of Technology. They explained what they had to offer—and they won the order. In fact, that was the beginning of a long and profitable relationship with Solomon Brothers, an important relationship that sent Cisco on its way into the ranks of the top Blueprint firms.

> The Cisco team's strength of will and determination exemplifies what is required to uncover higher-order unmet needs. This Cisco example demonstrates that it is critical to move development resources to the front line to quickly respond to customers.

Marquee Customers Shape the Revenue Powerhouse

When I share the three trajectories of the Blueprint Companies (four, six, and twelve years to reach $1 billion revenue), I am often asked how these stellar companies achieved their exponential growth. Let me tell you their secret: It is not just about the number of transactions a company completes; it is not even about just selling hard. Rather, *it is about securing deep relationships with a limited number of valued customers who become the rising tide for exponential revenue growth*. To be sure, they will not account for all revenues. However, at Blueprint Companies, these deep relationships account for a disproportionate share. These are the Marquee Customer™ relationships—like the booster stage on a rocket going into orbit, they supercharge revenue growth.

In sports, marquee players are superstars who lead the rest of the team. Blueprint Companies find that Marquee Customers exist for them as well. Marquee Customers are people or companies with such sparkling reputations that their glow extends to whomever they do business with. Marquee Customers give companies credibility and instant status—sort of like having Michael Jordan or Shaquille O'Neal dropping by your driveway to shoot hoops with you. In the case of Cisco, Terry Eger knew that Solomon Brothers would provide more than sales: Solomon would be the Marquee Customer that could help Cisco establish its credibility.

Marquee Customers help companies in three ways:

1. *Product Consumer: They test and deploy the product.* Marquee Customers give a company's product a test. If the product is deficient, they will say why, and if it is good they will place an order. For instance, when Performance Foods started, Outback Restaurants gave the company a trial run as its primary food supplier to four restaurants. When Outback was satisfied, it told Performance Foods to expand distribution services to more restaurants. Pretty soon, Performance Foods supplied them all. Similarly, eBay invited (and continues to invite) feedback from its top customers.

> **Marquee Customer =**
> Product Consumer ×
> Value Proposition Shaper ×
> Lighthouse Reference

2. *Value Proposition Shaper: They codevelop the value proposition.* Marquee Customers can tell you if your value proposition is good for them, regardless of how good it seems to you—and how to shape it to maximize its value. When eBay launched its business to bring buyers and sellers together, the community of buyers said, "You can be more successful if you broaden your range of goods." Brian Swette, eBay's former COO, revealed, "We have 1,000 key Power Sellers in the Gold Club and another 10,000 to 20,000 in the Silver. These are the people who do the most business with us and we make sure we run everything by them. They get to vote

on all the things that happen on the site. We are really as customer-centric as possible."[1] eBay is prototypical of the process required to enlist a few customers from the mass market to shape each of its lines of business. As the company evolved into other markets, such as small businesses, the company has followed this approach. Today, eBay has over 30 "Voice of the Customer" groups. It calls on these groups to meet with the company when eBay is redesigning its Web site, repricing, or making changes to its service offering.

> Marquee Customers fundamentally help the management team shape the business. Therefore the choice of which customers to sell to is critical to early execution of the company's strategy.

3. *Lighthouse Reference: They serve as a reference and sell to peers.* Marquee Customers act like lighthouses, drawing attention to up-and-coming companies by offering recommendations and references to their peers (no different than tipping a friend off to a good painter or plumber). In this way Marquee Customers become more than a customer; they become an *extension* of the company's salesforce. Ron Markezich, Microsoft's Chief Information Officer, noted that he would not necessarily respond to sales pitches from companies that wanted to do business with Microsoft. Nor did he want to be mailed any more golf club covers that required him to make a telephone call to get the free golf club! He would respond if he heard about the company and its products from one of his peers. "The CIO community is very tight," he told Information Technology Vendors at a Churchill Club forum. "Instead of sending me golf club covers with a coupon for a free golf club, get me a reference from one of my CIO peers. We all have the same problems." Markezich wants to do business with companies that have proven themselves with his peers.[2]

Toby Redshaw, Motorola's Corporate Vice President, IT Strategy, Architecture, and eBusiness, who reports to Motorola's CIO, is a Marquee Customer and serves the role of the lighthouse reference for multiple companies. He explained his motivations this way:

> When a company is solving a critical problem for us, I want them to be successful. I believe they are an up-and-coming company, so creating a long-term win-win relationship is important. I know that when I call my peers in support of these firms, I am helping companies shorten their sales cycle and reduce their sales costs. It's a win-win because I am sending my peers a winning solution that will help them with their problems. In return, I want a preferential seat at the table of the up-and-coming company. When they are successful and I need something, I can call and get what I need before others. I am more than an important customer with a known brand.

Marquee Customer buyers not only give Blueprint Companies "instant credibility," they increase their revenues dramatically. Time and again, as we read through corporate histories, we were struck by the number of times the Fortune 500 heavyweights helped up-and-coming Blueprint Companies. Siebel Systems, for instance, had Schwab as an early Marquee Customer, as well as Cisco, Compaq, and Andersen Consulting. For eBay just over half a million customers make their livelihood from doing business on eBay. This is a very important Marquee Customer segment for this Blueprint Company.

Joe Scarlett, CEO of Tractor Supply, described his company's Marquee Customer relationships: "We have a small percentage of customers who are not only important but very loyal to us. This small percent of customers accounts for a significant percentage of our business." These customers come back time and time again. These are the customers people talk about when they refer to "word-of-mouth advertising."

To understand this unique customer-company relationship, we developed the Revenue-Powerhouse Framework that is shown in

Figure 4.1. This framework is best summarized as an approach to understand and manage predictable exponential revenue growth. It is an iterative process that frames solution creation and delivery in partnership with customers.

> Marquee Customers are not just adequate engines of revenue—they help Blueprint Companies become revenue powerhouses. The more effort a company puts into becoming a revenue powerhouse, the greater the chances of getting to $1 billion revenue.

Blueprint Companies do four things right. First, they secure a customer beachhead. They find a customer champion that buys their product for the first time. Second, they capture the mind of the customer with intangible benefits. Third, they develop Marquee Customers. Fourth, they develop a unique revenue-building approach. They maximize customer life-cycle revenues.

FIGURE 4.1

The Revenue-Powerhouse Framework

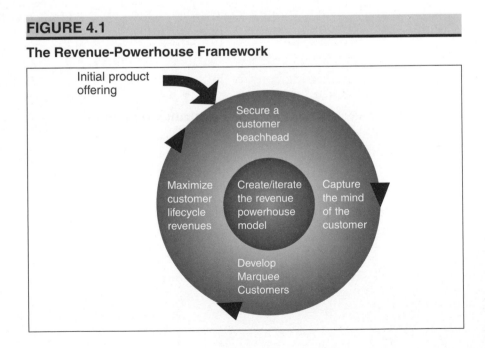

The elements of the Revenue Powerhouse are described in detail in the following sections.

Start by Securing a Customer Beachhead

Early on, a company needs to secure a beachhead with their Marquee Customer from which to launch their long-term relationship. The product does not have to be great, or the final iteration; it just has to give the company a toehold. In Cisco's case, the beachhead was created by the simple fact that HP 3000 and 9000 servers needed a Cisco router to communicate. That was the start; from there, Cisco could extend its product line into other applications.

To secure a beachhead you do not have to have the greatest product at the outset. In fact, Roger McNamee shared this with us:

> Sales teams with "quick and dirty" solutions often win out over those with better solutions. They're not only there first, but they are willing to listen as the customer engages with them about how they can make their solution better. Far better to jump in fast than to create a more sophisticated product that may not be what the customer really wants.

Once Blueprint Companies gain their beachhead, they quickly begin to develop their long-term relationship with their Marquee Customer, that, in turn, shapes them and their success. Here are three strategies that we have seen Blueprint Companies use time and again:

1. *Uncover a latent or unmet need by asking a lot of questions.* By asking deeper questions through exhaustive research and even through sheer intuition, they uncover unobserved needs—needs that exist but are not readily apparent. No one realized that they needed a comfortable place to drop in and drink a cup of coffee—Starbucks' Howard Schultz did. Rigorously asking questions helped identify the underlying intent of these needs as well as understanding the *real* problem (often not the apparent one). This was the case when

Terry Eger met with Solomon Brothers and discovered that
100% availability was the unmet need. Oftentimes this
requires understanding either the customer's attitude
toward a need ("bidding on eBay makes shopping more
fun") or the context of specific situations ("I prefer using
Amazon when I am purchasing a gift") or a combination of
the two. Identifying the customer's unobservable needs
enables the application of the most distinctive and innovative solutions. The Cisco story of Solomon Brothers illustrates an example of the value created by uncovering an
untapped need, then reshaping the solution to meet that
need with a unique solution.

2. *Identify an innovative solution to that unmet need.* Who would
   have thought that airline customers wanted a little TV screen
   in the back of each seat? JetBlue did. But JetBlue not only recognized the significance of the unmet need, it allied itself
   with Harris Corp. and Sextant In-Flight, companies that had
   developed a clever satellite TV service for airliners.[3] Finding
   an unrealized need and coupling it with an innovative solution gave JetBlue a knockout punch.

Probing to identify an important but unmet need unlocks higher-
order needs. Providing unique solutions for these needs can provide a unique win-win opportunity for you and your customer.

---

3. *Implement a vision.* Blueprint Companies do not just look for
   a transactional sale; they fulfill a higher-order need and in
   this way maximize the customer revenues over a period of
   years. Remember when Amazon only sold books? It gained
   early customer trust and has earned customers' permission
   to expand thereby becoming the definitive online shopping
   destination. Similarly Yahoo! began as a mere search engine
   and has now expanded its vision, gaining "permission" to
   become a complete community destination. When Cisco got

its first order from Motorola, it was to connect computers at Motorola's Austin, Texas, facility. Cisco knew that Motorola had more than 100,000 employees spread across four campuses in Illinois, Texas, Florida, and Arizona, along with offices in multiple countries. Cisco's vision was not for a single campus network but a global network for all of Motorola.

In each case, these Blueprint Companies found that their future business with their Marquee Customers would be shaped by what they did at the beachhead. They knew that they had limited resources, but recognized that their investment in customer relationships would have a long-term payoff.

Capture the Mind of the Customer

Blueprint Companies not only act differently than slow-growth companies, they also think differently. They are truly guided by a mission. They have a "big picture" that motivates management, electrifies the brand, and excites customers. Capturing the mind of the customer adds significant value to why they will want to do business with a company for the long haul. It underscores:

- A compelling emotional benefit.
- A roadmap of new services or products to come.
- The company's potential to serve a "greater good."

What is remarkable about the big ideas of Blueprint Companies is that they are synthesized into a simple, crystal clear concept. In fact, it is more than a concept; it is aligned with a higher-order benefit that encompasses functional and intangible benefits. These intangible benefits create permission from customers to rapidly extend and add new products or services and importantly provide endorsement to other customers. This is the highest step on the benefits hierarchy (see Appendix B).

For eBay, the Big Idea is building a global community where buyers and sellers can exchange goods, built on a core value of trust. For Google it is "to organize the world's information and make it universally accessible and useful." (Mary Meeker, Morgan Stanley's Internet analyst, has been calling Google the "eBay of information" for three years. She may be right.[4])

Roger Boeve, Founder and retired CFO of Performance Foods, defined his business as not being in the food distribution business, but being in the service business to be on time with 100 percent order fill. Its restaurant customers count on Performance Foods to provide high quality and consistent services so that it serves fresh food with a minimum of inventory.

The Big Idea is shared by customers. In fact, it not only captures the minds of consumers, but in most cases, their hearts as well. Have you ever noticed that many Harley-Davidson customers wear the company's brand as a tattoo!

> Blueprint Companies used the power of a customer-centric vision to align employees and customer development to be consistent with this focused direction. This vision was a clear articulation of higher-order benefits—a combination of functional and emotional benefits.

Cisco's and Performance Foods' Marquee Customers

To appreciate the importance of a Marquee Customer, consider how Cisco developed one beachhead opportunity into a long-term and very powerful Marquee Customer relationship.

Cisco sold its first product to this Marquee Customer in-the-making with a purchase of less than $1 million. Over the following years, the customer increased their investment in Cisco products and services at an exponential rate. The total investment in Cisco equipment and services is now hundreds of millions of dollars (see Figure 4.2).

Creating Marquee Customers takes time. As Terry Eger and his team sold routers to enterprise campuses, a need to integrate them rose. This required upgrades and additional capabilities. For exam-

FIGURE 4.2

Marquee Customer Life-Cycle Revenue: The Cisco Example

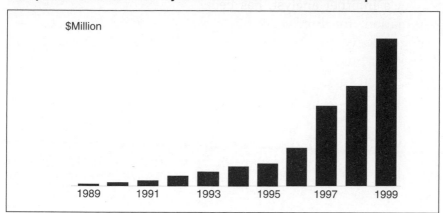

Note: Illustrative customer example.
Source: Interviews

ple, users wanted remote access to the network, so access capabilities needed to be added. In Cisco's case with this customer, it spent four years evolving from selling routers to divisions to selling a global corporate network to the Chief Information Officer (CIO).

In 1993, when this customer made creating a global Internet protocol network a strategic initiative, it agreed to set up a Cisco product-testing lab to test all Cisco's products. In return for early exposure to new products, this customer tested and fed back product requirements for the deployment of Cisco routers in their global network. Over the years, Cisco used this customer lab as a demo center for other customers. This customer often shared their testing results with other Cisco customers who visited their lab. At this point, this customer became a global lighthouse reference for Cisco—a quality Marquee Customer.

Coincidently, this same Fortune 100 Company was a Marquee Customer for Oracle, Dell, and Sun Microsystems. Guess what we found? Their sales to this customer exhibited similar exponential growth rates.

> A company's business model can be seen and its sales effectiveness measured in its exponential revenue growth with each of its Marquee Customers.

Performance Food Group (PFG) is another example of a company tailoring its services for Marquee Customers. PFG markets, processes, and sells food and related products. In 1991, Performance Group formed a Customized Distribution Division to serve Cracker Barrel Old Country Store. The division immediately aligned to provide customized services to Cracker Barrel to achieve operating efficiencies, timely delivery of food, and improved order accuracy—all tailored to Cracker Barrel's menu and operations requirements. To reduce mileage and time, the division aligned distribution locations with restaurant locations. Truck-routing software optimized distribution routes. New systems, utilizing an Internet-based ordering system, gave restaurant managers real-time access to orders, inquiries, and histories. As a result sales grew to 16 percent of total company revenues in 2000.[5]

Since the division's launch, PFG has added Outback Steakhouse, Ruby Tuesday's Restaurants, and Mimi's Café to their list of Marquee Customers. Setting up a division to customize services for a few Marquee Customers is an effective business model to generate a unique customer-centric competitive advantage.

Finding Your Marquee Customer

The concept seems simple, but execution is not. How do you get a Marquee Customer? There was no better way to find out than to ask Marquee Customers and interview companies that are trying to develop them. Finding Marquee Customers has two parts: identifying them and getting access to them.

1. *Identifying Marquee Customers should be obvious to the industry-knowledgeable executive.* Marquee Customers are regarded as:

- The thought leaders of the industry. These customers are not necessarily the largest but are regarded for their innovation and problem-solving skills. They may be identified either by name of company or a leader's reputation within a company.
- Industry giants that drive or set industry-leading standards. Their commitment to a supplier is the testament required for others in the community to follow their lead. For example, being a supplier to Wal-Mart is a testament that these companies are of a price, quality, and supply-chain standard worthy for others to consider.
- Blueprint Companies in-the-making. These become a new generation of Marquee Customers. For example, Siebel sold its sales automation software to Microsoft (which served the role as the Marquee Customer) a few years after Microsoft had become a Blueprint Company.

Executives often underestimate the time needed to develop deep customer relationships. Comparing this cycle to the product-development cycle, which can be much shorter, can be a reality check for managing priorities and lead times.

---

2. *To access Marquee Customers, try to become friends of their friends.* Determine who their advisors are. Get to know them and ask for a recommendation. Go to the professional associations in order to meet their executives.

Clearly, Blueprint Companies developed deep relationships with Marquee Customers so that their customers became their best sales force—a sales force extraordinaire! Unlike the conventional approach to allocate resources broadly, Blueprint Companies moved the executive team, marketing, and the development team to the front line to work with Marquee Customers. They sold a larger promise and realized it by iterating the way solutions were created and delivered in order to meet customer requirements.

Types of Marquee Customers

To find a Marquee Customer, companies must be careful to align themselves with the right kind of business. In pursuing a Marquee Customer, make sure that its appetite for risk versus return is similar to yours.

We have identified four kinds of Marquee Customers that align along the exponential revenue growth curve (see Figure 4.3):[6]

- **First Movers.** A precious few Marquee Customers are *First Movers* in that they like to stay on the cutting edge of innovation. These Marquee Customers know the solution when they see it and manage the higher risk given the potential payoff. They are willing to invest in order to apply the solution. They are often regarded as industry thought leaders.
- **Fast Followers.** Other Marquee Customers do not want to be the first over the edge, but they do want to work with companies that have already stress-tested a product or service. I call them *Fast Followers*—Marquee Customers that rely on the First Movers to pretest cutting-edge technology. They approach the issues just like First Movers, but have a much higher degree of inspection with the implementation. For Cisco, these were customers such as Motorola and Boeing. In the financial industry, Charles Schwab was such a Marquee Customer for Siebel Systems.
- **Mainstream.** These firms want to be sure that the product is proven and has a performance track record. They evaluate the company to ensure it can scale and provide service and innovation that will outpace their future requirements. Innovative banks and insurance companies fit this profile. Mainstream Marquee Customers will not introduce new technologies into the core of their systems unless the product or service is well proven. For Broadcom, the manufacturer of DSL broadband chips for telecom equipment, Nortel Networks was one of these customers.

- **Utilitarians.** Even slower to adopt than Mainstream Marquee Customers are what I call *Utilitarians*. They adopt innovation as long as there are no "smoking craters." They demand rigorous product testing, customer references, and a business case.

We derived this granularity of Marquee Customers after we found a growing frustration in a number of sales teams. Sales executives found customers asking for detailed business cases and references before the company had a chance to build a track record. It was not about what the customer was asking for, it was about timing. The sales executive had not found the first-mover and fast-follower Marquee Customers before finding the Utilitarian customers.

FIGURE 4.3

Marquee Customer Types

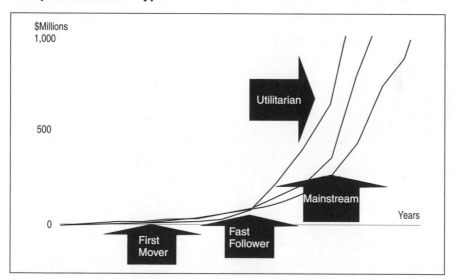

Source: Blueprint analysis

When Marquee Customers test the product and shape the value proposition and provide valuable new customers, the impact is more than 10 + 10 + 10. It is more like $10 \times 10 \times 10$. That's 1,000 versus 30. The *smaller* impact is particularly true when a Marquee Customer does not serve as a lighthouse and does not recommend you to others. This customer may be a big one, may help shape your product or your value proposition, but it is not truly a Marquee Customer. To truly be a Marquee Customer, it must be a lighthouse reference and an extension of your sales force.

The Math of Marquee Customer Life-Cycle Revenues

Now that you know to find a Marquee Customer and build a long-term relationship, there is another important lesson to be derived from Blueprint Companies: They created exponential revenue growth with these customers. Underlying per-customer exponential revenue growth is a set of variables that maximized customer lifecycle revenues.

These variables represent the more blocking-and-tackling aspects of per-customer exponential revenue growth. To identify these variables, let us examine how Microsoft, the number one Blueprint Company, executed them.

1. *Product scalability.* This variable describes the size of the initial product sold—small or large size. Because the customer has a choice of which size to buy, marketing and sales can influence this decision. For example, a Cisco router could scale from small to large. Starbucks lattes can be acquired in the Tall, Grande, or Vente sizes. The price range between the small to large size can be over three times. In contrast, buying donuts come as one size/one price.

   Microsoft launched MS-DOS 1.0 in 1981 with IBM. Besides the upgrades to MS-DOS, Microsoft launched Windows 2.0 in 1987, Windows 3.0 in 1990, and Windows 95 in 1995. Along the way, there were various smaller releases. Microsoft demonstrated with its core operating system dramatic

> **Life-Cycle Revenues =**
> Product Scalability ×
> Revenue per Unit ×
> Number of Customers ×
> Purchase Frequency ×
> New Product Extensions ×
> Geographic Coverage ×
> New Lines of Business

improvements in functions and graphic-user interface capabilities that resulted in a very sophisticated product on the customer's desktop.[7]

For each of its product lines, languages, versions of Microsoft Office, databases, and the like, Microsoft followed a similar approach.

2. *Revenue per unit.* Independent of size, revenue per unit is critical. If the price per unit is low, then volume is more critical in order to generate the revenue required. Discounting at the point of purchase affects this variable. The ability of the sales force to negotiate the best price per unit is critical to maximizing gross margins.

In Microsoft's case, software was priced in the $100 to $500 range. The revenue per unit of software was maximized over the customer life cycle by the sale of upgrades.

3. *Number of customers.* The ability to attract and retain customers varies depending on the value proposition, target market, and effectiveness of the sales force. This variable can have a broad range of outcomes. For Ciena, the maker of optical equipment, Sprint and Worldcom were its two primary customers in 1998.[8]

For Microsoft, it was millions of customers with a PC. Success is measured by share of available customers. To maximize the penetration of software on every PC, Microsoft developed two primary paths to market: the Original

Equipment Manufacturers (OEMs) and the retail market. Microsoft worked with Apple and PC manufacturers to bundle software with new computer shipments. Simultaneously, it pursued retail channels. Both strategies were executed on a global basis.

4. *Frequency of purchases per customer.* If companies have low-priced products, then along with a high number of customers, high frequency of purchase is important to generating high revenues. eBay relies on a high volume of auctions/customer. On the other hand, buying a home at a high price offsets the low frequency of purchase.

   Microsoft approached frequency per customer with two strategies. First, the team quickly focused on diversifying across languages, operating systems, applications, hardware, and books. By focusing on a diversified product line that could be bundled, Microsoft increased frequency and revenue per customer as each one bought multiple products with upgrades over time.

   Second, to recruit enterprise customers who had a large installed base of PCs, in 1992, Microsoft launched an innovative marketing campaign with its Marquee Customers, organized geographically and by line of software. For instance, Telecom Australia, the main supplier of phone services across Australia, standardized Microsoft solutions for Windows on more than 25,000 desktops. At that time, Telecom Australia was one of the largest buyers of Windows in the Southern Hemisphere.[9]

5. *Number of new product extensions.* Maximizing a company's portfolio of products or services increases the number of customers and the revenue per customer. Compare the menu at a Starbucks against a Krispy Kreme store—the diverse versus the narrow. Most Blueprint Companies developed a diverse portfolio over time by introducing a high number of new products per year. Revenue from new products in any one year can exceed current products for high-growth companies.

As Microsoft approached $1 billion revenue, it continued to leverage new products or extensions to fuel exponential growth. In 1989, Microsoft shipped 53 new products or new versions of existing products. Internationally, Microsoft released 256 localized versions of software in 16 languages.[10]

6. *Geographic coverage.* Companies need a diverse geographic coverage to increase the number of customers served or increase the revenue per customer (in the case of serving global corporations). Typically, companies measure this variable as revenue per geography. JetBlue would measure this metric by cities served. For companies with products that are applicable on a global basis, it is number of countries served and the revenue per country.

In 1989, Microsoft's domestic revenues accounted for 57 percent with international sales the remainder.[11]

7. *New lines of business.* Companies expand into new lines of business to grow revenue or create pull for their core business. This variable applies equally to stand-alone and large companies. For example, when Apple became successful with the iPod, it found sales of Macintosh computers increasing. Oftentimes Blueprint Companies made acquisitions to extend their lines of business offerings.

As early as 1983, for instance, Microsoft started laying the foundation for revenue diversification (see Figure 4.4). That year it launched Microsoft Windows, Mouse, and Word. In 1984, MS-DOS became popular as 200 microcomputer manufacturers licensed the system. In parallel that year, File and Word software packages for the Macintosh were developed and Chart and Project for the PC were launched. Word became immensely popular and sold 20,000 copies at $395 per copy.[12] (Software Digest rated Microsoft Word 5.0 as one of the top word processors in 1989.[13]) Also, in 1987, Microsoft acquired Forethought Inc., the developer of PowerPoint.[14]

For Microsoft, being in the hardware business making mice and

FIGURE 4.4

Microsoft Product Lines

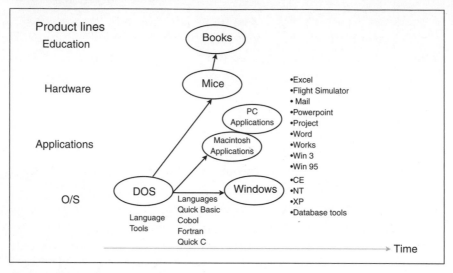

Source: Microsoft annual reports

the like and the publishing business by printing how-to computer books helped software sales and provided new areas of revenue growth. The Microsoft hardware group's principal products were the Microsoft Mouse and the BallPoint mouse pointing devices. Demand for these was linked to the deployment of the Windows operating system, which is enhanced by using a mouse.[15] At that time, Microsoft conducted a survey of users to find that eight of ten Microsoft Mouse owners used their personal computers in the work environment, with the majority being in the engineering and consulting fields. The hardware business continued to blossom as the company sold its one millionth mouse by 1988.[16]

In terms of Microsoft's revenues from its lines of business in 1988, software accounted for 47 percent of revenues, applications 40 percent, and hardware and books 13 percent.[17]

Number-one Microsoft is a classic example of how Bill Gates and Jon Shirley, then President and Chief Operating Officer respectively, were masters at applying a version of this framework (see Table 4.1).

Going to Battle to Win Marquee Customers

When a company is second in its market and is looking at an incumbent with dominant market share, there is only one place to go—into battle to win Marquee Customers. The battle is on the opponent's home turf—to take their Marquee Customers.

In 1987, Microsoft's Excel was the dominant spreadsheet on Apple's Macintosh. However, Excel was *Second-but-Better* compared to Lotus 1-2-3 in the IBM compatible personal computer market. Lotus had 80 percent share of the PC Spreadsheet market.[18] Microsoft had to break the Lotus 1-2-3 dominance in the spreadsheet market: a classic situation for a Second-but-Better.

Scott Oki, then Microsoft's VP Sales, led a taskforce to develop a strategy to break into the PC market with Excel. The plan would

TABLE 4.1

Microsoft Life-Cycle Revenues

Variables	Description
1. Core-product scalability	Evolution of MS-DOS to Windows
2. Number of customers	Bundle software with Apple, IBM, 200+ OEM PC manufacturers
3. Revenue per unit purchased	Add applications, mice, books for each operating system purchase
4. Frequency of purchases per customer	Upgrades and new products
5. Number of new products or extensions	High number of extensions across all products
6. Geographic diversification	Early global coverage to Europe and Asia
7. New lines of business	Diversify from operating systems into applications, hardware, and books

Source: Microsoft annual reports, Blueprint analysis

be to find a way to capitalize on the paradigm shift from command prompts to graphical interface with the release of Windows 3.0. But that was not enough. Oki's taskforce had to capture Lotus's Marquee Customers at the same time. There was a "window" of opportunity.

Microsoft launched a two-pronged attack. One was a grassroots effort to sway users. At the same time, the attack identified corporate customers. An aggressive launch of seminar marketing, demonstrations, and building of an Excel Evangelist team created high awareness and conversion of end users to the new, simpler-to-use Excel.

The challenge was convincing large corporations to convert from their corporate Lotus standard to Microsoft. One such targeted Marquee Customer was 3M. 3M had standardized on Lotus 1-2-3 across all of its 42 divisions as the preferred application to measure financial performance. To roll up the financials across multiple divisions, Lotus had developed, along with 3M, a macro program that would interconnect the divisional spreadsheets into one. This macro was not simple; it was in excess of 500 pages long! Lotus had created a barrier to entry, in partnership with this Marquee Customer (3M). Microsoft could not invest the resources to recreate this macro—the time and cost were prohibitive.

This became a real dilemma for Microsoft because it could not break into 3M without being compatible with 3M's corporate financial system. What could Microsoft do? The Excel team invested six months in creating new technology to convert the Lotus 1-2-3 macros to Excel. The beauty of this approach is that instead of rewriting the macro, the team built a translator that could be applied to any customer situation. As Windows 3.0 was launched and Microsoft could demonstrate its lead with a simple-to-use graphical user interface, the Excel team could now offer their Marquee Customer a compatible migration from Lotus 1-2-3 by coexisting as a corporate standard. Being macro compatible gave 3M a turnkey approach to migrate from Lotus 1-2-3 to Excel. Being a Second-but-Better product gave Excel the edge once the playing field was leveled—and Excel soon became the corporate standard at 3M.

> The battle to win Marquee Customers is one of the most critical battles to be fought by an up-and-coming Blueprint Company.

To win Marquee Customers, the battle planning and execution must occur with focus on the customer. Winning the competition's Marquee Customers is critical to taking share. The Microsoft team demonstrated that breaking down barriers set up by the incumbent was the critical success factor. Product alone was not enough to win.

Revenue Building at Starbucks and Toll Brothers

Along with Microsoft, Starbucks is another six-year trajectory company that applied these variables to maximize customer revenues. In 1992 and 1993, Starbucks launched a three-year store expansion strategy to attract a large number of customers. For each targeted region, Starbucks selected a big city to serve as a "hub" where teams of professionals were located to support the goal of opening 20 or more stores over the first two years. Once stores blanketed the hub, it then opened stores in the smaller, surrounding "spoke areas." By 1995, stores generated an average of $700,000 revenue in their first year, up from $427,000 in 1990.[19] As revenues approached $1 billion, Starbucks had opened 1,412 stores.[20]

The company's retail sales mix was roughly 61 percent coffee beverages, 15 percent whole-bean coffees, 16 percent food items, and 8 percent coffee-related products and equipment. The product mix varied in each store, with larger stores carrying a variety of coffee beans, gourmet food items, teas, coffee mugs, and coffee-making equipment.

With 5 million customers per week patronizing Starbucks stores in early 1998, loyal customers patronized a Starbucks store 15 to 20 times a month, perhaps spending $50 monthly. (I am one of those customers!)

To extend into new geographic markets, Starbucks expanded into licensing agreements for areas in which it did not have store locations. The company had an agreement with Marriott Host International, United Airlines, Horizon Airlines, Barnes & Noble, and Wells Fargo Bank to operate coffee bars in their locations or to have coffee served as part of an airline's service. Internationally, Starbucks' strategy was to license a reputable and capable local company with retailing know-how in the target host country to develop and operate new stores. In some cases, Starbucks entered into joint venture partnerships. Going into 1998, Starbucks was in Japan, Singapore, and the Philippines, and was exploring opening stores in Europe and Latin America.

Through product joint ventures, Starbucks expanded its product line. PepsiCo and Starbucks entered into a joint venture to create new coffee-related products through the Pepsi channels. Sales of the Frappuccino drink reached $125 million in 1997. In October 1995, Starbucks partnered with Dreyer's Grand Ice Cream, another Blueprint Company, to supply coffee extract for a new line of coffee ice cream made and distributed by Dreyer's under the Starbucks brand.[21]

Toll Brothers

Toll Brothers, a leading U.S. builder of single-family homes, made it to $1 billion revenue on the 12-year trajectory by excelling with three of the variables: price per home, number of homes built, and geographic expansion (see Table 4.2). In the late 1990s, the company was the 12th-largest home builder in the nation by sales, and the biggest company involved primarily in the construction of luxury dwellings. Toll, a family-owned and operated company, is distinguished in its industry by a long record of profitability and revenue growth.

Toll Brothers billed itself as a designer of luxury homes, not cus-

TABLE 4.2

Toll Brothers Life-Cycle Revenues

Variables	Description
1. Core-product scalability	Range of homes from $100,000–$500,000
2. Number of customers	• Number of customers in proportion to number of homes built • Targeted the 35–55 age group with high incomes
3. Revenue per unit purchased	High
4. Frequency of purchases per customer	Low frequency
5. Number of new products or extensions	• Limited extensions to standard plans • Bought land during downturns
6. Geographic diversification	• Regionally focused initially • Expanded to a broader set of cities
7. New lines of business	• Focused on home building • Mortgage unit to serve customers buying their homes • Set up a consulting business in 1990 to help other developers with problem projects.

Source: Thomson/Gale Business & Company Resource Center, Blueprint analysis

tom homes. Instead, it offered customers a variety of floor plans with customized options. Thus, Toll effectively brought the efficiencies of the mass homebuilding sector to the luxury segment. Toll could build the luxury homes for less money than custom builders because of its high-volume purchasing power and computerized construction cost controls.

Once the brothers established the Toll Brothers name in an area with their Executive homes, the company would start building its lower-end and high-end models. Its low-end line of houses, which were also considered move-up homes, had 1,700 to 2,000 square feet of space and were usually situated on lots of about 10,000 square feet or less. Dubbed the Glen line, they were priced from $120,000 to $170,000. In contrast, the high-end, or Estate line, of homes were often priced around half a million dollars and ranged in size from 3,000 to 4,500 square feet. They were located on three-quarters to three acres of land and offered such features as two-story foyer entries, curved staircases, walk-in closets, and whirlpool master baths.

Toll managed to boost construction activity during 1995 and increase sales and profits. It accomplished that feat by pursuing the same basic strategy that it had followed for several years: build large numbers of high-quality, upscale homes at the lowest prices, and keep a close eye on costs. By 1995 the average cost of Toll's home line had increased from a range of $175,000 to about $400,000, while its midrange Executive homes were going from about $230,000 to $425,000. Its high-end Estate homes sold for as much as $665,000, or more in some instances. The company also constructed some attached homes, including townhouses, "carriage homes," and "villas" priced from $100,000 to more than $400,000.

Toll geared its homes to high-income move-up buyers between the ages of 35 and 55. That segment of the population continued to post household income gains and was increasing its proportion of national wealth going into the mid-1990s. Furthermore, those buyers were less affected by interest rate volatility because they typically had large amounts of money to put down on a new home (from equity in their previous home). That cash also made it easier for them to qualify for a new mortgage loan.

Encouraged by gains in its core markets in the Northeast, Toll made plans in 1994 to expand out of the Northeast and into Orange County, California, and Raleigh, North Carolina. In early 1995, moreover, Toll announced its intent to expand into Palm Beach County, Florida; Charlotte, North Carolina; and Dallas, Texas.[22]

The company had two side lines of business. The company also maintained a separate mortgage affiliate to serve its clients. Toll began operating a subsidiary called Toll Advisors in 1990. Toll Advisors was set up as a consulting firm to help other financiers and developers work out their difficult development projects.

Tracking to a Trajectory

When you look at the three revenue trajectories to $1 billion revenue, you may think that the probabilities are highest on the twelve-year trajectory, and that's partially correct because creating exponential revenue growth is hard to do. But look at the case studies we just discussed: They each pursued different revenue trajectories (see Figure 4.5).

FIGURE 4.5

Comparative Blueprint Companies

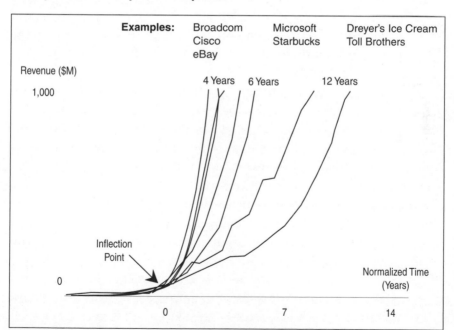

Source: Standard & Poor's Compustat, Blueprint analysis

What are the odds? Are they as dispiriting as one might think?

Of the set of Blueprint Companies we studied, we found that 75 percent of the companies followed one of the three trajectories. The remainder switched between the trajectories as they grew. Of those that followed the trajectories, the odds of making the four-year trajectory were 14 percent, the six-year trajectory 38 percent and the twelve-year trajectory 48 percent.

> Once companies are experiencing exponential growth, they are as likely to make the four- or six-year as the twelve-year trajectory. The odds are better than one might intuit them to be—very good news!

Chapter Summary

Key Points
- Customers that partner with suppliers to shape their company and products are Marquee Customers. They serve a unique and valuable role by:
  - Testing the product and providing requirements feedback.
  - Codeveloping a customer-centric value proposition.
  - Serving as a lighthouse reference—that is, as an extension of your sales force by calling peers and endorsing your product or service.
- Four types of Marquee Customers exist. Each aligns with a phase of the customer life cycle.
- Blueprint Companies develop Marquee Customers to create exponential revenue growth utilizing the Revenue-Powerhouse Framework, which has four fundamental components: (1) secure a customer beachhead; (2) capture the mind of the customer; (3) listen to Marquee Customers to shape the business; and (4) maximize customer life-cycle revenues.

- Securing an initial beachhead is very hard work; it is a test of will. It requires uncovering unmet needs, ensuring consistent delivery of the solution, and extending the frame of reference to create deep customer relationships.
- Capturing the mind of the customer provides an intangible benefit about why customers will want to do business with a company for the long haul. It underscores:
  - A compelling emotional benefit.
  - A roadmap of new services to come.
  - That the company has the potential to serve a "greater good."
- The intangible benefit can provide a customer "sponsorship" by giving permission to rapidly extend and add new products or services. Also, it importantly provides endorsement to other customers.

Unexpected Findings

- Many believe that customers cannot articulate their requirements for breakthrough innovation. Not true. There is a small set of First Movers who understand their unmet needs and options to resolve, and can engage up-and-coming companies that have breakthrough value propositions.
- Many executives underestimate the time required to develop deep Marquee Customer relationships, especially compared to the product development cycle.
- The Marquee Customer who calls peers to spread the good news and good reputation of a supplier is much more powerful than any marketing program or sales pitch. The positive impact on sales cycles and marketing costs is often underestimated.
- The probability of achieving exponential growth on the four- and six-year trajectory is surprisingly better than we thought—*over* 50 percent.

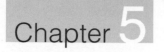

Leveraging Big Brother Alliances for Breaking into New Markets

Who is your ally? Big or Little Brother?

Bill Gates may not need any more awards or honors. But if he does, we have one for him and his company: Microsoft is the all-time number-one Blueprint Company. But as we stand to applaud, it is easy to forget that Microsoft might have meant nothing today if Bill Gates had not had the help of a Big Brother. In Gates' case, it was a company-creating opportunity.

If you remember the late 1970s, and even if you do not, Bill Gates was a young man with a young company in Redmond, Washington: Microsoft. He was trying to develop an 8086 software program and not having much luck. Another software creator, however, in nearby Seattle, Tim Patterson, had it nailed. In fact, in 1979 Patterson created an operating system for the 8086 card, which he called the "Quick and Dirty Operating System."[1]

Meanwhile, mighty IBM, the king of mainframe computer makers, was beginning to realize that the microcomputer business was becoming too big to ignore. IBM had to get into the market—and fast. In 1978, a special task force headed by IBM's Paul Rizzo, then Vice Chairman, assessed how the company could best enter this market. Rather than run the project through the normal channels, Rizzo decided to create a special group in Boca Raton, Florida, to

105

build the first IBM PC. As the IBM engineers brainstormed the new IBM PC, they realized they would need to outsource two key pieces of software: the operating system and the programming languages.

The logical move for IBM was to use the CP/M operating system from Digital Research because it was the standard at the time. Dr. Gary Kimball, a founding father of desktop computing, wrote CP/M—the first mainstream microcomputer operating system. While Kimball had the early lead, two events came to change his momentum and destiny: He was late with operating system upgrades to the Intel 8086 processor and Digital Research did not negotiate business terms with IBM.

Frustrated, IBM turned to Microsoft, which had already provided BASIC and a few other languages to IBM. The engineers at IBM knew Gates and his partner Paul Allen. Did they have an 8086 operating system as well? Gates did not but he knew where to get one. Microsoft promptly acquired all rights to Tim Patterson's software—for $50,000. IBM subjected the operating system to an extensive quality-assurance program. In October 1981, the IBM Personal Computer DOS 1.0 (PCDOS 1.0) was ready for introduction with the IBM PC.

The rest is history. Because Microsoft's agreement with IBM permitted selling the MS-DOS system to other PC computer manufacturers, Microsoft soon shipped its product to almost every PC manufacturer. Within a few years MS-DOS had become the standard. By the time MS-DOS 3.3 came out, Microsoft and IBM were working under their Joint Development Agreement in which Microsoft was IBM's exclusive software distributor.[2]

This Big Brother alliance was one of the critical essentials that enabled Microsoft to break into the new personal computer market. Many may think Microsoft was simply lucky, but from IBM's perspective, it had a gap in a very significant product line opportunity and only one partner got a deserved seat at the IBM table.

Microsoft demonstrated that when a small company enters into a relationship with a big company, an asymmetric relationship is structured. As a result, to provide the ingredients and value to the larger company, the smaller company has to be flexible and fast to respond not only with a product, but to solve for and deliver on the win-win relationship equation.

> The best alliances are formed when Big Brothers have a high need and motivation. When the Little Brother is quick and capable of adapting to the Big Brother's needs, it can become the preferred alternative. Relationships between the companies are as important as the innovation being offered.

If You Can't Do It All, Get a Big Brother Alliance

Building new businesses requires assembling a host of new capabilities such as manufacturing, emerging technologies to complement the core value proposition, channels to market, geographic expansion, and systems integration. Certain companies, especially those requiring exponential growth, require speed and flexibility in order to access the capabilities of others. Creating alliances requires less capital commitment and risk than do acquisitions—a big advantage when the company lacks scale and management capabilities. According to a recent McKinsey study, the market tends to favor alliances in fast-moving, highly uncertain industries.[3] The study found the market richly rewarded alliances in industries such as media, entertainment, and software.

Happy Together

Blueprint Companies abound in "Big Brother–Little Brother" relationships: Microsoft had IBM; Siebel had Microsoft and Andersen; eBay had AOL; Genentech had Eli Lilly; and Yahoo! had AT&T WorldNet. What do these relationships have in common? In each case, the Blueprint Company, the Little Brother, created a company-shaping alliance with an established Big Brother, an industry giant. This relationship helped the Little Brother get on its feet and enter a trajectory for one billion dollars in revenues. Similarly, the Big Brother benefited in a significant way from its Little Brother, often in its help in solving a critical strategic or operational challenge.

> We found this alliance pattern unchanged across boom-and-bust economic cycles. Little Brothers and Big Brothers *need* each other.

The number of alliances formed en route to $1 billion among companies in our dataset was highly variable. Highly volatile industries such as software, semiconductor, hardware, Internet retail, biotechnology, and consumer products are areas where we found asymmetric alliances prevalent.

Knowing that Blueprint Companies succeed in creating and capturing measurable value from alliance, regardless of the industry type or the kind of innovation involved—confirms that Blueprint success is neither random nor the result of luck. Blueprint Companies leverage their success by forming successful alliances.

Execute Moves Aligned to an Alliance Strategy

Alliances, however, are difficult to create—and even more difficult to execute. Most people would guess that half of such alliances fail and, in fact, they are right.[4] Yet the Blueprint Companies executed alliances with a higher success rate. They seemed to understand alliances and make them work. How did they do it?

As we talked with Blueprint Company leaders, we came to see that the "asymmetric" alliance between Little Brother and Big Brother falls into two categories: *business-model* and *revenue-centric alliances*.

Business-Model Alliances optimize the business model. They may focus on the supply of low-cost product or services, fill critical gaps in the product or service offering, or create channels to market. These variations in business-model alliances are discussed in the following sections.

Supply Chain

In many cases, as we saw with Microsoft, small companies get their start supplying a Big Brother with products or services. Little Brothers are not necessarily coddled by their Big Brothers. They are expected to jump very high hurdles to win the more established company's respect. But when they do, they can start working with some of the benefits of an outsider.

Lowe's, Home Depot, Office Depot, and AutoZone, for instance, are among the top retail Blueprint Companies aiming to link members of their supply chain electronically, eliminating paper invoices and enabling the tracking of documents.

Wal-Mart, always a tough Big Brother, expects its Little Brothers to strictly follow the rules. For instance, Wal-Mart sent a letter to about 20,000 suppliers saying it expected them to send all their product data to the stores electronically by January 2004.[5] The Little Brothers that made the cut have a chance of getting even more orders.

To illustrate a different supply chain alliance, the semiconductor companies, to offset high capital cost for foundries, typically outsource the fabrication to large global concerns such as Taiwan Semiconductor. Broadcom, one of the fastest growing Blueprint Companies in this sector, was on the four-year trajectory by designing broadband chips for cable modems. To get to market quickly with low-cost product and high-manufacturing capacity, Broadcom outsourced its manufacturing early to Taiwan Semiconductor.[6]

Product/Service

To set standards or to fill critical innovation gaps, big companies often create focused Big Brother–Little Brother alliances around a core innovation. Consider Google. In May 2000, Google partnered with Netscape, then a division of AOL, to augment Google's standard Web search results with hand-selected listings from Netscape's Open Directory Project (ODP). This resulted in Google's directory being different in two significant ways. First, directory search results are ranked according to Google's proprietary PageRank relevance system. Second, Google uses the technology to search across all the content of Internet sites.

"The ODP has very useful information," said Sergey Brin, President and cofounder of Google. "But it's tedious to browse. So we put our technology on top [to make it easier to find relevant results without having to scan through often lengthy alphabetized lists of links]." Google pioneered the use of assessing the *importance* of a Web page as a measure of relevance. In essence, Google seeks to identify the most highly regarded pages on the Web by analyzing both the quantity of links pointing to a page and the importance of the sites providing those links. "It's almost like a peer-review process for the Web," said Larry Page, Google's other cofounder.[7]

Channels to Market

Access to channels help growing companies reach market segments at a lower cost. For biotechnology companies, such access is critical, particularly for the first major product launch. In 1982, the U.S. Food and Drug Administration approved Genentech's human insulin product, the first recombinant DNA drug to be sold in America. Genentech did not want to compete with Eli Lilly & Co., which held 75 percent of the American insulin market. Instead, Genentech approached Eli Lilly with its potentially better version of insulin, hoping to arrange a licensing agreement. Eli Lilly agreed to market the new product and sold it under the name Humulin.[8]

Microsoft's alliance with IBM, while it started as a product alliance to fill a critical gap, evolved into a channel alliance in 1984 as IBM bundled PC-DOS with the its personal computers. In parallel, Microsoft arranged for channel relationships with the other PC manufacturers—and by 1985, as Microsoft approached $140 million revenue, it achieved most of its revenue through channel alliances.[9]

Revenue-Centric Alliances

To grow revenues with a customer-centric focus, Blueprint Companies shape their alliances to complement the *Revenue Powerhouse*, a suite of alliances that accelerate revenue growth shown in Figure 5.1.

1. *Product alliance to secure a customer beachhead.* Career Education, the Little Brother at the time, reached a major agreement in late 1998 with the French culinary arts school Le Cordon Bleu to offer its first sanctioned programs in the United States through Career Education schools. Le Cordon Bleu had been founded in Paris in 1895 and was renowned as one of the finest institutions of its type in the world. The Cordon Bleu training program emphasized classic French cooking techniques that can be applied to any cuisine. Le

---

FIGURE 5.1

Alliances Complement the Revenue-Powerhouse Framework

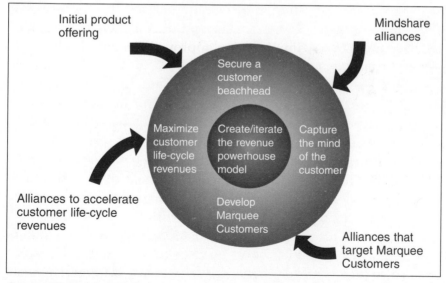

Source: Blueprint analysis

Cordon Bleu had schools in Paris, London, Tokyo, Australia, and Ottawa. The first U.S. programs would be offered at Career Education's Brown Institute campus in Minnesota, where the new Midwest Culinary Academy opened January 1999.[10]

2. *Mindshare alliances.* Forming complementary alliances to a Blueprint Company's core value proposition can help to provide higher-level benefits. As Starbucks transform their locations from being a coffee location to a "third place to home and work," they have developed alliances for high speed wireless Internet access (T-Mobile). Another recent development is Starbucks' alliances to provide music listening in the store.

3. *Marquee Customer alliances.* Consider Siebel Systems, a software company founded in 1993 with the objective of becoming the global market leader in sales-force automation software. Siebel formed its first systems-integrator Big Brother alliance with Andersen Consulting to ensure that it brought its best-in-class software to Marquee Customers. In return for investing in Siebel and helping the company sell the software, Andersen opened a sales-force automaton practice and deployed Siebel internally.

4. *Alliances to maximize customer life-cycle revenues.* Referring to the Revenue Powerhouse, there are different types of alliances aligned to each of the customer life-cycle variables discussed in Chapter 4. These alliances have a direct impact on the revenue trajectory of the Blueprint Companies. For example, to increase volume, AOL/Netscape selected Google as its Web search service, helping push daily traffic levels to over three million. In 1998, eBay entered into a three-year marketing agreement with America Online Inc. that featured eBay to customers as the exclusive provider of person-to-person auction services in the general merchandise category of AOL's classified ads and in several areas of the hobby section. Under the agreement, eBay would guar-

antee AOL $12 million.[11] The following year, eBay and AOL entered into a broader agreement for eBay to rollout auction services to regional and international markets. AOL gained rights to market AOL advertising to many of eBay's loyal users. In addition, eBay agreed to pay AOL $75 million. In return, eBay gained access to AOL's 16 million paying subscribers as well as CompuServe and instant-messaging customers. AOL also agreed to assist eBay in its effort to expand into overseas markets.[12] For eBay this was a very strategic Big Brother alliance.

Multiple examples of these kinds of revenue alliances exist. To increase geographic coverage, for instance, Cisco expanded internationally, entering into an OEM arrangement with British Telecom and establishing commercial relations with Siemens AG of Germany and Olivetti of Italy.[13] eBay partnered with PayPal early to offer easy payment methods, thereby increasing volume.[14]

When Yahoo! wanted to increase revenue per customer, it partnered with network providers such as AT&T and SBC to provide Internet access and broadband portal services.[15] And when Starbucks wanted to expand into new lines of business, it partnered with PepsiCo and Dreyers Grand Ice Cream to develop and distribute coffee and ice cream through alternative channels.[16]

Who to Partner With

The Big and Little Bothers' table seats only a few. For that reason Blueprint executives (and their Big Brother counterparts) must find the most suitable partner and move swiftly to shape the best fit and highest quality alliances.

In the software industry, where alliances abound, companies may partner to form multiple complementary Big Brother alliances such as with a PC or server manufacturer to bundle software; an operating system provider to ensure compatibility with platforms;

a database provider to ensure compatibility and value added capabilities; and a system integrator to deploy software solutions to common customers or telecom equipment providers for the wireless markets (see Figure 5.2).

Within each segment of the software industry, typically only three or four large providers occupy significant share and customer coverage. For operating systems it is Microsoft, IBM, HP, and Sun Microsystems. A finite set of Big Brothers exist, therefore, from which to choose—in other words, a limited set of seats at the table.

In the case of Siebel Systems, for instance, its complementary alliances include Microsoft for operating systems, Compaq (now HP) for server platforms, and Accenture for Systems Integration services.

FIGURE 5.2

Finite Set of Big Brother Alliances in Software

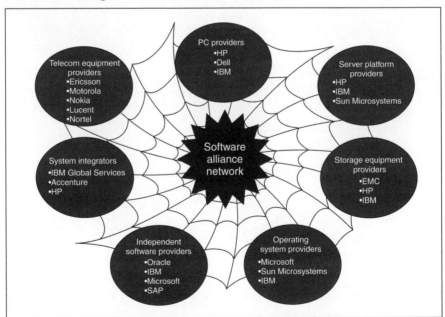

Source: Blueprint analysis

Our case studies showed that Little Brothers can have multiple Big Brother alliances by creating complementary alliances from different market segments. For example, in the software industry, a company could create complementary alliances across the operating system, independent software provider, and systems integrator segments.

Execution Can Be Challenging

Asymmetric relationships are challenging. "None of us *want* Little Brothers," one seasoned Big Brother executive explained, "but we all recognize that for certain pieces of the portfolio, we'll have to turn to someone else and Little Brothers are the best ones to turn to." Another Big Brother executive had to warn his managers not to spend too much time nurturing Little Brothers. (After all, they are sometimes irresistibly bright eyed and bushy tailed and can be a real time sink.)

Big Brothers have other problems with Little Brothers. Big Brothers do not want to take others products and services too seriously because they "are not invented here." And they certainly do not want to encourage more Little Brothers to knock on the door, resulting in a flood of phone calls. Nevertheless, Big Brothers realize that they need Little Brothers. They fear being left out of emerging markets or not being able to fill critical gaps in their portfolio with the latest innovation. As one executive at a global technology company explained to us, "If I am not in the game of partnering with leading edge companies, then I am out of the game. I'll be reading about innovation and then I'm behind the curve. It is about making the news not reading it."

For Little Brothers, alliances are attractive because they create access and scale into new markets as well as establish market credibility. Smaller companies gain access to much-needed customers across markets by partnering with industry giants. In addition, they often access benefits in innovation and product development through access to their partner's platform and range of products and services. In marketing and sales, benefits typically result in lower cost access to Marquee Customers.

Successful partnerships between innovation-centric partners give the Little Brothers a unique opportunity to exploit an additional source of value: intelligence. When effectively pursued and executed, partnerships provide insights into customer demand, bottlenecks in the current market offerings, and the evolution and emergence of new webs or business ecosystems. Effective companies translate this visibility into competitive advantage to be jointly exploited by the partners as they deepen or broaden the relationship.

Alliances are hard to set up and difficult to maintain but the results are well worth the effort. I hope you will enjoy the interviews in the next section. They are a showcase of what these rewards are all about.

How One Successful Big Brother Masters Alliances

No company has mastered the art of the Big Brother–Little Brother relationship better than Procter & Gamble. P&G thrives on innovation—and in the fast paced world of consumer products, it has learned how to cultivate relationships with Little Brothers that bring energy, fresh ideas, and capabilities to the table. That is why A. G. Lafley, P&G's President and CEO, is well known for stating that he wants to source half of P&G's innovation externally—not just innovation in products, but in processes and business models as well. P&G does not care where ideas come from. What is important is that good ideas find their way to P&G and they are successfully commercialized to benefit consumers and create shareholder value.

Okay. How do you do that? How do you get a small company with big ideas through the corporate portals? Penetrating a large corporation can be difficult and time consuming. P&G addressed this problem by calling on Jeff Weedman, Vice President of External Business Development, who leads an entrepreneurial group inside P&G whose two-fold mission is to build value through taking P&G's intellectual assets outside and help bring external innovations into P&G. One of the strategies to accomplish this is to build relationships with Little Brothers who have big ideas.

I first met Weedman at a McKinsey & Company/Conference Board seminar on alliances where Weedman was a featured speaker. One point that he made was to let any Little Brothers, that might be in the audience, know that they should feel free to call on him first. "P&G used to be called the Kremlin on the Ohio. We didn't want to talk to anybody," he joked. "Nothing annoys me more then finding out an opportunity was taken to one of my competitors because they didn't think P&G would be interested. I always want people calling me first."

Later, when I had the opportunity to explain my Blueprint thesis to Weedman, he treated me like a Little Brother, grilling me on every aspect of my value proposition. As you might expect, he quickly got my attention and earned my respect.

Finding the Right Fit

When Weedman discusses the fundamentals of an asymmetrical relationship, it sounds similar to the fundamentals of an alliance between two big companies. Says Weedman, "You have to ask: Is this something that is truly needed by both parties? Are there complementary capabilities that, put together, make the sum of the two parties much bigger than either individually?"

But it is not just a practical fit; it is an emotional one as well, one about building relationships. "First, you've got to spend a lot more time getting to know the people," says Weedman. "You need to understand their principles, what their goals and ambitions are. Quite often a small company may have multiple owners and, interestingly enough, they may not all have the same vision. One partner may be willing to play for the long term and the other may want money up front."

He adds, "To get a Little Brother, you have to structure the relationship so that it 'scratches the itch' of the smaller party. On the other hand, you have to have the guts to walk away if there is no way to achieve that." Indeed, in some small companies the owner/inventor/founder may have difficulty giving up total control. In that case, the Big Brother has to decide if the relationship really can work and if the value creation is large enough for both parties.

"It is only after P&G determines that the outcome has the potential to be really big, and the other party is someone we can do business with from the standpoint of culture, capability, and goals, that we sit down and start talking about what is the right legal structure for the relationship in order to capture the most value," says Weedman. The deal structure itself comes last. It could be an acquisition, a license, a revenue share, or a joint venture. "In addition, we tend to structure the contract to incent appropriate behavior from both parties," Weedman explains. "It is not unusual for our contracts to stipulate that P&G do X, Y, Z by a particular time, and if we don't, here are the consequences. This ensures that the smaller party is protected."

Weedman adds, "What we spend the most time on is figuring out how to structure the relationship so that our interests are aligned. What I've learned is the importance of negotiating contentious issues up front. This allows us to spend our time building the business together, instead of wasting time in 'negotiation hell.'"

To make the transition as smooth as possible, Weedman requires a champion within an operating business who will serve as the Big Brother and who will treat the external business as an internal client. "There has to be ownership by the business so the alliance is deeply imbedded and the people who have responsibility for that particular business own the relationship," he explains.

Cover Girls and Other Benefits

What are the big benefits for P&G's Little Brothers? Plenty. For example, they can uniquely access advertising resources from

P&G. Suppose P&G has hired a few top models for its Cover Girl cosmetics photo shoots. At the end of the shoot, the company that licenses the Cover Girl name for, say, eyewear. The licensee uses the same models and high-priced photographer, thereby saving time and money. "All of a sudden, instead of being just another eyewear company, they're able to tap into a Cover Girl commercial shoot and get photographs you otherwise could probably not afford," Weedman explains. "In addition, the brand equity is maintained—the look and feel of the Cover Girl brand is consistent across all the product touch-points to the consumer."

What about an introduction to the bigger retailers? "How long would a small company have to work to get an appointment with the appropriate buyer at Wal-Mart or Safeway?" Weedman asks. "For many it could be forever. Our customer team can jump in and help our partners schedule an appointment next week."

Some other current examples of P&G's Big Brother–Little Brother relationships are equally illustrative. P&G's External Business Development uses a small financial company for contract compliance and revenue tracking. As Weedman explained, "They can do it better and more cost effectively." For trademark licensing, P&G utilizes the services of Nancy Bailey and Associates. They have the expertise in the field and the dedicated resources that really know the industry. "They often come across a lot of neat ideas," said Weedman. "In the past, they might have had trouble getting to the right person and making the connection. Through our ongoing relationship, we've eliminated all that and established a much more efficient process."

Another example is a company called Changing Paradigms. "They have taken some of our brands, like Downey Wrinkle Releaser, that are not big enough for P&G, and have provided the critical mass to take them to market. They use our name, our logo, and our formulas. For them these are big brands," Weedman said. "By opening up the possibility of taking our brands to external partners, we have a perfectly acceptable way of deriving value from a project that wasn't doing so well inside P&G. You have to realize that these are projects that someone invested their heart and soul in, and now, by utilizing companies like Changing Paradigms, it allows P&G to move to a higher yield and a more efficient way of getting in market."

Weedman's Corollary

To speed up the pace and success rate of relationship building, Jeff Weedman invented a new rule to manage deal-making:

> You may have heard of Moore's law [regarding computer chips]: speed doubles; costs halve every 18 months. We have the "Weed's Corollary." Simply put, the second deal with the same company takes half as long as the first. The third takes one-third less time, etc. I get a ton of repeat business. And interestingly, we now have an addendum to the "Weed's Corollary." The addendum states that deals that follow the first are often unpredictable at the outset but usually end up bigger and create more value than what was originally envisioned.

As it turns out, there is also a networking dynamic to the Weed's Corollary. "For example," Weedman continued, "one of the potentially biggest returns of my relationship with Changing Paradigms is not the amount of money I've made because they've been successful with some of our products. It is what I term the virtuous cycle: Changing Paradigms has started bringing us opportunities that they think are too big for them."

How does Weedman keep track of it all? He says it becomes a process.

Weedman's team has a wheel diagram they use. On it they post external relationships—universities, research institutions, companies, competitors, partners, suppliers, and retailers. They view all of these relationships as part of a large access pool. They have found that when P&Gs people are encouraged to look externally, they more frequently make the kind of connections that lead to value creation for all parties involved.

Furthermore, Weedman finds there are certain kinds of courtesy to use when small companies call P&G. He explains, "First, we aspire to always get back to them. I would guess 98 percent of the time the answer is 'no thank you'. But it's not just 'no,' or even 'no thanks'—it's 'no thank you, please call again.' The fact that we actually get back to these small companies impresses them. Many of them thank me for turning them down because at least they have received a definite answer."

Even if Weedman's team turns them down as a P&G Little Brother, they often direct them to someone else who may be interested—that even includes competitors. "The reason is not because we necessarily think it will benefit or mess up the competitor," Weedman said. "It's because when someone has an opportunity, I *always* want them to call me first. I want them to know that the best chance of creating value is to bring it to P&G first."

As I noted earlier, Jeff treated me like a Little Brother when we first met. Since then, like my real little brother, he is a real friend.

How One Little Brother Masters Its Alliance with P&G

You might be thinking that Little–Big Brother alliances are 1:1, and involve products or services that fit a gap in a company's product line. That is not entirely what this story is about. P&G is a world-class marketer and is an example of the potential that a Big Brother can realize from alliances. Weedman mentioned that P&G's CEO wanted him to help source some of P&G's innovation externally. This did not mean just finding innovation and bringing it into P&G. The unique opportunity that a world-class marketing company has is to leverage its intangible assets—its brands. How can P&G use Little Brother alliances to create value from its brands? To help me understand, Weedman sent me to Nancy Bailey & Associates—a Little Sister with a special relationship with P&G.

Nancy Bailey is the Chairman of an 11-person firm that specializes in trademark licensing. Nancy describes her job as a matchmaker. As one of the top trademark licensing firms in the country, her company has alliances with top marketing honchos; P&G, Alcoa (Reynolds Wrap), General Mills, and Crayola to name a few. As a matchmaker, her team works to license a trademark for use on closely related products. The licensee gets to market branded products that have strong consumer awareness; customers and consumers have access to a broader line of branded products; and the licensor benefits from expanded brand awareness and royalties.

Why is Nancy Bailey & Associates so special to P&G? Bailey and her team had to earn their way into today's special relationship. It started with Bailey taking the initiative to add value to the Hawaiian Punch brand. "When we first met with Hawaiian Punch, we recommended they extend their brand into food products like fruit snacks, but they initially weren't interested in food brand extensions. After a competitive brand licensed a company to make candy and fruit snacks, we quickly moved to help Hawaiian Punch structure a licensing program built around the brand's unique 'one of a kind fruit taste.' Soon after, we helped the Vicks brand team launch Vicks Vaporizer in partnership with Kaz Products. Kaz had invented the vaporizer, but it had no brand recognition. When Kaz came out with the Vicks Vaporizer, it became the number-one product in the category and achieved a 25 percent market share. That initial product has since spawned a whole line of health care products that are available in many markets around the world."

For Jeff Weedman and his team, Bailey proved that her firm could move quickly, add value, and overcome P&G's initial perception that Bailey & Associates was expensive. Weedman and his people were surprised to see how flexible this Little Sister was in making the relationship work. "One of the original challenges was our pricing," said Bailey, "as P&G didn't want to use the standard licensing compensation structure. We negotiated a win-win financial arrangement that has allowed us to work effectively together. In our initial relationship, P&G thought we would just bring them trademark licensing deals and walk away. But we didn't walk away because our own philosophy is that the work begins once the agreement is signed. We manage the relationship and ensure that the program runs smoothly and is maximized for both parties. And we are very good at what we do."

Creating a Family Affair

A few years ago, Bailey got a call from Weedman. "Nancy, why don't you take the Mr. Clean brand and see what you can do with it. Mr. Clean is a single-product line and we aren't focusing enough on it." Bailey reached out to another Little Brother, Jordan Glatt, the President of Magla. Magla was about a $30 million revenue un-branded company making gloves at the time, primarily as a licens-ee for Stanley Tools. Bailey and Glatt worked together to make a licensed deal for Mr. Clean gloves happen in record time—about 60 days—just in time for the 2000 Housewares Show. Little Brother and Sister teamed up to create a huge booth at the entrance of the hall of the trade show. Immediately, their credibility soared with their strategic line extension of the Mr. Clean brand and their asso-ciation with P&G.

Magla's relationship with P&G was off to a great start. Glatt was thrilled by the win-win relationship:

> What the Mr. Clean brand did for us was move us from selling a commodity product to a highly differentiated and branded product with a lot of marketing muscle behind it. Prior to P&G, we had been selling unbranded commodity gloves to Wal-Mart. This move enabled us to break into a category against the Playtex brand that was on the decline and with little marketing investment.
>
> An added benefit from working with P&G is we could hook in to their national FSCIs (free-standing coupon inserts) that appear in newspapers, which made the P&G and Magla products look like a seamless Mr. Clean product line. A company our size could never afford this type of investment. That's a lot of marketing dollars going into our category that

our retailers just don't see. What makes this so unique is we are bringing a consumer product name into a category where there wasn't one before.

While Magla is using the Mr. Clean trademark, the company is separate from P&G and sells directly to the big retailers of the world. The great news is Magla expanded its customer base and distribution channels as a result. "The year after the launch," Glatt reflected, "we got an end-aisle display of Mr. Clean gloves and other products at Target and broadened distribution of Mr. Clean's core products into the cleaning aisle at Home Depot. On the flip side, as P&G extended Mr. Clean into the automotive channel, we were able to expand into this class of trade as well."

Success leads to more success. The next year, Magla launched reusable wipes for the kitchen. Bailey added Mr. Clean brooms, mops, and cleaning accessories to the brand offering through another licensee.

Common Incentives

How do three alliance partners stay focused on the same goal? They structure the relationships so, as Bailey sees it, "the work really starts once the deal is done." For P&G, it receives royalties from Magla, and Bailey & Associates receives a percentage of P&G's royalties. For Magla, it gets to grow its business—a lot. While the company is private and the numbers are confidential, Glatt did share that over "the past few years, the company has been growing at an exponential rate." Today, it is estimated that Magla has about tripled in size. The value of a Big Brother alliance cannot be clearer than that.

"It's About Being a Great Partner and Loving the Work You Do"

Asking Bailey what this means to her, she summed it up as her firm's going the *second* mile to suggest ideas and help P&G wherever it can:

We have a very special relationship with P&G. They are our biggest client. They view us a part of their internal trademark licensing team rather than an outside agency. We are in sync with how they think and understand how important it is to find the right companies and products to complement their brands. When they have issues, we reach out and find a solution. We want to be a great partner to such a great company.

For more information on this Little Sister/Little Brother–Big Brother alliance, visit http://www.magla.com and http://www.baileylicensing.com.

What You Need to Get Alliances Right

In an era of great uncertainty and rapid market evolution, here are the elements for a well-structured alliance agreement.

- **Choose the right agreement.** It is not always desirable to invest in a formal contract before the value of the partnership is clear to both parties. Choose a "type" of agreement acknowledging uncertainty and nature of contributions.
- **Avoid granting exclusivity—but always push for exclusivity.** Hedge your bets by relying on multiple partners. Allow market forces to define de facto exclusivity.
- **Use equity to encourage mutual performance.** Contrary to popular belief, equity does not guarantee performance. Think of equity as an incentive one may pay out in the long run if the partnership is effectively executed. Andersen took an equity stake in Siebel and got a board seat. Effectively communicate the prospect of significant value within each partner's organization.

(continued)

- **Commit Business Unit heads along with the CEO of the small company to champion the alliance.** Senior executives on both sides should be champions of the alliance. Their names should be written into the agreement.
- **Have an exit strategy.** This includes triggers that may be pulled depending on performance or market conditions; also, how assets and intellectual property created during the partnership will be distributed. We have identified three typical evolution paths: (1) buy the company, (2) buy the intellectual property, and (3) grow together or grow apart. Effective contracts include provisions for all of those options.

Scale Alliances Based on Success

In order to increase the odds of success, we noticed that many Blueprint Companies institutionalize their successful alliances so that other companies can also participate.

In 1998, for instance, Siebel launched a formal alliances program modeled after its Big Brother alliances with Microsoft, Andersen (now Accenture), and IBM. The program featured a comprehensive set of technical and marketing programs that enabled new partners to develop and promote their products in conjunction with Siebel Systems.[17]

The alliance program was divided into three categories:

- *Consulting Partners*—Siebel's partnership with Andersen Consulting (now Accenture) established the standards for their program. The program enabled partners to provide services to customers—much like the services Andersen provided to its customers—in terms of systems integration, consulting, training, and process re-engineering.
- *Software Partners*—Independent software companies were given the right to provide Siebel customers with software

applications and products that inter-operate with Siebel software.

- *Platform Partners*—Providers of hardware, database, and operating systems were certified to offer joint benchmarking, tuning, sizing, and configuration with Siebel.

■■■■■■

Chapter Summary

Key Points
- Blueprint Companies used Big Brother alliances as a company-shaping strategy.
- When a small company enters into an alliance relationship with a big company, an asymmetric alliance is structured: a Big Brother–Little Brother alliance.
- Asymmetric alliances are more challenging than "typical" alliances. Therefore, it is important for both parties to be flexible and look out for each other's interests.
- Alliances can often be interconnected with Marquee Customers. Marquee Customers can play a key role by pulling the partners together as well as helping to shape the combined value propositions.
- For the Big Brother, alliances with Little Brothers can fill important capability gaps. For Little Brothers, alliances can provide credibility for their product or services as part of a larger offering or provide a valuable channel to market. This forms a "win-win" relationship where each party looks out for each other's needs and interests.
- For Big Brothers, creating alliances requires less capital commitment and risk than internal initiatives or acquisitions. Alliances can also improve time to market.
- The best alliances are formed when there are strong management relationships combined with a strong need and motivation within both parties.

- It is fundamental that senior management of both enterprises drives the shaping of the alliance strategy on an ongoing basis. They provide continuity of relationships and a win-win perspective to the equation.

Unexpected Findings
- Asymmetric alliances are more difficult to execute than symmetrical alliances.
- Blueprint Companies are more successful than average companies at leveraging Big Brother alliances to shape the company.
- There are fewer "seats at the table" than most perceive. There are a limited number of Big Brothers and they can only handle a few alliances for any given space.
- Big Brothers need Little Brothers more than many perceive. Big Brothers find it challenging to identify the best Little Brothers.
- There can be an all-too-human gripe that Little Brothers require too much time, but these same Big Brothers know they can't continue to innovate without Little Brothers.

Part THREE

SEIZING THE OPPORTUNITY TO CREATE EXPONENTIAL RETURNS

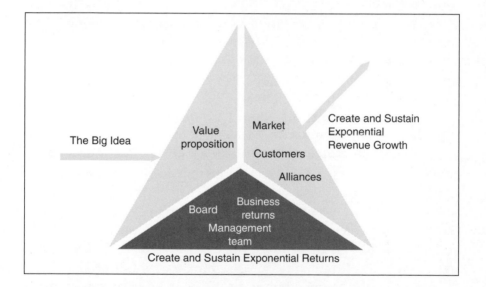

While exponential revenue growth is the distinguishing character-istic of Blueprint Companies, most of them seized the opportunity to create and sustain *exponential returns*. The companies with the highest returns tended to have the highest return on investment. Achieving these returns is unique in the history of American busi-ness building. For example, remember the four-year trajectory companies shown in Figure 1.4 (on page 7)? These companies delivered an average 87% per year return to their shareholders as they ascended from the inflection point to $1 billion revenue.

How did they do it? By the early and consistent execution of three key prerequisites: (1) a business model that creates and sustains returns that grew in proportion to exponential revenue growth; (2) a leadership team that could manage all 7 Essentials simultaneously; and (3) a board of essentials experts. The next three chapters give you an in-depth perspective into the companies that exemplify these qualities.

Chapter 6 reveals Blueprint Companies that defied the conventional wisdom of overinvesting and being cash flow negative in order to grow. The highest valued companies generated a high return on investment—driven by high earnings and positive cash flow—significantly greater than the cost of capital. Looking at the tech sector, the highest valued sector, these companies became cash flow positive before the inflection point and *continued to be* as they ascended to $1 billion revenue—in contrast to the approach that prevailed during the 2000 bubble.

Blueprint Company leadership is not a CEO who leads and manages the 7 Essentials at the same time; that is, there is not one brand-name leader who does it all. My research shows that it has to be a dynamic leadership duo—an Inside-Outside pair. The Inside-Outside pair became relevant in the 1990s with Microsoft, and it is still alive and well in new Blueprint Companies such as Tractor Supply. In Chapter 7 we highlight two Inside-Outside pairs—Jon Shirley and Bill Gates in the formative years of Microsoft and a newer pair, Jim Wright and Joe Scarlett of Tractor Supply.

Finally, board composition is another indispensable ingredient for growth. Some companies do not leverage this essential—the best ones, though, do. Companies that struggled or grew at a low rate tended to have a board packed with investors and management members. In contrast, Blueprint Company boards had members who were customers, alliances, a Blueprint Company CEO, and a community member. Chapter 8 gives you a quick overview of these findings.

Chapter 9 links what has been learned about all 7 Essentials described in the chapters preceding it. It also ties together the frameworks in which to create your own exponential growth with returns.

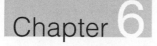

Chapter 6

Becoming the Masters
of Exponential Returns

What's the bottom line?

When Breakaway Solutions went into business in the mid-1990s, this e-commerce provider looked like another high-tech sure-shot. After all, revenues were $10 million in 1998, $25 million in 1999, and, by 2000, $102 million. As investors saw Breakaway heading onto the four-year trajectory, they jumped in, lifting the firm's market cap to over $1 billion.

Underneath these successful numbers, however, things were not nearly as reassuring. As Breakaway grew to its $10 million revenue in 1998, it also posted a loss of $3 million. That might have been acceptable for a high-tech startup, especially then, but the following year Breakaway lost more money—and by 2000 net income had plummeted to a $101 million loss. Return on invested capital? A staggering negative 835 percent. Even worse, the company had created a cash flow drain of $321 million.[1]

The Importance of Positive Returns

In the high-tech boom of the late 1990s, we were treated to a rare cultural phenomenon: Companies actually thought they could succeed without profits, and there were investors—for a few giddy months—who seemed to agree. That phenomenon did not last long. In the case of Breakaway, investors finally awakened and fled. By 2001 Breakaway was in Chapter 11 and its assets were sold by the end of the year.[2]

The story of Breakaway, precisely because of its dismal ending, is instructive in highlighting one of the most critical characteristics of Blueprint Companies. Unlike companies that fail, Blueprint Companies *expect* to make a profit. In fact, they demand it early.

To answer why companies like Breakaway Solutions failed while Blueprint Companies succeeded, we sought the advice of a good friend, Dick Campbell, who is the former Senior Vice President of Financial Management at PepsiCo and former CFO of PaineWebber.

Based on Dick's experience, there are three fundamental drivers —or rules—of market value:

1. *High spread of Return on Invested Capital above the cost of capital.* Companies that create the highest market value (shareholder value) are companies that create the greatest spread between the Return on Invested Capital (ROIC) and the cost of capital. Companies that create business models that generate high returns for capital deployed create a unique opportunity to reinvest in the business as the most attractive option.

2. *Revenue and revenue growth rate.* Companies that create high revenue growth give the management team the opportunity to reinvest at the high rates of return being generated by the business. These above-market-rate investment opportunities are available only to the company, not the market in general. This allows the company to create value unavailable to ordinary investors.

3. *Sustainability of drivers 1 and 2.* The greatest risk to the business, more important than one thinks, is sustainability. Companies with high market share and high returns have the greatest probability of success.

This process is shown in the following equation:

$$ROIC = NOPAT/Invested\ capital$$

where

$$
\begin{aligned}
NOPAT &= \text{Net-operating profits less adjusted taxes} \\
Invested\ capital &= \text{Operating working capital} \\
&\quad + \text{Net property, plant, and equipment} \\
&\quad + \text{Other assets}
\end{aligned}
$$

Breakaway Solutions violated all three of these rules. While sales increased and gross margins remained somewhat attractive, its net-operating profit margins were increasingly negative. The team was spending more than they were earning from gross margin! While losing more as the company grew, the situation compounded as Breakaway's capital expenditures had to increase in order to support a growing business.

This seems perfectly logical (at least during the 2000 bubble) until the return on invested capital is calculated. Returns became increasingly negative. As a result, the company ran out of cash and the investors could see no path to a positive return on their investment.[3]

Revenues, of course, are very important. Revenue growth provides management the opportunity to generate earnings and cash flow. Dominant market share is important as well, as it often helps generate the highest returns. In fact, companies with both high market share and high returns have the greatest probability of sustainability (driver 3 in the previous list). That is why return on invested capital is so tightly linked to a company's chance for survival.

As Dick Campbell pointed out, companies need to grow their revenue line to enable them to reinvest at high returns. However, not being profitable enough to generate returns above cost of capital means that growth requires reinvestment since returns are negative. Investing at negative returns only lasts until the capital runs out. Unfortunately, Breakaway Solutions broke away from the rule and lost.

That sounds too basic to ignore: But of the 7,454 companies that went public since 1980, 25 percent do not exist today. While we did not perform an exhaustive analysis on the failed companies, it was not hard to find plenty of companies like Breakaway Solutions in terms of low revenue growth and negative returns.

The Importance of Return on Invested Capital

Earlier in this book, we discussed the importance of revenues. They *are* important: We have even based the trajectories of the Blueprint Companies on their revenues. Following these three revenue trajectories (four, six, and twelve years), Dick Campbell's Rule 2 is achieved, as well as part of Rule 3, sustainability.

However, the other half of Campbell's discussion is about generating the spread of returns over the cost of capital. This provides the best opportunity for management to reinvest in the business. We need to drill deeper into the significance of return on invested capital (ROIC) to Blueprint Companies.

What is it that makes analysts and investors eagerly buy into what we call the top Blueprint Companies, and hold them for years? In *Valuation: Measuring and Managing the Value of Companies*, a team of McKinsey & Company authors stress that the true drivers of value are growth and ROIC.[4] In fact, according to the authors' studies, ROIC is the primary difference between a company that languishes on the exchanges and another that is a stock market superstar.[5]

As we reviewed our top Blueprint Companies, we saw that the best managed companies increased their value in one or more of the following ways:

- They increased their ROIC.
- They ensured that ROIC exceeded the cost of capital.
- They grew the company, but only when the return on new capital exceeded the cost of capital.
- They strove to reduce the cost of their capital.

FIGURE 6.1

Market Value Drivers

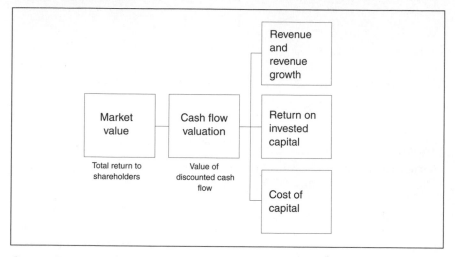

Source: Blueprint analysis

Where is cash flow, the traditional measure of shareholder value? A company's cash flow and ultimately its market value stem from its long-term growth in revenues and profits and from its return on invested capital relative to its cost of capital.[6] It is important, therefore, to understand drivers of cash flow as well as return on invested capital, which can be seen in Figure 6.1.

Why Blueprint Companies Create Disproportionate Value

In Chapter 1, we showed that the market value of Blueprint Companies was highly disproportionate (see Figure 1.6). Microsoft was number 1 with a normalized market value of $42 billion, while others were as low as $300 million at $1 billion revenue. To look into why one top Blueprint Company is so highly valued, consider Cisco Systems, the number 15 Blueprint Company (see Figure 6.2).

From its very beginnings, Cisco was not only a Revenue

FIGURE 6.2

Cisco's Return on Invested Capital and Growth Rates

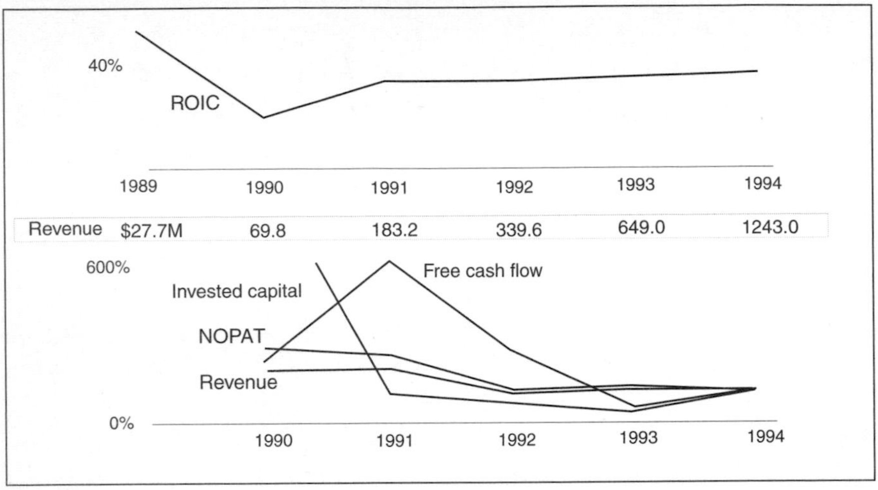

Source: Standard & Poor's Compustat, Blueprint analysis

Powerhouse, but a cash machine as well. As Cisco grew from $27 million in 1989 to over $1 billion revenue in 1994, its earnings margin averaged in excess of 30 percent. Combined with capital efficiencies, this enabled the team to deliver incremental profit and free cash flow growth rates in excess of 300 percent per year. While Cisco acquired numerous companies throughout its trajectory to $1 billion revenue, the management team managed to consistently maintain an average return on invested capital of 35 percent. Finally, their growth was consistent and sustainable. Cisco is a showcase of the three value creation rules Dick Campbell shared.

The Financial Profile of the Blueprint Masters

We identified the group of industries that delivers the highest market value at $1 billion revenue: High Technology, which includes hardware, software, peripherals, and semiconductors. These industries may not be the most numerous in the Blueprint list of 387 companies—that distinction goes to the Specialty Stores industry with 18—but the high-tech companies, of all the Blueprint Companies, are the most highly valued by shareholders (see Table 6.1).

Because the tech industries consistently outperformed, we wondered how they did it. What are the common lessons that one could learn from their success? We identified four key principles to creating superior value:

1. *Create attractive gross margins early.* Blueprint Technology Companies not only achieve high margins (60 percent or

TABLE 6.1

Highest Valued Blueprint Industries

Rank	Industry	Number of Companies	Market Value/Company ($ millions)
1	**Systems Software**	8	15,519
2	**Internet Retail**	3	13,238
3	Biotechnology	7	10,138
4	Specialized Finance	1	9,931
5	**Internet Software & Services**	4	9,847
6	**Semiconductors**	9	7,651
7	**Communications Equipment**	6	6,904
8	**Application Software**	8	6,854
9	Health Care Equipment	4	6,356
10	Diversified Metals & Mining	2	5,927
11	**Computer Storage & Peripherals**	4	5,402
12	Paper Products	2	5,063
13	**Computer Hardware**	2	5,041
14	Diversified Commercial Services	7	4,920
15	Apparel	5	4,801
16	Multi-Utilities & Unregulated Power	3	4,501
17	**Semiconductor Equipment**	3	4,483

Note: High-tech industries are shown in bold. Market value is normalized to 2004 values. (See Appendix D for the methodology.)
Source: Standard & Poor's Compustat, Blueprint analysis

more) early in their history, but remain at that level throughout their journey to $1 billion in revenues (see Figure 6.3).
When Cisco just started out—with $27 million in revenues—
its margins were 58 percent. Several years later, when the
company hit revenues of $1 billion, its margins had climbed
to 69 percent.[7]

2. *Contain expenses to achieve 20+ percent EBITDA.* On average,
   Blueprint high-tech companies spent selling, general, and
   administrative expenses (SG&A) and research and development (R&D) equal to the difference between the gross margin and 20+ percent Earnings before Interest, Taxes, and
   Depreciation—EBITDA. They generated this level of earnings as early as $25 million revenue and consistently main-
   tained this level of earnings. They rarely overinvested.

3. *Become cash flow positive early.* Contrary to what you might
   expect, Blueprint Companies do not wallow in red ink. From

---

FIGURE 6.3

**Blueprint Technology Companies Consistently Delivered
Positive Earnings**

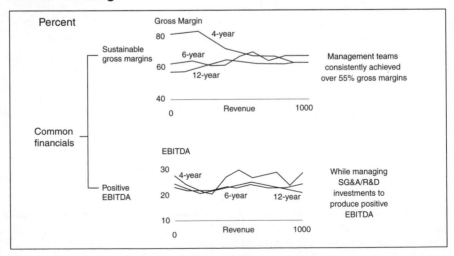

Source: Standard & Poor's Compustat, Blueprint analysis

the time they achieved between $20 million to $30 million, most Blueprint Companies are cash flow positive—and remain that way. To be sure, they may stray occasionally, but for the most part they deliver consistent cash in proportion to revenue growth. For example, let's examine Cisco's cash flow performance (see Table 6.2).

> Blueprint Technology Companies create a positive earnings and cash flow business model early so that exponential revenue growth creates exponential returns for shareholders.

4. *Utilize incremental gross margins to self-fund incremental investment*. Not all gross margins are equal. Many investors assured us that market structures and pricing were the primary determinants of gross margins. This may be true but we found that of the four-year trajectory technology companies, most demonstrated higher gross margins than average in their early years of growth, with margins converging to

TABLE 6.2

Cisco's Free Cash Flow

Year	1989	1990	1991	1992	1993	1994
Sales ($ millions)	27.7	69.8	183.2	339.6	649.0	1243.0
NOPAT	4.2	13.9	43.2	84.4	172.0	314.9
+ Depreciation–amortization	0.1	0.8	2.7	6.5	13.3	30.8
= Cash flow	4.3	14.7	45.9	90.8	185.2	345.7
− Extraordinary items	2.1	5.2	1.9	34.7	9.2	28.1
= Cash flow from operations	2.2	9.5	44.0	125.5	176.0	317.5
− Capital expenditures	0.3	4.1	11.3	21.6	33.9	59.6
− Dividends	0.0	0.0	0.0	0.0	0.0	0.0
= Free cash flow	1.9	5.4	32.7	103.9	142.1	257.9

Source: Standard & Poor's Compustat

the mean of 64 percent as revenues approached $1 billion revenue (see Figure 6.4). Furthermore, they managed to maintain high margins as they scaled to $1 billion revenue. Yet, when we looked at their earnings, their bottom line was similar to that of the six- and twelve-year trajectory firms. What happened to these incremental margins?

It turns out that these four-year companies incrementally funded increased SG&A and R&D with their incremental margins. We benchmarked their results to their 12-year trajectory peers and found that the four-year trajectory company's SG&A was 50 percent higher and the R&D was double!

> Achieving above-average gross margins provides a unique opportunity to incrementally self-fund a higher level of investment in sales and marketing as well as product development. This reinforcing cycle accelerates growth.

Management teams that can achieve incremental margins can incrementally self-fund product and sales investments. The higher

FIGURE 6.4

Incremental Margins Drive Self-Funding of Incremental Investment

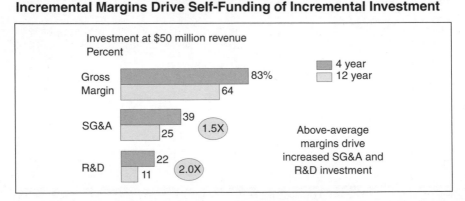

Source: Standard & Poor's Compustat, Blueprint analysis

the value a salesperson can sell a product resulting in higher incremental margins, the management team can incrementally fund the development team so that they can accelerate the design of valuable new capabilities. It is a win-win-win situation.

Deliver Consistent and Superior Financial Performance

We wanted to test Dick Campbell's contention that *Blueprint to a Billion* management teams must consistently outperform their non-Blueprint competitors and peers. So we compared eBay's performance to its industry peers as shown in Table 6.3.

eBay grew to $1 billion revenue—as it did, its sales rank in the Internet Retail industry moved from the eleventh position to third. While maintaining this growth rate on the four-year trajectory, its management team *consistently* delivered on earnings, cash flow, and return on equity. Indeed, eBay did this while moving successfully in cash flow growth, going from fifth position in 1997 to second in 2002 when it had achieved $1 billion revenue.

Delivering Shareholder Returns

While a firm's return on invested capital guided its market valuations, another perspective of market valuation of Blueprint Com-

TABLE 6.3

eBay Peer Ranking

Year	1997	1998	1999	2000	2001	2002
Revenues ($ millions)	6	47	225	431	748	1214
Rank						
Sales	11	9	6	5	4	3
EBITDA margin	1	1	3	1	1	1
Cash flow	5	5	2	2	2	2
Return on equity	2	5	3	3	6	6

Source: Standard & Poor's Compustat, Blueprint analysis

panies delighted us: Average shareholder returns were proportional to the revenue trajectory followed. In fact we derived that the companies that achieved $1 billion revenue in four years averaged 87 percent annual growth in market value. Those that reached it in six years averaged 41 percent annually. Those that reached $1 billion revenue in 12 years averaged a market value increase of 21 percent annually. Stepping back, we observed that the pattern continues to be consistent as the average shareholder returns are proportional with time. The 12-year trajectory average of 21 percent, for example, is half the six-year trajectory average, which is 41 percent.

This seems to agree with what we learned in our discussion with Roger McNamee, that analysts tend to average out expectations driven by financial modeling versus driving to understand demand curves and when a breakthrough value proposition is "hot." That is, the four-year trajectory companies outperformed expectations 80 percent of the time and 20 percent for six-year trajectory companies. Clearly, it is easier for management teams to manage expectations when growth exceeds what the typical financial models predict!

> Blueprint Companies on the four- and six-year trajectories exceed shareholder expectations while generating the highest returns. They offer the best risk/return compared to companies on the 12-year trajectory—a counterintuitive insight.

Applying These Principles to a Different Kind of Hardware Business

Fastenal, which became a Blueprint Company in 2004, is another consistent hitter. Fastenal sells nuts, bolts, screws, and about 195,000 other pieces of hardware through its company-owned stores throughout the United States and Canada.

The centerpiece of Fastenal's strategy is attracting customers willing to pay a premium for dependable service—a contractor, for instance, who is paying employees $30 an hour and cannot afford to delay a project for lack of a special fastener.

By the early 1990s, 50 percent of Fastenal's sales came from manufacturing companies and 30 percent from the construction industry. By then, each Fastenal store was offering 30,000 items. Four thousand items were in stock, while the rest could be delivered within 24 hours from regional distribution facilities. Store operators were trained to answer any question posed to them by a customer because a key emphasis of this Fastenal strategy is customer service. This strategy worked: Stores typically had profit margins of between 50 and 80 percent, far above the industry average of about 37 percent. Costs were kept low by locating stores in low-rent districts and minimizing other kinds of overhead.[8]

Fastenal may have grown more slowly than eBay, but it is interesting to note that its financial results were just as consistent. Fastenal became solid in terms of return on investment, with an average over 20 percent as shown in Figure 6.5. The company ranked number 102 as the most-valuable Blueprint Company at $1 billion revenue. This achievement is even more significant when

FIGURE 6.5

Fastenal Exponential Performance

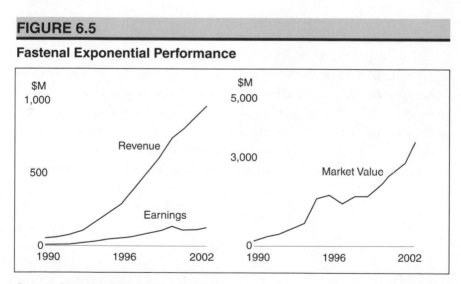

Source: Standard & Poor's Compustat

you consider that when Dell achieved $1 billion in sales in 1992, it ranked as the 138th most-valuable Blueprint Company.

How the Blueprint Masters Delivered Returns

The math sounds simple enough. The real question now becomes how did they *do it*? While no single answer exists, our interviews identified that these management teams executed a process that maximized the drivers of value. After reading these interviews, you might consider it more than a process—an end-to-end system aligning functional processes with metrics and incentives. Within each of the Blueprint CEOs whom we interviewed, we found an overwhelming conviction that you had to be making money almost from the get-go, that no consideration was more important than cash and ROIC. After all, you might have the greatest value proposition in the world, but it would not fly without cash.

The Mantra of Performance Food Group:
Cash First, Revenues Second

A memorable discussion hammered this lesson home during an evening spent with Roger Boeve, a founder and recently retired CFO for 15 years of Performance Food Group (PFG).

Founded in 1988 through the merger of three family-run food distribution companies, PFG took the fast track from $150 million in sales in 1988 to a billion in 1997. The remarkable part of the PFG story, however, is that despite slim gross profit margins, the firm generated consistent cash flow and a positive and consistent return on invested capital throughout its ascent. Repeatedly, *Fortune* named PFG one of the fastest-growing companies and one of the "most admired." More significantly, in 2000, *Barron's* named PFG number three in its list of 500 companies that had achieved the greatest increase in shareholder value over five years.

How did PFG do it? "From the very beginning," explained Boeve, "we ran the business for cash. Cash was king. That's the key to success: cash flow." When Boeve mentions cash above every thing else, he is serious; Performance Foods would acquire no company unless cash flowed almost immediately from the deal. The company would not even keep a customer who could not give them a targeted return on investment. As for sacrificing a certain level of ROIC to make gains in market share—forget it.

PFG kept up a blistering 25 percent compounded growth rate throughout the 1990s and early 2000s—a rate four or five times that of the industry—yet still had only 3 percent of the total $300 billion food distribution market. Would Boeve have sacrificed profitability to nudge that market share upward? Not for a minute, he says. He would rather step back to a 2 percent market share and be profitable. Boeve knew that PFG could not sacrifice profitability for scale even though scale could eventually help returns by lowering costs. "We observed that in this business," Boeve said in hindsight, "our largest competitors had much higher returns on investments primarily driven by lower food costs."

A Profit at All Costs

According to Boeve, an account *had* to be profitable:

> . . . and if it didn't meet certain standards you met with the customer and explained that we had to make this a profitable account. With us, this started right from day one. When a customer did not produce the profitability that was required, we worked with the customer to reconfigure the arrangement. Maybe the customer was getting a delivery every day. Every time you dropped a load at the back door it was a cost. We said to the customer, "If you could buy all of your product from us—we could become your prime vendor, which would increase our profitability." Second, we might say instead of three deliveries a week, we could make two deliveries a week.

Anyone in business who has struggled to retain a difficult customer has got to be sitting up straight by now—and saying, "You've got to be kidding." Go to the customer and explain you need a certain level of profitability? To comprehend this, one must understand that the top Blueprint Companies *earn* the right to negotiate a profitable agreement with their customers. They do not leave ROIC to chance—they do not even leave it up to the customer to set the level of profit. Rather, they set up the metrics for success themselves.

Okay, how do they do that?

First, Performance Food made sure that every manager understood the critical importance of ROIC. Boeve was happy to explain:

> Shortly after we formed the company, we sent our top management team to attend a Stern Stewart value added seminar. We designed our executive management bonus incentive system around the value added concept. We assigned the cost of capital to each unit and then the spread—the difference between the return and the cost of capital— we called value added. The executive got a percentage of that. A certain amount went into a pool so that they would average out over a time period. There were some quarters, for example, where the return for some reason was below par. You could then draw some bonus out of the pool and then another quarter the bonus went back into the pool. It was a kind of moving average. We paid these bonuses quarterly. In another quarter, if you were ahead of target, you replenished the pool.

Performance Foods also offered a generous ESOP (employee stock ownership program) for all its employees. Boeve believes that, in the early days of the company, the ESOP was perhaps the greatest reason for its success. "We wanted to remind the employee that he or she was a shareholder or owner of the business," Boeve recalled. "The employees even wore caps that said 'Shareholder.' Something magical happens when a person transforms from an employee mentality to an owner mentality."

PFG also tracked vendor float—the relationship between payables and inventory. Before long the company had managed this so that its suppliers provided all of its inventory capital and a good portion of its receivable capital. In some of the business units, PFG did not have to put in any of the working capital. These numbers and many others were communicated weekly to headquarters. "We looked at the numbers daily," Boeve continued. "The minute we saw a trend developing, we'd call the general manager of the business and ask what's going on? If it was a sales issue, the general manager would call in his sales VP or his distribution warehouse manager and we'd get it fixed right away."

Measuring Profitability

Performance Food also set targets for every aspect of its business. The company had targets for each unit and managed those numbers. Most companies manage their receivables and inventories, which PFG did, too. However, it also managed its payables intensively.

"One thing that we insisted on was that we measured account profitability." said Boeve. "We developed our business model on that basis." There were other important numbers to track such as Day Sales Outstanding tracked receivables. The company then could tell that it was doing a better job than its competitors. PFG also tracked sales per delivery, and even more precisely, cases per delivery. Boeve believes that these were "the key to profits."

"It all starts on the front line." Boeve asserts. "You have to measure customer profitability."

Making Happy Customers

PFG recognized the critical importance of customer service. "In reality, we weren't in the food distribution business," said Boeve. "Our business was customer service. And that meant getting the food to the restaurant when they wanted it, with a 100 percent order fill." With its motivated workforce, and its control and analysis systems in place, PFG could do that. "I remember we called Outback Steakhouse in 1993, and talked to them about servicing [supplying] a few of their restaurants. We wowed them. They couldn't believe that service could be that good. So they gave us more restaurants. Today, I believe PFG services all of the Outback restaurants and concepts. So it's the level of service that really grows the business."

Of course, PFG measured its customer service just as it measured everything else. According to Boeve:

> If customer service is our objective, and this is what the restaurant requires, we need to measure it. There's no reason to have a goal if you don't measure it. So we put in place a customer service index, in terms of timely delivery and order fill. That was reported daily by every unit. Performance surveyed its own customers for their level of satisfaction—and even the customers of its competitors.
>
> Outback has a saying: "No rules; just right." That was our motto, too. We had a superior workforce that would do anything for a customer. Not sell at a loss—but anything in terms of servicing the account.
>
> If you service the customer—if you exceed expectations— the customer is going to be happy, and they will buy more from you.

It's not rocket science but it does turn the company into a Blueprint winner.

In the case of Performance Food Group, Wall Street watched eagerly as the company charted an annual 25 percent compounded increase in the top line, of which approximately 10 percent was from acquisitions and 15 percent from internal growth. Its internal rate of growth was four to five times the rate of the industry.

How PFG handled its numerous acquisitions is more impressive, perhaps. "We could acquire mom-and-pop distribution companies in the $80 million to $100 million dollar sales range at perhaps six [or] seven to nine times P/E," said Boeve. "When those earnings came on stream that would then trade at 17 to 18 times P/E." PFG could also assist the local manager, boosting profits dramatically in the first few years after the sale. "We looked at every acquisition from a strategic standpoint." Boeve observed. "Is it a growing market? Our philosophy was to leave the current management in place. We said, 'You can continue to run the business. We will be at your elbow. We will show you how to do it better.' That's why they wanted to sell to us, even though we, in some cases, didn't offer the highest price."

By the way, Performance Food Group is *still* growing at $6.1 billion revenue and is 328th on the Fortune 500 list of America's largest companies. As they drive for the benefits of scale, the management team continues to use the principles that Boeve described to us.

At Columbia Sportswear It's an End-to-End System

If you wear casual outerwear, then you should know Columbia Sportswear. One of the largest manufacturers in the world in its sector, Columbia Sportswear Company designs, manufactures, and markets outdoor apparel and footwear, and distributes its merchandise to more than 12,000 retailers globally. Columbia's rise to the top began during the 1980s, when Gertrude Boyle and her son, Tim, orchestrated the remarkable growth of their family-owned business nearly 50 years after the company began doing business as Columbia Hat Company. At year-end 2004, Columbia achieved $1.1 billion revenue at a market value of $2.4 billion. ROIC averaged 22 percent over the past five years.

We asked Tim Boyle, now CEO, what was Columbia's secret to generate such positive returns in the garment business. Tim summed it up nicely: "Give your customers what they want; you go make it and you sell a lot of it." Actually, there is more to this simple axiom. Reflecting on Columbia's difficult rise, Boyle admitted:

> We really weren't good at making clothes. The capital cost to open factories was high, we weren't good at manufacturing, and the utilization of the factories was too low. We discovered in the early 80s how important Asia was as a sourcing point for textile products.
>
> There is a cultural bias about Asia that if you send products

over there they will be knocked off. What we have learned is that the percentage of individuals with ethical business activities over there is the same as here—it's high. We have someone at the company spending half his life over there learning the process and becoming good at judging character. Early on we hired ethical and highly motivated people.

Our sourcing approach allowed us to be cash flow positive as we grew. We had a relationship with one of the seven merchant trading firms in Japan that established a financial arrangement whereby they would place an order with a factory in Asia for us. In exchange for a fee, the merchant firm would open a letter of credit to the factory. The factory would send the merchandise to us and we would ship the merchandise to the customer. We would then pledge the receivable as collateral and borrow from our local bank. That provided us with the cash flow to allow us to grow as rapidly as we could place orders and manufacture the product. The challenge was then about making sure our infrastructure in Asia was up to speed.

The capital demands were primarily working capital. We ran the business this way up to the early 1990s. Our total fixed asset base during that period of rapid growth was about $30 million. We delivered innovative products that were high margin but we weren't very timely with delivering merchandise.

Beyond low-cost sourcing, the Columbia Sportswear equation had a number of other important variables. Boyle identified them for us:

First, our breakthrough ideas were in our products. We had a great start with the Quad Parka; you could wear the shell with the liner, reverse the liner, and wear the liner with the jacket. Surprisingly, real opportunity for this parka was for customers who weren't hunting because there aren't very many hunters. When we put it together with a ski jacket, the Bugaboo, this was our big home run.

The Bugaboo, which ranked as the greatest selling parka at its price point in the industry by the end of its debut year, put the company on the map, touching off prodigious growth that elevated Columbia into the elite of nationally recognized contenders. As the product line evolved, so has the Big Idea. Boyle explained the Columbia's core value proposition: "When people are wearing casual apparel, they want to reflect what they do in their spare time: surf, hang around at the beach, be a fisherman, skier, or hunter. The product has to perform technically appropriate and still be worn casually."

Boyle and his team planned for high returns right from the start of the design process. Boyle explained it this way:

> The product development process that we use is to take last year's successes and have them vetted by a group of customers. Customers will tell you what additions need to be made to be successful in the future. It is then a question of how to price the product line to have high returns. To set the right price is a function of how different the product is and what our sourcing team can do to bring the costs in with high margin.
>
> The advantage we have is our customers are placing orders with us it before we have the inventory made. If we offer a product that is not successful, it means customers don't order it and we don't have to make it.

Of course, with the greatest assets in working capital and inventory, managing the complexity between sourcing and distribution is absolutely critical. As the larger retailers have demanded higher levels of service, this complexity has increased. As Boyle shared with us:

> Making a product is one thing, delivering it is another. The garment business is different from other businesses as we sell 10,000 to 15,000 items with derivatives of colors and size. Matching demand to production is highly complex; multiple countries to multiple customers across multiple currencies.

When we buy, we buy from multiple factories and match the customer's demand with production on a rolling forward basis. We manage this complexity with our own software that we developed.

While the system to generate positive returns at Columbia sounds simple, Boyle and team have developed a process to generate high returns and remain cash flow positive by managing the process from design through to the distributor.

A Helpful Assessment Framework

While talking over our findings with Dick Campbell, he suggested an assessment framework he used to use during his career (Figure 6.6). As he explained to us, this simple two by two grid basically measures businesses with high revenue growth and high ROIC and groups them into actionable categories.

If the business has high revenue growth and high returns on investment, get behind this business or division! On the other hand, if revenue growth is high and returns low, fix the business model. Businesses with low revenue growth and high returns become great sources of cash—known as cash cows in the consulting industry. If you find a business with low growth and low returns, you better think twice about this business.

Dick found it useful to apply this approach when he managed across a broad portfolio of business units. This is great for stand-alone business assessments as well.

FIGURE 6.6

Value Assessment Framework

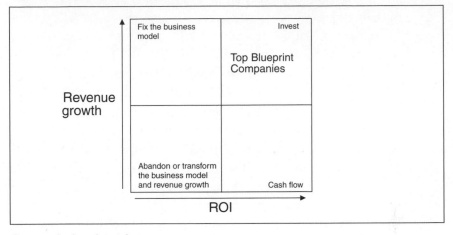

Source: Author, interviews

Chapter Summary

Key Points

- Companies that create the highest market value are those that create the greatest spread between the return on invested capital and the cost of capital. A corollary exists, however: When managers generate high returns for capital deployed, they give themselves a unique opportunity to reinvest in the most attractive option—their own business.
- Revenue and revenue growth are significant drivers for cash flow, which is another driver for maximizing shareholder value.
- The technology industries are the grouping of industries that generate the highest average value per company at $1 billion revenue. The key lessons learned from these companies are:

- *Create a business with attractive gross margins early.* We found that gross margins were established early and remained fairly consistent.
- *Contain expenses to achieve 20+ percent EBITDA.* Companies spent SG&A and R&D equal to the difference between the gross margin earned and 20+ percent EBITDA. They generated this level of earnings as early as $25 million revenue and consistently maintained this mean.
- *Become positive cash flow early and scale.* Contrary to conventional wisdom, these companies became cash flow positive early and remained cash flow positive. While they deviated from the mean at times, the mean trend indicated a consistent performance of generating cash directly proportional to revenue growth.
- The management team consistently delivered on earnings, cash flow, and return on equity. Cisco, eBay, and Fastenal are great examples to follow.

Unexpected Findings

- The highest valued Blueprint Companies, with technology companies being dominant, created a positive cash flow and ROIC business early and continued to deliver consistent performance as the company scaled to $1 billion revenue.
- Companies that generated higher gross margins could self-fund incremental investment in R&D and SG&A to accelerate growth. The four-year trajectory companies are examples of companies that self-funded incremental investment to accelerate growth.
- The market returns for the four- and six-year companies average 85 and 41 percent per year, respectively. Also, the four-year trajectory companies outperform analyst expectations 80 percent of the time.

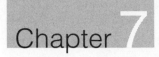

The Management Team

Inside-Outside Leadership

■■-■■■

It takes a dynamic duo!

In 1994 Jerry Yang and David Filo, two doctoral candidates in Stanford University's electrical engineering program, spent as much time surfing the newly created World Wide Web as they were pursuing their doctoral studies. They even created their own Web site, "Jerry's Guide to the World Wide Web," which linked Internet users to their favorite places in cyberspace.

"Jerry's Guide," however, did not make the Yang and Filo site sound very interesting, so one night they changed the name. Teeing off the phrase Yet Another Compiler Compiler (YACC)—a favorite among Unix computer code programmers—they came up with Yet Another Hierarchical Officious Oracle—or YAHOO! for short because Yang and Filo considered themselves a couple of major yahoos after all, and thus a famous brand name was born.[1]

Then in 1995 Marc Andreessen, cofounder of Netscape Communications, invited Yang and Filo to move Yahoo! from the Stanford University computer system, which Yahoo! had outgrown, to Netscape's big facility. Commercialization soon followed. Advertising revenues began to rise—and Yang and Filo soon realized that they could not manage the business by themselves anymore.

That is when they recruited an experienced technology professional and former Stanford PhD, Tim Koogle, to serve as CEO. Koogle, in turn, recruited Jeff Mallett as COO, who had already cut his teeth at Reference Software and WordPerfect and was Vice President and General Manager of Novell Inc.'s consumer division. Together, Koogle and Mallett began transforming Yahoo!, turning it into one of the most popular stops along the information highway.

While Yang and Filo would arrive at work wearing T-shirts and sneakers, Koogle and Mallett preferred suits. Many viewed the foursome's working relationship as one of children with ideas and their parents who could turn their children's ideas into action.[2] As analyst Andrea Williams of Volpe Brown Whelan & Co. noted, "Americans are captivated by the idea of two college kids like Yang and Filo starting an incredible service. But Mallet and Koogle have turned it into a business that advertisers and investors understand and respect."[3]

Indeed, the relationship between Mallett and Koogle helped turn Yahoo! into a winning Blueprint Company for the first five years of its development. Mallett was a strong inside leader and responsible for running operations. Koogle was an ideal outside-facing CEO. In the first 12 months on the job, Koogle took a start-up and signed 50 alliances, hired a sales team and several crucial top management team members, and took the company public.[4] Koogle essentially guided the company through tremendous growth as he contributed to building its management team, creating its adventurous organizational culture, and signing up alliance partners. Together the two men made Yahoo! into one of the few profitable, high-growth Internet companies of the late 1990s.

After the dot-com meltdown, however, and Yahoo!'s well-chronicled falters, another team turned around the company and got it onto its present track. Current Chairman and CEO Terry

Semel and COO Dan Rosensweig have also made a compelling team—with all the requisite external and internal skills needed to get Yahoo! onto the fast lane of the enormous Internet search-and-advertising industry.

To pin all the early success of Yahoo! on Koogle and Mallett—and where it is today on Semel and Rosensweig—would oversimplify a complex corporate history. But teams of such effective pairs do, in fact, perform much of the work that catapults their companies to record-breaking success. The following sections explain why.

The Importance of Dynamic Duos

Among Blueprint Companies, we found that "dynamic duos" drove many of the star-performing companies. These are two individuals who worked tightly together to build the firm from dreams to a billion dollars in revenue.

> Dynamic duos are the stuff of corporate legend: Sears and Roebuck, Roy and Walt Disney, Hewlett and Packard, and the like. What we found is that in Blueprint Companies it is more than corporate myth—Blueprint Companies *do* spring from such pairings.

More surprises surfaced as we drilled deeper into this finding. We learned that for the duo to be dynamic, one of them had to excel in the *outside* part of the effort—in marketing and sales. The other had to be the *insider*—keeping the operations purring or, perhaps, inventing new products. Together, they had to explore and innovate continuously—whether it was in product innovation or marketing innovation. They had to make swift decisions—and often quick and nimble correction of their mistakes. Most important they had to have complete trust in and respect for one another.

The Koogle-Mallett combo at Yahoo! is typical of what we found in the top Blueprint Companies: an Inside-Outside leadership pair (working in partnership with the founding team) who managed to execute all the essentials simultaneously. This particular pair, like others we have seen repeatedly in Blueprint Companies, had a unique chemistry. They had a unique *synergy* that electrified the evolution of their service. Cisco, eBay, Nike, Starbucks, and many others have applied the same pattern as shown by the list of dynamic duos in Table 7.1.

There is one other thing that struck us. These dynamic duos who lead Blueprint Companies are not just colleagues or even just friends. They have a remarkable chemistry between them, built on a very high level of respect and trust. They benefit from having complementary skills and talents. They are the yin and yang, the weave and warp, the bacon and eggs—and without this dynamic of compatibility their companies could not have made it to the top. Their relationship is dynamic in the way that they use their complementary strengths. Any individual weaknesses or flip-flops went unseen by outside observers because they used each other's strengths in ways that compensated for what the other

TABLE 7.1

Inside-Outside Leadership Pairs

Company	Leadership Pair Examples
Yahoo!	Jeff Mallett and Tim Koogle
Microsoft	Jon Shirley and Bill Gates
Tractor Supply	Jim Wright and Joe Scarlett
eBay	Maynard Webb and Meg Whitman
Siebel Systems	Patricia House and Tom Siebel
Starbucks	Orin Smith and Howard Schultz
Broadcom	Harry Samueli and Henry Nicholas III

Source: Company reports

lacked or could not do. As a pair, they were the highest of performance teams.

The Essentials of Blueprint Leadership

To get from an early blueprint to an actual billion dollars in revenue, you need a breakthrough value proposition, Marquee Customers, and a powerhouse business model. What about leadership? What kind of management does it take to propel a company from a blueprint to a billion dollars in a few years? What are the roles of the CEO in a Blueprint Company, the COO, the engineering team—even the founders themselves?

To answer these questions, we—in collaboration with Peter Robertson of the London-based consulting firm Human Insight—took a closer look at the best Blueprint Companies.[5] With Robertson's help we assessed a sample of the top Blueprint Companies (see Appendix C). There we found patterns in—and answers about—Blueprint Companies leadership.

In addition to these assessments, we studied published interviews and articles that featured the leaders of top Blueprint Companies. Their statements gave us clues to the best management practices. We conducted our own interviews with numerous founders, CEOs, COOs, and investors. These individuals helped identify the elements of management that they believed drove their success. After a year of this kind of exploration, we had a much clearer understanding about this unique set of leadership dimensions.

Three Leadership Dimensions of the
Inside-Outside Leadership Duo

Blueprint leadership, it turns out, has three dimensions:

1. *Focus on relationships and products.* One member of the dynamic duo is focused on company-shaping relationships—

that is, building relationships with Marquee Customers, Big Brother alliances, strategic investors, board members and outsiders such as other Blueprint CEOs, suppliers, and community leaders. The other half of the duo focuses on logical ideas concerned with product development, processes, and systems that fuel the company's product or service pipeline.

2. *Drive to innovate and explore.* While one member of the duo manages for internal structure, that is, problem solving for disciplined and predictable responses, the other is forward looking by exploring and shaping opportunities. This is a delicate balance between preserving the past and exploring in order to innovate. That said, there is a useful back-and-forth and, sometimes, even a brief exchange of roles that keeps this chemistry dynamic and replenishing.

3. *The ability to manage the 7 Essentials simultaneously.* Most important, we learned the importance of management's ability to balance the execution of each of the essentials. In such a high-powered environment, there are always many balls to juggle and it takes a particularly talented, collegial team to keep those balls in the air. Dropping one can cause a Blueprint Company to risk falling off trajectory. Successful Blueprint management teams learn how to do it all—how to deal with the simultaneous execution of the 7 Essentials— and still keep the corporate trajectory heading rapidly toward a billion dollars and more.

These initial two leadership dimensions, focus and drive, form the basis for clearly defining the roles of the Inside-Outside leadership pair (see Figure 7.1).

When we started our research for this book, we sensed that Blueprint Companies had a unique management style. After all, only 5 percent of IPO companies make it to $1 billion revenue. What we learned was that *Blueprint to a Billion* management is unique. With limited resources these teams execute "1 + 1 = 3" miracles. What can we learn from these impressive leaders?

FIGURE 7.1

Inside-Outside Leadership Pair

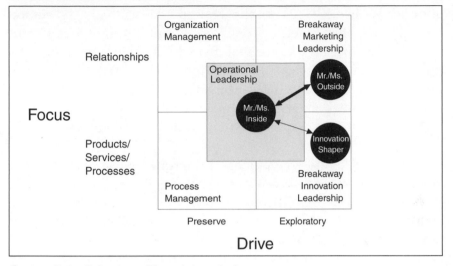

Source: Peter Robertson, Blueprint analysis

Breakaway Marketing Leaders

First, Blueprint leaders are superb communicators. They possess the personal chemistry, even charisma, that lets them bridge the gaps between alliance members, Marquee Customers, community leaders, and important investors. They are accomplished at finding, qualifying, and shaping the deals and relationships that ultimately shape the company.

One member of the leadership pair, typically the CEO, fills this role. The CEO could be an external hire, typically brought in early —or a founding member. Meg Whitman was brought in early; Bill Gates, Howard Schultz, and Phil Knight are founding members.

The role of the leader depends on the value proposition of the company. Nike's Phil Knight was a showcase of breakaway marketing leadership. Knight constantly pushed the boundaries— and changed the ground rules. Instead of marketing shoes, he marketed the athletes who wore the shoes and what they achieved in their Nikes.

As new market segments emerged, Knight tried to be the first to spot them. In 1984, when the National Basketball Association (NBA) games began televising in prime time, Knight was instrumental in getting an endorsement from Michael Jordan, then just a promising player. The Air Jordan shoes helped make Nike's basketball shoes into a $500 million business by 1990.[6] No wonder that a recent *Fortune* magazine cover read: "Nike After Knight: The maverick built a company like no other. Can anyone fill his shoes?"[7]

Tom Siebel aggressively shaped Marquee Customer relationships with Charles Schwab and General Electric, shaped a Big Brother alliance with Microsoft and Andersen Consulting, and shaped his board by adding Charles Schwab and the head of Andersen as a result of an investment in Siebel.

> Outside-facing CEOs are highly exploratory—particularly with relationships and creating opportunities. This forward-thinking style is critical to proactively developing Marquee Customers and Big Brother alliances, securing the right board members, and evangelizing the company's vision to employees and the community. This leader affects the forward-thinking approaches of the person whose role is focused more primarily on the inside, who is usually responsible for innovation leadership.

Breakaway Innovation Leaders

While the dynamic duo is evangelizing customers, conceiving a brilliant marketing strategy, and managing the business, a third critical leader is what we call *Breakaway Innovation Leadership*. These leaders, typically the founders of the company, focus more on the product rather than on outside relationships. They are often highly creative, with a broad range of interests, perhaps skipping from mathematics to biology to music in a single thought. They have a need for innovation because they have a passion for extremely creative inventions. They work with others, but mostly because of a mutual interest in the subject. Rather than personal charm or charisma, they often use brilliant new ideas and the lure of exploration to keep their teams working together.

Company founders often assume this leadership role. They are pivotal in shaping the innovation-based value proposition, creating and leading the core engineering team, and contributing to the fundamental principles by which the business model is based. They serve to provide a consistent trajectory of innovation aligned to the company's core value proposition.

These leaders are an important link to customers, partners, and markets in terms of getting product feedback from them. They are highly regarded by their specialist colleagues, who exist as customers and partners in the same technical community, who breathe the same air. As corporations grow with new employees, these product-centered innovators act as a critical adhesive element by spurring the team on to higher levels of innovation.

More Key Roles in Blueprint Management

If you relied on the covers of the business magazines, you would think that it takes only an individual or two to run a Blueprint Company. No single CEO can possibly keep all of the essentials in motion without help. In fact, the more our team debated the unique qualities of Blueprint Companies, the more we realized that the successful corporation was much more like an *ecosystem* than a cult of personality or personalities.

Blueprint Companies need steady-handed managers who bring stability to the enterprise. These individuals exhibit control, discipline, and predictability. With this keel beneath them, Blueprint marketing and product innovators can feel secure enough to keep their minds out on the cutting edge.

Three Surprising Insights

As we looked into the histories of the Blueprint Companies, three counterintuitive insights dawned on us:

1. Most people assume that most Blueprint leaders had previous experience working in smaller companies. That, we found, is not true. Of the top companies that we studied, the Inside-Outside leaders came from varied backgrounds.
2. There seems to be a belief that the founders rarely stayed with the company all the way to the $1 billion revenue mark. That is not true with these companies. A significant number of the original leaders were still at the helm when the Blueprint startup crossed the billion dollar line: Bill Gates, Larry Ellison, Tom Stemberg, and Pierre Omidyar to name a few.
3. The third misconception is that Blueprint founders are of the same breed, that stereotype of the young, tousle-haired, pizza-gobbling, brilliant college dropout—or some variation of the theme. However, Blueprint leaders did not have a common background. They came from all walks of professional life—from college dropouts to college grads, from small company leaders to large company leaders. They came as business professionals or customer advocates with little marketing and sales expertise or with a lot of it.

Process Managers, for instance, typically are the captains of supply chain leadership. They are controlling and process focused. They can either operate within existing boundaries or shape new boundaries within which to operate. They tend to be the key team to support the COO and CEO. Of course, not every Blueprint Company needs to invest in its own supply chain to get to the top. Many of them, on the faster four- and six-year trajectory, tended to outsource manufacturing. That allowed them to grow quickly, to minimize capital costs, and to achieve lower product costs. Cisco, for instance, outsourced its manufacturing early. Broadcom also outsourced its semiconductor manufacturing. Nike moved its manufacturing to several Asian footwear producers.

Organization Managers are another role. These leaders are at home in the caring role. They foster a more congenial atmosphere in the organization and will do their best to maintain it. Especially important in high-growth and services companies, these leaders believe that caring for employees is fundamental for the company to provide a highly differentiated service to customers. This leadership style is typically humble. They are leaders by example, great listeners who pick up on feedback and quickly resolve issues. Typically, they support the CEO and COO.

A third role is *Operational Leadership*, the Chief Operating Officer. This role forms the complementary half of the Dynamic Duo—and is the inside counterpart to the outside-facing CEO. COOs are known as Mr./Ms. Inside and are at the right hand of the outside-facing CEO. Operational leaders are centered and well balanced. Often, they are so far behind the scenes that you hardly hear about them in the business press or notice them when you walk in the door of a company. As shown in Figure 7.1, they are highly versatile across all of the leadership styles. They have a trust-based relationship with a very high propensity to effective and efficient problem solving. They are real partners. If you can envision a high-performance team of two, this would be it.

The Number-One Inside-Outside Pair of the 1990s

Today, people often think of the prototypical Inside-Outside pair as Bill Gates and Steve Ballmer. But another great example of the Inside-Outside dynamic pair can be found in the evolution of Microsoft. Back in 1983, when Microsoft was at the inflection point, the company outgrew its small-time style faster than Bill Gates could handle it. Gates had tried to take charge of five product lines.

As a result, he paid little attention to tailoring programs to meet customers' needs. Key planning decisions were often delayed or not made.[8]

Gates recognized his own shortcomings. He tried to hire a president, but that individual did not work out. He tried again in August 1983, and this time he hit gold—Jon Shirley, a 25-year career veteran at Tandy Corp. who had known Gates as a customer (see Figure 7.2).

Shirley recalled, "The company lacked a lot of systems that it needed to grow to become big. It was nothing like an ideal organizational setup and it had no MIS system. They were using a Tandy Model 2 for the general ledger." Shirley also discovered that Microsoft lacked key statistical data about its products, its markets, and its sales. "We were totally out of manufacturing space, and we had no one who knew how to run the manufacturing side," he said looking back, adding that he threw himself into developing "a whole lot of structures and systems that would give us the tools we needed."

Shirley had performed many of the same operations for the much larger Tandy and felt comfortable operating within Micro-

FIGURE 7.2

Microsoft's Original Inside-Outside Pair: Jon Shirley and Bill Gates

Source: Courtesy of the Microsoft Archives

soft's "get-it-done" corporate culture. Shirley viewed his role as one of building up the support side of the business, hiring the chief financial officer (Francis Gaudette, who would later play a critical role in shepherding Microsoft's initial public offering through Wall Street in 1986), and honing the management team, whose members had almost all been hired from within the company.

In August 1984 the management team took serious action. It reorganized around two divisions: (1) systems software, the programs that control a computer's internal operations; and (2) business applications, programs that tell a machine to do specific tasks, such as word processing. Four years later, in 1988, Microsoft restructured the Applications Division into five business units. The business units would have profit and loss responsibility for their product lines and would be responsible for marketing and documentation of their products, said Shirley. "It gave them a great deal of control to run as a small business," he noted.[9]

Analysts give Shirley credit for quarterbacking many of the key strategic alliances that helped catapult Microsoft to industry prominence (though Shirley said they naturally evolved from simple customer relationships). In contrast, Gates played the market and standards leadership role, shaping the technologies for various product areas. "Gates and Shirley absolutely occupied different ends of the business," said Arthur Block, Manufacturers Hanover Trust VP in charge of end-user support. "Bill focused on the IBM alliance while Shirley focused on Hewlett-Packard (HP). Gates talked to user groups while Shirley talked to the financial community. Gates linked product/market opportunities to technology, while Jon applied structure and process to the business so that it could scale."[10]

On the day-to-day level, Shirley mirrored a management style that was supportive and didactic, well-suited to Microsoft's campus ambiance. "I believe in delegation and teaching," Shirley said. "You've got to give people sufficient authority to make mistakes."[11]

Shirley retired in 1989—after Microsoft passed $800 million revenue (on the way to $1 billion next year). He had essentially guid-

ed the company from the inflection point to $1 billion as Bill Gates'
"Mr. Inside."

A Leading Inside-Outside Pair Today

Tractor Supply is a wonderful case study of a similar management
pair in today's management world. Tractor Supply is the number-
one U.S. farm and ranch store, with sales of $1.7 billion and over
7,000 team members. The company is known for its great customer
service, which it provides to full- and part-time farmers and ranch-
ers as well as the general public. Tractor Supply carries a complete
line of livestock and pet products; maintenance products for agri-
cultural and rural use; hardware and tools; lawn-and-garden
power equipment; truck, trailer, and towing gear; and work cloth-
ing. Despite the wide variety of products that Tractor Supply
offers, the most popular item it sells harkens back to the roots of the
business: the simple lynchpin, that basic item that connects the
farm tractor to what it pulls.

While Joe Scarlett's official title is Chairman, he is more often
described by those he works with as coach, cheerleader, company's
conscience, and chief missionary of the gospel at Tractor Supply.
Scarlett provided us with a unique perspective on the dynamic-
duo leadership paradigm. During his tenure, he worked with an
Inside counterpart—and without one:

> Before I became Chairman and my right hand, Jim Wright,
> became President and CEO in 2004, we served as the CEO and
> COO team [see Figure 7.3]. Then and today, we are on the
> same page at all times. We share the same values. We finish
> each other sentences. Just the other day someone remarked
> that we are "like an old married couple." The chemistry
> started during the interviewing process.
>
> When I hired Jim, we spent hours interviewing. We went to
> Florida and walked the stores for hours at a time. We attended
> a manager's meeting in Florida together. We spent two days
> walking through Wal-Mart, Lowe's, Home Depot, and a score

FIGURE 7.3

Tractor Supply's Inside-Outside Dynamic Duo: Jim Wright and Joe Scarlett

Source: Tractor Supply

of other stores learning from them. In each of these settings, we asked questions of one another, we talked strategy, we discussed values, we discussed the competition, we problem solved. We would ask each other "How would you handle this situation?" in merchandising, operations, logistics, competition, people, and training. We got into each others heads so well that when we are in meetings today and look at each other across the room we often know what the other is thinking.

Today, when Jim and I get the same email and I send a follow up I often find that Jim independently sent a similar follow up to the same people.

What makes us successful is that we have similar but different backgrounds. We each managed a lot of different parts of the business over the years. We both have merchandising and operations experience, which we believe are critical factors for leadership success in high growth retailing. We both have run businesses before. Jim was previously the CEO of a smaller company. We are honest with one another. We are quick problem solvers. No problem lingers.

Scarlett explained that Wright is process driven and more internally facing. He can take a problem and determine the right priority, the right person, and the right process to get it solved. In contrast, Scarlett said he is more focused on big picture strategies and people issues. He spends much time preaching the message and interacting with employees—even though he is ostensibly more externally facing. "Of course," said Scarlett, "both of us are committed to our people first. Leadership in each store is our top priority." Scarlett spends 50 percent of his time coaching, mentoring, career planning, and training. Together they just brought in their 22 top high-potential store managers, with whom Scarlett spent two days discussing the business and customers. In fact, Scarlett personally visits about 150 stores a year.

Scarlett continued to elaborate on the differences of style in Tractor Supply's leadership pair:

> In contrast there was a time before Jim [was at Tractor Supply] when it was a struggle. I am not process oriented. We found ourselves talking a lot and didn't execute. I would unrealistically expect people to do things based on how I thought it should get done. We would "take three steps forward and two back." He could get things done realistically. He could break down problems into tasks with a process. With Jim on board we take three steps forward and stay there. I found that when I wore both hats, I simply did not have enough time for it all!

There was another aspect of this Blueprint winner that impressed me. "We are very close to our suppliers," Scarlett said and continued in some detail:

> I am on a first-name basis with our 50 top supplier CEOs. We bring the Presidents and CEOs in each year to share leadership, business strategy, direction, plans, philosophy, and values. We share confidential information with them so

that they can partner with us to innovate and be first to market. We count on our suppliers to help us offer products that are both key to our target customer and not part of the offering from the big-box retailers such as Wal-Mart and Home Depot. We work with our suppliers to serve as a guide for them so that we are first to market. We become their "test kitchen." Today we are very proud of the fact that 35 percent of our business is from new products that weren't in the product line three years earlier. We listen to our customers carefully to offer them higher quality and better lifestyle products.

Finally Scarlett explained that his company espouses some down-home, old-fashioned values (see Figure 7.4) and they have paid off. Scarlett said the company mission statement is "Work hard, have fun, and make money by providing legendary service and great products at everyday low prices"—and there is not a meeting where he or Jim do not discuss the values of the company in terms of everyday decision making. "When I visit stores, I am consistently preaching our values," he explained. "For example, we will discuss ethics with the store teams, what are breaches, how not to get in these situations. I preach and repeat our values consistently."

"Why preach and repeat?" I asked.

"We continually have a lot of new people," he replied with a country man's grin, "and people naturally only retain a small portion of what they hear!"

Calm in the Midst of the Storm

In contrast to the intense stress environment that typically comes with high-energy innovation for both products and marketing, Blueprint Companies share another trait: The ability to remain calm in the midst of the storm, to stay consistent and fairly unflappable even under the onslaught of chaos and ever increasing change. The "secret weapon" is having consistent values with the ability to self-correct.

FIGURE 7.4

Tractor Supply's Mission and Values

Source: Tractor Supply Company

One of the most important tasks of management is ensuring a climate in which people feel safe to explore. Exploration can only be achieved if leadership values are consistent. Leadership values are not one action, but a demonstrated set of actions over time in all kinds of situations that demonstrate consistency of values. There are two equally weighted drivers of consistency.

Consistent Behaviors, Communications, and Messaging

Marshall Goldsmith, world-renowned executive coach whose skills are in demand by many major CEOs, shared his perspective on this important leadership aspect. "What matters in leadership," Goldsmith said, "is not the words hanging on the wall; it is the behavior demonstrated in the hall." This is the case in Blueprint Companies, given the consistent nature of the communications that we found in which CEOs are always "on message."

For Joe Scarlett, Tractor Supply's Mission and Values are integrated into all of his communications and messages. This leads him to be consistent and aligned with communicating corporate values. As already mentioned, Scarlett spends much of his time with employees discussing the application of values to behaviors and customer service.

Consistent Values at Defining Moments

Consistency means that personal values and organizational aims will largely dictate what a manager does. These are best illustrated during defining moments—times when an organization is facing a crisis. All eyes are on the leader. Consistency is tested when there is a worrisome opportunity for the leader to act in *opposition* to stated values—and a broader sense of ethics. If he or she demonstrates consistent values, they are not only proven a good leader, they have reinforced the culture of the company and, hence, the conditions for continued growth.

> Leaders who lay out a consistent communications plan and vision—and act with upright values even in crisis—are critical to mobilizing an organization into consistent behaviors.

We found often that, early in the company's trajectory, many leaders of Blueprint Companies are pretty unimpressed by the wealth and fame that might follow. They are focused on the business—or even how it might help the community. eBay's IPO, for example, established a charitable fund. Instead of focusing on themselves, Blueprint leaders focus on the company. Mark Leslie, who built Veritas software to over $1 billion in revenue, came to this understanding: "I wasn't a great CEO until I realized it was about everybody *but* me."[12]

Blueprint leaders are goal and results oriented. They manage for long-term results. They know how to leverage customers and alliance partners to shape products and services, thereby creating exponential revenue growth. In certain sectors, software for example, it was paramount that these companies dominate their markets. These leaders, therefore, placed a high value on beating the competition.

We found that Blueprint leaders communicate consistent messages about the company's value proposition. Their passion is aligned to the value proposition and the priorities that they must execute, as in the case of Meg Whitman.

In 1999, when eBay's Web site crashed for 22 hours, Meg Whitman stepped up. She called this event eBay's "near-death experience"—the young company risked losing its entire trove of customer and transaction data. The outage exposed a glaring weakness for an Internet company—and eBay did not have the in-house talent to fix the site. What saved her, and eBay too, was a new technology chief. "I was like a crazed woman on a mission," she recalled about her meeting with Maynard Webb, then Gateway Computer's tech boss, a few days after the outage. Whitman successfully pleaded with him to come over to eBay— and the infrastructure that he built now handles, in a typical day, more transactions than NASDAQ—with no major outages in almost six years.[13]

The defining moment does not stop there. Everyone at eBay was given a list of 100 customers to call and apologize to. It turned into a defining moment of another nature. The customers were genuinely touched and the company reconnected to the community. If you ask any eBay employee, this defining moment is one that is often described as part of the company's lore. In 2005, six years later, when the pricing changes were not understood by the community, the employees again picked up the phone to call the com-

Passion over Pain

Although the management world has been taught that pain, crisis, and the need to overcome deficiencies motivate change, Blueprint Companies reveal a different picture. Top Blueprint Companies innovate because they have an inner drive to explore. This exploration is not limited to products. It includes new markets, new alliances, new customers, and new business models. Although pain can drive change, it often comes too late to be of much use.

munity and Meg Whitman joined the town hall meeting that week to explain the changes to customers.

Having your values in place also means that you can move fast to acquire an opportunity. For Tractor Supply, this happened in the summer of 2001. A competitor had gone bankrupt, and Tractor Supply had the chance to buy its stores. The problem was that the investment banker for the creditor said that Tractor Supply would have to buy all of them, not the 40 that Tractor Supply wanted. Tractor Supply could have lost the opportunity, but instead it came up with what CEO Joe Scarlett described as Project 110, in which the company had to open up all 110 stores by the end of 2002, with 87 of them opened in 110 days.

"Project 110 galvanized the whole organization," recalled Scarlett. "We brought the top 20 leaders in Tractor Supply together. Jim Wright ran the project. The teams met every week to readout the status: on target, nearly on target, or screwed up. No one wanted to report screwed up. This lifted the confidence of the management team. We opened 87 stores in 110 days—when the maximum we had ever opened was 30 in a year. Jim and I spent hours in each of the 87 stores talking with the entire team, sitting around in a circle on those five-gallon buckets and talking about the values of our company, relationship with our customers, our value over Wal-Mart, and the things we can do to continue making our culture very special. Since then, we have never looked back."

A change in leadership can also become a defining moment. It may be the need to change senior management or the search for a successor when "the shoes are hard to fill." The spotlight is on the board, founders, or CEO at this defining moment. Yahoo!'s founding team was wise to recognize early on that they could not shape the business themselves. Their defining moment—bringing in Koogle as an Outside leader—brought increased talent and structure to the business. Koogle then brought his Inside counterpart, Mallett, into the company. And what would eBay be without Meg Whitman brought in as CEO in 1998? Not nearly as big a success.

The Ability to Quickly Self-Correct

When growing to $1 billion, whether you are a four-, six-, or twelve-year trajectory company, at the inflection point you should expect revenues to double every 4, 9, or 24 months, respectively. The speed at which four- and six-year companies double revenues particularly requires that these companies exhibit the ability to not only self-correct—but to do so with speed. Failure to correct quickly increases the likelihood that a company can fall off trajectory.

Joe Scarlett passed this lesson on to other leaders at Tractor Supply. "Drill down if you don't know a lot about a problem or opportunity. Ask a lot of questions," he said, describing his style of self-correction. "Once I failed to do that when we bought a computer system. We bought too large a system when we could only manage a fraction of it. It wouldn't have happened if I had asked more questions." Scarlett says you have to challenge the status quo—and not "fall in love with your own thinking."

Scarlett offers another homily: "Get close to everyone in the organization—customers and suppliers, too. Any CEO spending over 50 percent of his or her time in the office is doing a disservice. Go where the action is."

The Third Leadership Dimension: Managing the 7 Essentials Simultaneously

We have already noted that Blueprint leaders must demonstrate breakaway marketing and breakaway product innovation leadership. Their third challenge is the toughest of them all: Managing the 7 Essentials simultaneously. Yet the leaders of our top Blueprint Companies have proven themselves to be shapers—leaders who can effectively shape their company's destiny in the face of intense uncertainty.

These leaders are problem solvers. But even more, they have a comfort level for problems with a lot of moving parts. Beyond that they have a superior capacity to recognize patterns—the pattern of Marquee Customer behavior, the pattern of Big Brother alliances, patterns of linkages between the essentials, to name a few. As in crewing a racing shell, all oars dip and swing simultaneously. The rowing team is comfortable managing scale, scope, and complexity—balanced in a single stroke and aligned.

Second, they are also *collaborators*. They keep the team, employees, customers, partners, and investors passionate about the company's direction and execution. They develop a balanced board (as an extension of themselves for the execution of the 7 Essentials).

These CEOs shape the company and its opportunity through their exploratory passion, which leads them to new markets, new strategic customer and alliance deals, and new standards. Just as Bill Gates shaped the IBM alliance, Tom Siebel shaped Marquee Customers early on with the Andersen alliance and Phil Knight shaped new markets for running shoes, the most notable being the game of basketball with Nike's groundbreaking Air Jordan.

Passion for the Company

In truth, passion is present in both Blueprint Companies *and* failed start-ups. In all of these cases, founders loved their companies. They were willing to sacrifice for their success. They poured their heart and souls (and real money) into the enterprise. So what's different?

> The Inside-Outside team is critical to linking the 7 Essentials. They determine the cross-functional initiatives. More important, they balance the mix of preservation of the past and exploration for the future as the company experiences exponential growth.

We found three big differences.

First, Blueprint Company leaders articulate their passion as one that is also relevant to customers, often in terms that will deliver higher-order benefits. By this we mean that their passion is tightly aligned with the value proposition; a pursuit for higher-order benefits. For Bill Gates it was "conceiving ideas to make personal computers easier to use and to program." Gates envisioned a computer on every desk and in every home."[14] He was known for having a one track mind—microcomputers.

For John Morgridge, Cisco's original CEO, it was "realizing Cisco had a solution in anticipation of customer demand." Morgridge passionately drove to be early and dominant in capturing the big advantage.[15] For Howard Schultz, it was about becoming the "third place" for the Starbucks community after home and work. In other words, the passion of the leader could also be viewed as a valued passion of the customer.

Second, such leaders had a consistent strength of will to execute. As Cisco's former VP Sales, Terry Eger said, "In the face of limited resources, you have to have superior strength of will to execute. You have to have superior energy to execute ahead of the growth curve."

Third, these leaders are intensely committed to the company, not to the position they fill. They are hands-on managers. They get involved in shaping deals with partners and customers. They serve as an important link between the engineering team and the customer. They work incredibly hard at the details.

Superior Problem Solvers

Blueprint leaders are superior problem solvers. They can navigate and execute in the context of a growth strategy. They can break problems down in the height of uncertain outcomes. They can best define and lead strategic initiatives enabling teams to link execution to strategy. These might sound like traits of all leaders, but they are not.

Blueprint leaders can qualify, shape, and execute deals with partners that shape the company. When Starbucks' Howard Schultz entered into a relationship with Pepsi to codevelop their first product together, it failed. So Schultz suggested they try working on another idea together: Frappuccino. It became a $500 million- plus business opportunity. Tenacity, stubborn optimism, and the ability to shape markets with their own hands mark Blueprint winners. When we interviewed companies that had failed or were on the slippery slope downward, we didn't pick up the same vibes. They just weren't closing in on the big opportunities.

The Bottom Line

To become a Blueprint Company, follow this handy leadership formula:

> **Blueprint Leadership =**
> **Focus** on relationships and products ×
> **Drive** to innovate and explore ×
> **Ability** to manage 7 Essentials simultaneously

Why should you multiply the three leadership dimensions rather than add them? We found that multiplication compounds the leadership effectiveness. The ideal leader would create a score of $10 \times 10 \times 10 = 1,000$ versus $10 + 10 + 10 = 30$. Alternatively, if leaders don't achieve the performance required on each of these dimensions, the business fails. Therefore, failing to execute a single leadership dimension results in a score of zero.

Ever see a "hands-off" leader who focuses only on process with little understanding of the details of the business? Ever find leaders who are focused only on cost reduction at the expense of growth? Ever find leaders who are simply maxed-out with no time to manage all the moving parts? Not the leader of a Blueprint Company.

Chapter Summary

Key Points
- Blueprint leadership is often in the form of a dynamic duo, a leadership team that pairs tightly together. These leaders characterize themselves in three ways:
  - The *Focus* on relationships and product
  - The *Drive* to innovate and explore
  - The *Ability* to manage all 7 Essentials simultaneously
- Leadership pairs are primarily inside and outside facing. In the majority of cases, the CEO serves as the externally facing leader (Mr. or Ms. Outside) who shapes the revenue-centric essentials. The COO serves as the internally facing leader (Mr. or Ms. Inside) who manages the operations- and innovation-centric essentials.
- Many founders assume the innovation leadership role. They are pivotal to shaping the innovation-based value proposition, creating and leading the core engineering team, and contributing to the principles on which the business model is based.
- The most effective driver of change is the ability to proactively explore and self-correct, and to do so quickly.
- In order to foster a culture of exploration, Blueprint Company leaders have a consistent set of values. This is accomplished through:

- • Consistent behaviors, communications, and messaging
- • Consistent values at defining moments
- The third dimension of leadership, the ability to manage all 7 Essentials simultaneously, is a key to differentiated leadership.
- Blueprint Leadership = Focus × Drive × Ability to manage 7 Essentials simultaneously.

Unexpected Findings

- The mutual respect that defines the relationship between the Inside-Outside pair was truly distinctive. Their relationship was dynamic in their use of their complementary strengths. The masking of their weaknesses was invisible to outside observers as they flip-flopped transparently to use each other's strengths to make up for weaknesses. As a pair, they were the highest of performance teams.
- The prevailing wisdom seems to be that founders cannot scale from start-up to $1 billion revenue. We found many examples where one or more of the founding team led the company to the top: eBay, Staples, Microsoft, and Oracle are just a few.
- Blueprint Companies exhibited a consistent exploratory behavior with the ability to self-correct. This exploratory behavior was critical to growth in many of the important parts of the business: innovation, market segments, customers, and business models. The impact of leadership behaviors during defining moments is often underestimated—and shouldn't be.

Chapter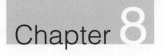

The Board

Comprised of Essentials Experts

Is the Board a leverage point for exponential growth?

We did not forget the board when considering the management team. We wanted to know if the composition of Blueprint Company boards was different from other companies. For our purposes, we limited the study to board structure so that the role of the board could be examined—as well as its interaction with management teams.

In order to understand the structure, we sampled top companies that were on the four-, six-, and twelve-year trajectories and assumed that these boards probably had many customers and investors represented on them. The results surprised us:

1. Of the four-year companies, 60 percent had an alliance partner on the board and 30 percent had customers. This ratio was reversed for 12-year companies.
2. A consistent set of big-name investors did not show up on these boards. We tended to see firms, but rarely the same partner. Instead, the CEOs from other Blueprint Companies were represented time and again.

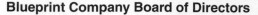

FIGURE 8.1

Blueprint Company Board of Directors

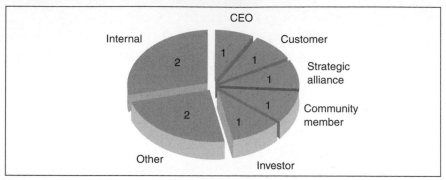

Source: Company reports and Blueprint analysis

3. The boards were, on average, quite balanced in terms of structure. The average size was nine with customers, alliance partners, community leaders, and CEOs from other large companies counter-balancing the investors and management team (see Figure 8.1).

Classic examples come to mind. Early in the life of Siebel Systems, Tom Siebel recruited Charles Schwab (the person) to his board. With the Andersen alliance and their 10 percent investment, they secured a board seat. With these two moves, Siebel had a Marquee Customer, a Big Brother alliance partner, and a CEO on his board by the time Siebel Systems made it to $1 billion revenue.

eBay paralleled Tom Siebel's example by recruiting Howard Schultz, Starbucks' CEO, and Scott Cook, the Chairman of Intuit. Both provided CEO mentorship from Blueprint Companies and invaluable market and alliance insights. Howard Schultz was an eBay board member as eBay ascended to $1 billion revenue.

Fifth Third Bancorp, the top Blueprint regional bank, has a 12 member board. On this board is another Blueprint CEO, the Chairman and CEO of Cincinnati Financial Corp., John Schiff. George Schaefer, Fifth Third's CEO, described his board's unique value to his company:

Our largest shareholder is Cincinnati Financial. Coming from the sales culture of the insurance business, Cincinnati [Financial] has been helpful in reinforcing our culture to stay close to the customer and in getting people to go out and sell. In addition, early on, they were advocates of stock options. We were leaders at creating options rewards. Today we utilize options or similar instruments like Stock Appreciation Rights [SARs] as an incentive very deep into our organization; 5,500 of 22,000 people in our company participate in some way. To provide other perspectives that inform and improve our aggressive sales culture, we also have had board members from good-sized companies such as General Electric and P&G to give us advice.

Tom Stemberg, former CEO and founder of Staples, appreciated Staples' seasoned board members who knew the business.

We were fortunate to have our investor from Bain Capital, who was also a brilliant business consultant, as well as Mitt Romney who is now the governor of Massachusetts, also a very smart business consultant. The Chairman of the Board was Leo Kahn who was one of the most successful retailers of all time. I competed with Kahn while in the supermarket business. This combination created a board that knew when growth was too fast and when to diversify. For us, managing growth was "like trying to knit on water skis. Trying to be precise to get everything right and moving like a rocket behind the boat." The board made a big difference.

Today, Stemberg plays the Blueprint CEO role on the board for PETsMART.

Cross-board relationships between Blueprint Companies can occur for strategic reasons. At the high point of the Internet Retail industry's growth in 1999, Tom Stemberg recruited eBay's Meg Whitman to join the Staples board.

Given the composition of the Blueprint boards, who then sat on the boards of struggling companies? These boards were dominated by investors and management team members! This suggests that the management team had probably not developed Marquee Customer or Big Brother alliance relationships. Also, they had not reached out to Blueprint CEOs for expertise. It would seem that if a Blueprint CEO agrees to sit on the board of a smaller company, you can probably bet that this person knows a Big Idea when they see it and believes in the potential of the smaller company's management team.

Because Siebel Systems had the profile of a typical Blueprint Company board, Tom Siebel could provide an inside perspective of the difference between having a board of, what I have termed, Essentials Experts versus one dominated by investors.

We gave a lot of thought to board composition. I wanted a proven and tested management team to build a billion dollar business. The board's job was to help build and inspire this management team. To do this, we were looking for people to be on the board who had been there and managed growth. We were looking for those values. All we were looking for were just several of the most accomplished entrepreneurs on the planet who had built large successful companies.

We recruited Charles Schwab who built one of the greatest [financial] service companies [our Blueprint Company 81]. George Shaheen had led Andersen Consulting from $1 billion to over $9 billion revenue. Eric Schmidt [now CEO of Google Inc.] was and still is one of the most powerful technology visionaries.

One of my primary goals was for the stature of this board to affect the standard of the management team's performance: perform at their better-than-best level. When the management team went to a meeting with this board, no one wanted to look bad in front of them. This required the team to perform higher than they had operated to date in their career.

Why do investor and management boards tend to be associated with lower-growth companies? While the reasons are varied, we heard a consistent theme.

When the board is dominantly composed of investors, the board's primary interest is managing to achieve the financial return from the investor's investments. If you put the board and the management team together, what you get is more of a "virtual" management team, which is sub-optimal. What often happens is that if the company's sales leader is weak, the investors put a sales coach on the board. If the CEO has skill gaps, they put a CEO coach on the board. At the end of the day, this type of board is a virtual management team, not the board required to build a billion dollar business.

It cannot be over-emphasized: Creating and maintaining a trust-based relationship between the board and the management team is paramount.

In the next chapter we discuss how all the 7 Essentials come together to create Blueprint Company performance.

Chapter Summary

Key Points
- Blueprint Company boards were heavily weighted with alliance partners, customers, and CEOs who had scaled a business. Companies with investor-dominated boards tended to struggle. Blueprint Company boards were a much-valued extension of the company's business strategy and management team.
- These external members provide cross-industry experiences that can greatly benefit the company.
- The presence of Essentials Experts on a board is a good indication that a company is executing the essentials required

for exponential growth. For example, a Big Brother alliance partner often takes a seat on the board if the alliance is strategic.

Unexpected Findings

- We thought that smart investors would dominate the most successful boards. Four-year companies were dominated with alliance partners, customers, and CEOs who had scaled to $1 billion revenue.
- Blueprint Company CEOs are the best source for experts who have experience with exponential growth.
- While exceptions existed, Blueprint Company boards predominantly featured some combination of customers, alliance partners, and CEOs (typically from Blueprint Companies).

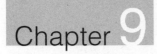
Linking the 7 Essentials

■■■■■■

Have we got it all together?

A space shuttle is poised for launch at Cape Kennedy. Mission Control is checking all systems for liftoff: Fuel temperature and pressure are a go, instruments check out, the crew is on board, and the weather has cleared. All critical functions are being monitored. Three . . . two . . . one . . . we have ignition.

To reach orbit, the shuttle must fly at a speed of 36,700 feet per second or 25,000 miles per hour.[1] This is the *escape velocity*. Achieving this velocity is critical—not enough and the shuttle's orbit is too low.

During liftoff, every part of the system endures unimaginable stress. Yet once orbit is established, less thrust is required. As the shuttle approaches outer space, the crew takes on many of the functions of mission control. The team on the ground takes on a new role: tracking the flight, monitoring systems, and proactive planning to self-correct in the event of deviations from plan.

Launch and Escape Velocity

Blasting into orbit is similar to what Blueprint Companies experience as they hit their inflection points and stretch skyward in growth. While the rest of us tend to simplify the picture and observe the graceful trajectory of rising revenues, inside the company critical, high-pressure decisions are constantly being made. The decisions at this stage—the value proposition, early customers, the leadership team—are critical to determining the difference between becoming a *growth company* and becoming an *exponentially growing company that achieves $1 billion revenue*. These decisions are the g-forces (multiples of the force of gravity) that can hold back management—challenging them to build the company fast and furiously enough to achieve "escape velocity."

We learned that most companies experience slowing growth as they get bigger. This tends to pull them back to earth. If the company is going to make $1 billion revenue, then it has to start with a surprisingly high growth rate. A company that expects to reach revenues of a billion dollars in just four years, for instance, must have an approximate compound annual growth rate of 110 percent. For six years, the growth rate must be 65 percent—and for twelve years, 30 percent. Achieving such incredible rates of growth is rare. What does it take?

To answer this, we compared two similar companies—each founded during the same period, targeting the same market with a similar product, and with exposure to similar resources. One became an *exponential growth* company, that is, a Blueprint Company, while one became a growth company. Within the technology industries, for example, there are numerous examples of one company that achieved exponential growth and a comparative company that did not: Oracle and Relational Technology, Sun Microsystems and Apollo, Juniper Networks and Avici, Xilinx and Lattice Semiconductor, and Siebel Systems and Onyx Software. The Blueprint methodology (see Appendix D) enabled us to examine the differences between growth companies and exponential growth companies in terms of execution of the 7 Essentials.

Growth is never perfect or without the need for self-correction. We illustrate this point in the following comparative case study of Siebel Systems and Onyx Software, with each company having real challenges along the way. These two companies are in the same customer-relations software business that started up at about the same time. The common positive aspect of these two stories is that these companies represent a more recent case study than the other comparative companies mentioned in the previous paragraph. Also Siebel, one of the fastest growing software companies, ascended the four-year trajectory making the contrast with Onyx Software more definitive. The downside is that both companies are off their highs. (*Note:* On September 13, 2005, Oracle offered to buy Siebel for $5.85 billion.)

To put this in context, if you are thinking that the best example of a Blueprint Company to conclude this book should be a company that continues to consistently excel, be aware that only 29 of the Blueprint Companies have surpassed $10 billion revenue! Microsoft, Cisco, and Oracle are such examples in the Information Technology sector with Nike, Best Buy, Staples, HCA, and Express Scripts being examples from other sectors. Clearly the Blueprint to $10 billion is an especially difficult one. In fact, the trajectory to $10 billion differs from the one taken to $1 billion revenue; over half of the Blueprint Companies are off their revenue highs! Therefore, consider the following comparison of Siebel and Onyx through the lens of the *journey to* $1 billion revenue: the period between 1993 and 2000. It is an illustration that compares *growth* versus *exponential growth*, not failure versus success. It also illustrates that though the concept of a trajectory is a central one in this book, escape velocity can be intensely difficult to achieve and falloffs are inevitable. And falloffs are not necessarily bad, because they are opportunities for shrewd recalibration and self-correction.

Siebel Systems and Onyx Software

Your first impression, as was mine, might be that this is another "tech bubble" comparison. Actually, the seeds for exponential growth of these two companies were sown between 1994 and 1998, prior to the bubble.

Siebel Systems reached its inflection point in three years and then rocketed to a billion dollars, launching from a revenue growth rate at the inflection point of *389 percent a year*. In comparison, Onyx Software did not quite achieve this escape velocity and flew a lower orbit; the company's revenues peaked at $121 million. Using the spaceflight analogy, this is like the difference between the space shuttle and cruising on an airplane at 40,000 feet. We may fly every day, but only a few make it into the outer space of revenue. Siebel Systems is the firm that became the number-nine Blueprint Company.

Siebel's revenue grew to $1 billion exponentially and consistently as shown in Figure 9.1. It achieved its inflection point of $39 million in revenues in 1996. By 1999 Siebel had achieved $790 million revenues, a net income of $122 million and a market value of $15 billion. The following year, it achieved not $1 billion, but $1.7 billion!

Onyx, however, reached its inflection point two years later in 1998 and its growth rate was only one-third of Siebel's. That was not enough "thrust" to send the company to $1 billion as Figure 9.1

FIGURE 9.1

Siebel and Onyx

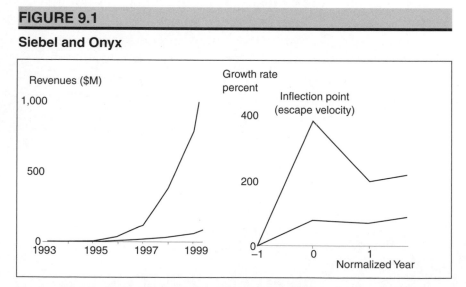

Source: Standard & Poor's Compustat, Blueprint analysis

shows. (The growth rates on the right-hand side are normalized so you can compare growth rates. The calendar years are two years apart.) Onyx's revenue peaked at $121 million in 2000 with a market value of $407 million. As of year-end 2004, both companies were down from their peak revenues; Siebel closed the year at $1.3 billion revenue, with a market value of $5.3 billion; Onyx's $59 million had a market value of $46 million.[2]

> Without high enough growth, or "escape velocity," at the inflection point, companies usually do not become Blueprint Companies.

What was the difference in the execution of the essentials so that one company had exponential growth to $1 billion revenue and the other became a growth company? An essentials "scorecard" is needed to determine this, one that can quantify how well companies perform the 7 Essentials—a scale of growth versus exponential growth.

The following analysis offers a comparison between the two software companies and their execution of the 7 Essentials.

Siebel Systems and Onyx Software were founded in July, 1993,[3] and February, 1994,[4] respectively. Each was targeting the multi-hundred million dollar market for sales force automation and customer relationship management software. Both developed their software on Microsoft operating systems. Both had access to capital. Both had the opportunity to make comparable choices regarding type of product, customers to serve, how to build their revenue powerhouse, alliance partners, and board members. The founding teams, however, came from different professional backgrounds. Tom Siebel and Patricia House came from a background at Oracle and having worked at a small company; Siebel having been on the sales fast track and House having been a marketing director. Tom Siebel had a big idea for new software but hadn't defined the product yet. The three Onyx founders, Brian Janssen, Brent Frei, and Todd Stevenson, came from

Microsoft. They came up with the idea to form Onyx Software after developing internal customer management solutions while at Microsoft.[5]

Essential 1—The Big Idea: A Breakthrough Value Proposition

Onyx was and is an impressive company, recognized as one of "The Best Companies to Work For" in Washington state and topping Deloitte & Touche's "Washington Fast 50" as the fastest growing company in the state in 1999.[6]

Onyx believed that customer functions should be managed from a single database, including sales, service, technical support, and marketing. Because there was only one database, customer information was always up-to-date—no matter who entered the data. What was once a difficult task on a mainframe could now be done much easier on server computing, using Microsoft platforms. "We've learned early on never to bet against Bill (Gates)," said Janssen in 1997. "By being at the forefront of Microsoft's NT Wave, we are very well positioned now."[7] Brian Janssen believed that the 1990s were all about managing customers for competitive advantage.[8]

Janssen and his other fellow Microsoft alumni at Onyx created their software on Microsoft Windows NT, an operating system that was one of the fastest growing platforms with medium-sized businesses.[9] Their focus was to develop software to merge a company's separate sales, customer service, technical support, and marketing databases so that employees could easily access all of the information on a particular customer. To do that, they also focused on Microsoft's database products (also known as SQL Server) to develop features and functions quickly.[10]

Onyx released its first product in 1995, called EnCompass. It ran on Microsoft's NT operating system and database server. Initially, the software required a high level of customization and, therefore, a high level of support.[11] Soon thereafter, in 1997, the company had grown from $2.1 million to $9.8 million revenue—and its biggest challenge was finding enough qualified employees to keep up with growth.[12]

By 1998, Onyx had released Customer Center 4.0 to rave reviews for being easy to use and highly customizable. Built from the ground up, the software was less expensive than that of competitors but lacked some flexibility. That year, Onyx won the Codie Award, one of the most prestigious awards in the software industry, for the best product in the enterprise client-server application.[13]

Though EnCompass was easy to use and to customize, it was not clear to reviewers whether Onyx could lead in the category, that is, customer management software, that it was creating. Onyx could collect and share knowledge or customer contacts from every department, but only if companies would consolidate their legacy platforms into an architecture based on Microsoft's Windows NT and SQL Database Server.[14] This meant that being on the Windows and Microsoft SQL Server platform, the *target market in large enterprises* was limited because their dominant operating system was UNIX and the database solutions were by IBM and Oracle.[15]

Meanwhile, Tom Siebel of Siebel Systems was also on his way to figuring out how to make Siebel Systems one of the fastest growing software companies. When we asked in an interview what initiated his Big Idea, he told us:

> The Big Idea for Siebel Systems started in the early 1990s. Corporations had effectively used information and communications technology to improve a lot of business processes and bring productivity increases to many processes: office automation, accounting, manufacturing, and general automation systems. And yet, as of 1993, the processes of sales, marketing, and customer services remained untouched by IT. Most people used notes, yellow stickies . . . there was nothing there.

However, no research to support that idea existed then for Siebel—or for Onyx. The global market for sales automation in

1993 was $100 million, and nearly 400 companies operating in this sector faced the same problem. How did Siebel determine if there was an opportunity inside this same pack? "We spent quite a bit of time interviewing customers," he reflected. Tom Siebel continues:

> Customers such as Oracle, Sun Microsystems, Amgen, Cisco, LSI Logic, Chevron, Unisys—we knew them well from our previous work lives. This was more like a consulting project than a software development project. In the process of doing the customer interviews, we learned about their requirements. We started with sales automation and asked them, "Ideally, what would it do? What would it look like?"
>
> After six months we wrote a product specification—we called it *Malibu*. This was to be the first enterprise-class, fully comprehensive sales automation system that could scale to meet the needs of the world's largest corporations. We developed a prototype and took it back to those customers. We asked them if this is what they meant and they said not quite but were quick to suggest modifications. We modified it and took it back. That is what we tasked engineering to build.

Siebel Systems quickly developed valuable insights for the new software: scalable from 50 to 50,000 salespersons, multilingual, and very adaptable to various customers' needs.[16] Additionally the software provided the sales force with up-to-the-minute data concerning products, customers, and industry information. Therefore, the salesperson could spend less time on back-office and administrative matters and more on "making the sale" instead.[17] Siebel staked out the domain for the "front office" to offer tools to make the sales process super effective and ensured that customer relationships were managed for maximum pay-back.[18] This was particularly important because companies had diminishing returns for squeezing costs from manufacturing, but sales force automation could significantly lower overhead while increasing revenue.

In 1994, Siebel released Siebel Sales Information System for companies with *large sales forces*—and achieved the remarkable by bringing its first product to market spending less than $1.8 million.[19] Later, in 1997, Siebel introduced a powerful development environment to allow applications developers and customers to more easily customize the software.[20] While Siebel's software also had the advantage of running on Microsoft's NT operating system, the Siebel Enterprise Applications 3.0 release was a major step to integrating the software with customers' enterprise systems.[21] Siebel focused on integrating their applications with the installed base of databases. For example, a hallmark alliance came in 1998 when Siebel announced a development partnership with IBM that would bring Siebel's Enterprise Relationship Management solutions to IBM's award-winning DB2 Universal Database. As Siebel acquired technologies to serve diverse markets, the team quickly integrated their technologies.

From the get-go, the Siebel team moved to shape a company that could scale faster by focusing on Fortune 500 enterprise customers with well-defined areas of high value. Siebel leveraged the interviewing process to presell those customers early. Tom Siebel explained:

> The first customers—LSI Logic, Unisys, Cisco, and Compaq (now HP)—were involved in the specification process. Every one of them wanted the product. The first revenue was $50,000 from LSI Logic in Q4 1994. LSI Logic beta-tested the product and then adopted the product on a large scale. Compaq was an early customer and that has led HP/Compaq to grow to 80,000 users—the largest deployment on the planet. Cisco has 30,000 users today. They were very happy to serve as references and told their peers in the industry that we had solved the problem. It was like viral marketing. It turned out that the demand for this technology was greater than we thought.

The scorecard criteria (for these two technology companies) frame the Breakthrough Value Proposition (see Appendix D for the list of criteria) as delivering higher-order tangible and intangi-

ble benefits in order to become an exponential growth company.
Siebel Systems highly researched these needs before designing the
product, and then delivered the high-order benefits. (To follow the
relative scoring, see Figure 9.2.) Siebel realized that the "front
office" of larger enterprises was where the most lucrative customers were located.

Essential 2—Exploit a High-Growth Market Segment

Both Siebel and Onyx had access to a large software market for
sales-force automation and customer-relationship management.
Their primary difference was in choosing customers. Onyx targeted medium-sized businesses; Siebel targeted Fortune 500-sized
corporations.

Both Onyx and Siebel saw the same overall high-growth market
in the same timeframe, but each had a different view of the market.

FIGURE 9.2

Siebel and Onyx Essentials Scorecard

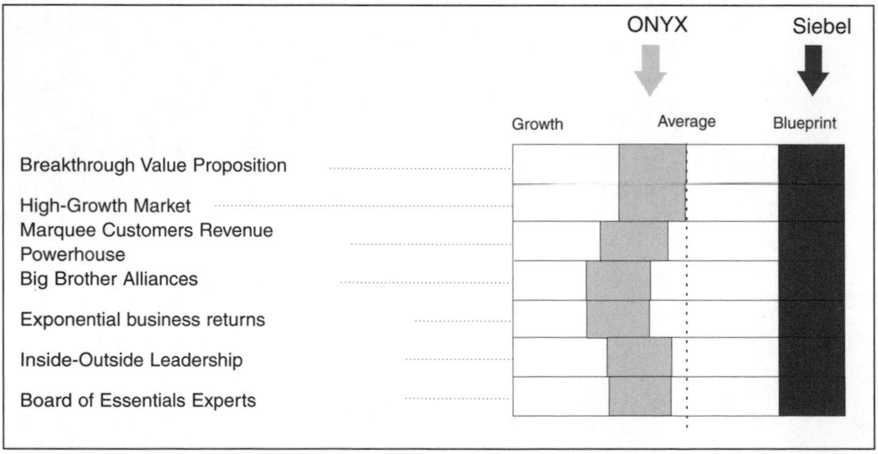

Source: Blueprint analysis

In 1997, sales-force automation software brought in $788 million, up from $100 million globally in 1995. Sales were forecasted by the research market firm IDC to grow at an annual compound growth rate of 42 percent to $4.5 billion by 2002.[22] By 2000, Forrester Research predicted that this market would be larger than the $2.1 billion spent on manufacturing software and the $2 billion on financial software.[23]

"Onyx is seeking a position in the medium-sized enterprise part of the market, beneath the area taken by competitors such as Siebel, but well above that of contact management," observed Brian Janssen.[24] Onyx's customers were medium-sized corporations that tended to be in vertical industries such as financial services, health care, high-tech, and telecommunications, which places a very high value on customer relationships.[25] The software targeted enterprises with 10 to 1,000 users.[26]

To access this market segment, Onyx targeted midsized, value-added resellers with the Microsoft-based platform. Onyx depended on the growth of Microsoft's Windows NT operating system for businesses.[27] After targeting the United States, Canada, and Australia, Onyx expanded to Europe in 1997 to focus on the rapidly growing European customer management market.[28]

Onyx's solutions could be implemented in two ways. It sold software and services that could be deployed internally within a company or could be purchased and deployed through third parties that added value (value-added resellers). In 1995, the company was challenged in sales and marketing; Onyx had no value-added reseller channel to carry its product into large corporations and this limited its access to large customers.[29]

Siebel, by contrast, executed a direct-selling strategy to large corporate customers to secure contracts that averaged tens of millions of dollars. This strategy evolved to include a vertical-market focus to win large corporations that needed a tailored product. For example, Siebel initially targeted sales-force automation to corporations with large sales forces and national and multinational corporations. Siebel expanded into vertical and horizontal markets.

In 1997, through the acquisition of Nomadic, Siebel expanded into the pharmaceuticals market[30] followed by expansion into the energy market in 1998.[31] That same year, it acquired Scopus Technology and expanded into the customer-service and call-center markets.[32]

Siebel's emphasis on sales-force automation in large enterprises led it to a bigger market segment than small- and medium-sized businesses. Siebel scored the highest in this High-Growth Market Segment essential because the largest contracts Siebel signed with Fortune 500 customers well exceeded $30 million. In contrast, Onyx targeted medium-sized business with a lower cost per user—which would have been a perfectly good strategy if the lower per-customer revenues had been offset with higher volume.

Essential 3—Marquee Customers Shape the Revenue Powerhouse

After getting a start through its value-added reseller channel, Onyx gained 65 customers by 1996. Most of these were medium-sized businesses that had adopted Microsoft's Windows NT operating system. In 1999, as Onyx shifted to Web-based solutions, this new approach helped them gain several new customers, including Cincinnati Bell and the Seattle Seahawks.[33] At this point their base had grown to over 550 customers.[34]

By then Siebel had several big Marquee Customers in its fold. In 1997, Siebel's revenue tripled to close at $118 million with customers such as Siemens, Compaq, and Charles Schwab accounting for a significant portion of their revenue. Charles Schwab, besides being a Marquee Customer, invested in the company and Charles Schwab himself became an active member of Siebel's board of directors. Through global marketing, Siebel Systems wooed multinational clients such as GE Capital, Ford Motor Company, Bank of America, and Hoechst Marion Roussel. Siebel solidly entrenched itself in the Fortune 500 class of customers.[35] As a benchmark, Nationwide Insurance, the Fortune 500 U.S. insurance giant, signed contracts valued at $32 million.[36] Using Siebel software,

Motorola established a customer-relationship management system that established seamless and interactive communications between its worldwide service centers and its sales groups.[37]

Onyx and Siebel both had Marquee Customers. Siebel's, however, were large Fortune 500 corporations that not only made a larger commitment to Siebel, they also served as lighthouse customers. Companies such as Nationwide and Schwab attracted their peers. Finally, Siebel simply had more Marquee Customers. The result was large deals at a much lower cost of sales.[38] Onyx had the right idea but the company did not get the scope or scale of Marquee Customers in comparison to Siebel. One reason: Tom Siebel was known for his aggressive sales background and techniques, whereas Onyx struggled early on to ramp up sales and marketing and targeted medium-sized enterprises.[39]

Essential 4—Leverage Big Brother Alliances for Breaking into New Markets

Onyx created its Onyx Software Value-Added Reseller Network. Partners included Trilogy, which resold its Selling Chain products, and TechnologyWorks, which sped the adoption and deployment of Onyx solutions.[40] In 1999, an alliance was signed with Arthur Andersen Business Consulting to co-market in the Asia-Pacific Region.[41] Not long after, Onyx teamed with both Yahoo! UK and Yahoo! Ireland to deliver Yahoo!'s popular Web programming and services to business users.[42]

Siebel Systems determined that large, strategic alliances were going to be critical to achieve its growth aspirations. Tom Siebel, in our interview, explained his rationale for utilizing alliances early.

> We were always looking to remove our constraint to growth. In the 1995 to '96 timeframe, we weren't constrained by the market, competitors, or availability of technology. We were constrained by delivering, configuring, and integrating the software. We looked at our largest competitors—Oracle, SAP—who were doing everything internally.

At that point in time, we took a radical departure from our competitors' approaches. If we built the capability to execute systems integration internally, we assessed that the overall growth rate would be constrained by the rate at which we could grow our professional services organization. That growth would be linear. On the other hand, if we could form long-term strategic business partnerships with the leading information technology companies in the world, we could remove that constraint. We chose to form strategic alliances with Andersen, IBM, Deloitte & Touche, and Cap Gemini. We were in the business of borrowing other people's brand equity. It brought us enormous credibility. Those relationships became a strategic advantage; they built a business around us and we had nine of ten salespeople from those strategic alliance companies selling our products.

The very next year, Siebel and IBM announced a development-and-marketing partnership that would bring Siebel's Enterprise Relationship Management solutions to IBM's award-winning DB2 universal database. The value proposition for large enterprises was highly differentiated. "The ability to implement these business-critical applications on a scalable, robust, cross-platform database is increasingly important to our customers," said Janet Perna, General Manager in IBM's Software Solutions. Under the terms of the agreement, IBM and Siebel agreed to:

- Jointly test, performance optimize, and support activities to help customers obtain maximum performance.
- Develop competency centers to ensure rapid and successful deployment.
- Certify Siebel applications with IBM Universal Database platforms.
- Jointly train their organizations to cooperatively market and sell to mutual customers.[43]

To provide structure and value to an expanded set of alliance partners, Siebel launched its Global Alliance Program in 1998. This program provided for partners to access a comprehensive set of technical and marketing programs.[44]

Onyx targeted alliances with value-added resellers—naturally, a set of smaller companies.

Siebel not only commanded best-in-class alliances with Accenture followed by IBM, these big alliances were also executed early in its revenue growth trajectory. Another important difference is that while Onyx had a Big Brother alliance with Microsoft, it was as a value-added developer. Accenture, on the other hand, built a sales-force automation practice around Siebel's software.

The good news for Onyx was that it leveraged alliances— many companies of this size do not. The big difference between Onyx and Siebel, however, was the size and timing of their alliances.

Essential 5—Become the Masters of Exponential Returns

As the companies grew with time, Siebel managed the drivers for positive returns typically profiled by Blueprint Companies. As a result of compounding cash flow growth by 2000, Siebel's market cap was $29 billion against Onyx's $407 million.[45]

Not only was the growth rate and cash flow different, the companies' performance at similar sales levels was not comparable. Onyx achieved key revenue milestones at least two years later than Siebel. All things being equal, when Onyx did achieve these levels, Siebel outscored Onyx on gross margins, higher investment in R&D, and SG&A (Sales and General Administration) effectiveness as shown in Table 9.1.

Even though Onyx placed a high value on being a technology leader, Onyx's higher investment in R&D, at $35 million revenue, did not drive a higher revenue growth rate. Surprisingly, Siebel's R&D investment was higher when both companies achieved $120 million revenue. In the early days, investment in sales and marketing was comparable. But Siebel's sales force and alliance partnerships, along with higher revenue per customer deals, were major reasons why Siebel spent 36 percent SG&A versus Onyx's 58

Table 9.1

Siebel and Onyx Financial Performance

	Siebel	Onyx	Siebel	Onyx
	1996	**1998**	**1997**	**2000**
Revenues (in millions)	$39.2	$35.1	$118.8	$121.5
Gross Profit Margin	97.4%	77.2%	94.9%	81.6%
Gross Profit (in millions)	$38.1	$27.1	$112.8	$99.1
R&D Expense	15%	26%	30%	17%
SG&A Expense	62%	68%	36%	58%
EBITDA Margin	20%	−16%	33.8%	7.3%
Net Income/Loss (in millions)	$5	−$7	−$2.4	−$2.5
Free Cash Flow (in millions)	−$3.9	−$6.1	$16	−$15.8

Source: Standard & Poor's Compustat, Blueprint analysis

percent when the companies each reached the $120 million revenue mark.

Essential 6—The Management Team: Inside-Outside Leadership

Both management teams at Siebel and Onyx had an inside-outside combination. Janssen, the Executive Vice President at Onyx, served in the Outside role while Todd Stevenson focused more internally on innovation as the Chief Technology Officer. Brent Frei, CEO, best summed up the management team's core values during the Deloitte & Touche Fast 50 Award. "We've focused on building the best products in the market, and having fun while we do it."[46] The company tried to recruit people not only on the basis of their skills, but also on how well their goals and personal characteristics matched the company's.[47] During this time period, Onyx was recognized for its technology, as a great place to work, and as a team-oriented culture.

In contrast, Tom Siebel and Patricia House came to Siebel Systems with an extensive sales and marketing background. While Onyx's challenge in the early days was sales and marketing, Siebel rapidly developed a marketing and sales powerhouse.[48]

Patricia House played the Inside role as "a world-class project manager and problem solver," as Tom Siebel shared with us. Tom Siebel, as Mr. Outside, established a reputation in the software industry as one of the most aggressive marketers. His management style created an organizational culture, based on early days of Oracle, with an extreme performance focus: fierce competitiveness, emphasis on product line management, and winner-take-all ethos.[49] Having an aggressive Mr. Outside turned out to be the reason that Siebel Systems secured Big Brother alliances and Marquee Customers early. Tom Siebel's role was a key propellant in the company's compounding revenue growth.

The combination of Patricia House and Tom Siebel demonstrated that they could out-execute Onyx across the three dimensions of Blueprint leadership: focus on product and relationships, drive to explore and innovate, and the ability to simultaneously execute all 7 Essentials as a team. Siebel finishes as a Blueprint Company, an achiever of exponential growth. Onyx, on the other hand, typifies a good growth company—aggressive about product, but not as productive in shaping Marquee Customers and Big Brother alliances.

Essential 7—The Board: Comprised of Essentials Experts

Onyx's board was composed primarily of management team members and venture capitalists including Orlando Ayala from Microsoft (alliance partner), and a VP of Operations from Interworld.[50] Siebel's board, on the other hand, stressed a team without investors, combined with a cohort that had experienced exponential growth in their own companies. In 1994, Charles Schwab joined the board and purchased a personal stake of 2.5 percent of Siebel's stock. Schwab, the experienced builder of his own Blueprint Company, helped guide Siebel through the journey to $1 billion.

Then, in 1995, Siebel brought Andersen Consulting's managing partner, George Shaheen, to the board. Andersen purchased a 10 percent stake in the company. Shaheen created a Big Brother alliance partnership between Andersen and Siebel, as we saw in Chapter 5. Also on the board were Eric Schmidt (then Chairman and CEO of Novell, Inc.) and Michael Spense who had served as the Dean of the Graduate School of Business at Stanford University.

Onyx scored around the midpoint in all 7 Essentials compared to Siebel, which scored similar to companies experiencing exponential growth (see Figure 9.2 on page 198). This case study is a real-world representation that demonstrates what it takes to be best in class across all 7 Essentials. There are three themes that cut across this two-company comparison:

1. The choices made regarding the value proposition have a significant impact on the direction and execution of the other essentials. Onyx's decision to target medium-sized businesses (with its limited sales channel) affected its product development, revenue powerhouse, ability to secure larger Marquee Customers, and the type and number of Big Brother alliance partners. These first decisions were critical to the company's fortunes. In contrast, the compelling value proposition from Siebel, the sales-force automation software, was the cornerstone of its early Big Brother alliance with Andersen and its initial Marquee Customers such as Charles Schwab.

2. The difference between growth and exponential growth companies, at times, is not a matter of technology. Both Siebel and Onyx used essentially the same software platform—Microsoft NT—though Siebel gained the flexibility of integrating with installed databases, for example, from IBM. The real difference came in the execution of the essentials.

3. Growth companies tended to score at or below the midpoint in many of the 7 Essentials, not just one or two. Exponential growth companies scored highly on all 7 Essentials.

Linking the Essentials

When you reflect on the Onyx–Siebel case study, see how the linking of the essentials gave Siebel a growth boost, like the second stage of a rocket pushing the space shuttle in orbit. Siebel had this boost because on its execution of all 7 Essentials. When you put the essentials together, they are more than the sum of their parts. Linking them, in fact, creates the dynamic "1 + 1 = 3" effect that accounts for exponential revenue growth and cash flow. One of the central points of this book is that executing all 7 Essentials average or above can make the difference between being a growth company and being a Blueprint Company.

The linkages that differentiate Blueprint Companies—exponential revenue growth and exponential returns—can be described as follows:

- *Link the Big Idea with markets and Marquee Customers.* Figure 1.4 in Chapter 1 shows that growth has two parts: before and after the inflection point. Before the inflection point, Blueprint Companies either did the market and customer research up front, as in the case of Siebel, or followed a journey based on market and customer feedback, as in the case of eBay. Similar to the advice that Roger McNamee shared with us in Chapter 4, both had a quick and dirty solution to get to market quickly—which, significantly, echoes the name of the first PC operating system, Quick and Dirty Operating System.

  The goal is to link the Big Idea with an initial value proposition and to get it to market quickly in order to shape the customer-centric value proposition. The second linking is the identification of unmet needs, not functional ones (such as a common database and being built on Micorosft SQL) but higher-order needs such as a scalable Sales-Force Automation system to provide a single global process for sales force management. Terry Eger demonstrated this skill set when he identified the unmet need to provide an "always up" network at Solomon Brothers.

- *Link the company's resources to the front line*: All too often, large companies, and even small ones, leave their greatest assets in the back room. But when companies link development teams to customers, as Terry Eger did, there is an almost chemical reaction that unlocks value. The result? Higher gross margins as measured per Marquee Customer. Roger Boeve highlighted that higher returns started at the customer. Chapter 7 showed that companies with higher gross margins could self-fund higher levels of investment in product development and sales and marketing.

- *Establish a board of Essentials Experts.* The board is immensely important though not in the way we have traditionally assumed. While investors can bring a particular brand of expertise, there is no substitute for a board that is balanced with Essentials Experts. These experts provide the external perspective and unique set of experiences regarding the execution of the Blueprint pattern. Their added value is about "having lived it" and then transferring those experiences. We also saw that these kinds of board members help link the company to marquee relationships. Finally, do not forget the role of the advisory board. Broadcom demonstrated that this board was critical to linking the company to new markets and new customers and for developing a roadmap for their development team.

The Linking of the Leadership Team

Interestingly, the grouping of the essentials in the Essentials Triangle (see Figure 1.8 on page 12) is a parallel framework to leadership (see Figure 9.3). The innovation leader leads the development team and links them to the value proposition (the Big Idea). At the same time, the outside leader shapes the revenue-centric essentials: securing Marquee Customers, forging a Big Brother alliance, and shaping the market. The inside leader, typically the Chief Operating Officer, is responsible for creating and sustaining

FIGURE 9.3

Leadership Links the Essentials

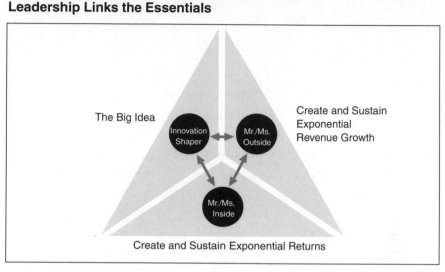

The Big Idea

Innovation Shaper

Mr./Ms. Outside

Create and Sustain Exponential Revenue Growth

Mr./Ms. Inside

Create and Sustain Exponential Returns

Source: Blueprint analysis

exponential returns. The essentials, combined with this leadership model, map to a company's financials. It is now not hard to understand what happens to financial performance if one or more of these leaders do not perform to the required levels or the leaders do not function as a high-performance team.

Are All Blueprint Companies Built to Last?

A recent *Fast Company* article on the best business books pointed out that a number of the companies identified by the authors of *In Search of Excellence* and *Built to Last* have lost their shine. Does that taint the conclusions of these books? Jim Collins, referring to his book, *Built to Last*, correctly noted that his writings are not about the performance of particular companies, but about the lessons learned.[51]

(continued)

For our part, we say upfront that Blueprint Companies inevitably do struggle. The odds are 21 percent that companies will fall off trajectory. We found that growth has two themes: (1) getting on trajectory and (2) correcting to get back on when companies almost invariably struggle or stumble. Success is often about what companies do to self-correct. Consider two key findings:

1. For the companies that achieved $1 billion revenue, 21 percent fell back below this mark and have revenues below $1 billion today. Some of this is mismanagement; some of it is due to external circumstances. For example, JDS Uniphase and Ciena have suffered as a result of the telecom "downdraft."

2. We said earlier in the chapter that only 29 Blueprint Companies have surpassed $10 billion revenue. Still, we analyzed 2004 Blueprint Company revenues versus their historical highs because we wanted to determine if Blueprint Companies were continuing to achieve new highs or if the 2000 bubble had affected growth. Surprisingly, 166 of the 387 companies were achieving new revenue highs, with an average growth rate of 17 percent over 2003. For the remaining companies, their 2004 revenues were, on average, 25 percent below their all-time previous record revenues.

Chapter Summary

Key Points
- There are few compromises regarding how well essentials are executed, particularly in Marquee Customers, alliances, market performance, and board composition. This is espe-

cially important early on in a company's life and as it approaches the inflection point.

- Blueprint Companies executed all 7 Essentials with above average performance.
- The impact of a CEO who secures large Marquee Customer relationships and contracts along with Big Brother alliances is not to be underestimated.
- The Value Proposition essential has a direct impact on the context, shaping, and execution of the other essentials. The Onyx–Siebel case study illustrates how Siebel benefited from board membership, alliances, Marquee Customers, and high-revenue contracts, especially in terms of shaping a company that could scale faster by focusing on large enterprise customers with highly defined areas of high value.
- The essentials scorecard can serve as a simple tool to identify the performance of each essential relative to how well growth companies versus Blueprint (exponential growth) Companies executed them.
- Inevitably companies do struggle. The odds are that about 20 percent of up-and-coming Blueprint Companies will not achieve their revenue trajectories! We found that growth has two themes: getting on trajectory and correcting to get back on it when the inevitable stumble takes place.

Unexpected Findings

- The Siebel–Onyx comparison illustrates that decisions made early in a company's life can greatly determine the achievement or non-achievement of Blueprint Company status.
- Consistent growth from the inflection to $1 billion determines a company's revenue trajectory: four, six, or twelve years. That said, the highest growth rate typically occurs near the inflection point. Therefore, not achieving high growth rates early is one of the chief reasons a company does not become a Blueprint Company.

- Comparative *growth* companies (as opposed to Blueprint Companies) in the same industry, founded in the same year and targeting the same market, tended to score midpoint or below in most essentials. We initially assumed that growth companies would be lacking in only one or two essentials.
- Revenue growth beyond $1 billion can have a distinctly different profile, even for four-year trajectory companies! Inevitably, growth will slow.

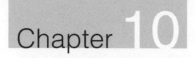

Chapter 10

Blueprint Companies for the Next Decade and Your Part in Them

An Epilogue

"For the first time in our history, we are going to face competition from low-wage, high-human-capital communities embedded within India, China, and Asia," Harvard's president Lawrence Summers told Thomas L. Friedman of the *New York Times*. In order to thrive, "it will not be enough for us to just leave 'no child behind.' We also have to make sure that many more young Americans can get as far ahead as their potential will take them. How we meet this challenge is what will define our nation's political economy for the next several decades. "[1]

As the sometimes controversial Summers pointed out, the world is more than changing: It is *restructuring* with new market shifts, shifts in human capital from North America to Asia, and the high cost of finding and developing talent. These are at the top of the megatrends list. The good news is that up-and-coming Blueprint Companies demonstrated that they can adapt quickly and effectively and that they can restructure the very way business growth occurs. I believe that business leaders and investors will truly benefit by considering the Blueprint success pattern in light of the megatrends sweeping the world of business building.

Economic Sector Rotation

In the course of our research, we learned that the United States is a business-building engine of consumer and services companies.

However, the icons of these industries indicate that this may not be sustainable. For example, Tom Stemberg, Chairman Emeritus of Staples, pointed out that the opportunity to create new Category Killer superstores is limited because there are fewer price-inefficient categories. So what economic sectors are most likely to generate the greatest number of next-generation Blueprint Companies?

In the 1950s, the top growth companies were in paper, steel, electronics, and publishing. In the 1970s they were gold and silver, catalog showrooms, hospitals and nursing homes, and oil. Of course, then the personal computer came on the scene in the 1980s, leading to the next era. Recently, top growth is in industries such as retail specialty stores, biomedical, oil and gas drilling, and financial services. A new group will undoubtedly rule the top tier in the coming years.

Which seems most likely?

Leisure products, nursing homes, energy, and natural resources seem to be industries aligning with the aging population, as well as industries in the sweet spot of the world's demand for more energy, commodities, and natural resources.

Silicon Valley investor Roger McNamee has made some good choices in the past in terms of putting his money on the right fast-growth technology companies. In looking for the Next Big Thing, McNamee uses the same approach that has already served him well. "It is very much based on having a top-down view of the major themes that were really social themes," he believes. "In the mid-80s I had three themes: mobility, connectivity, and interactivity. The essential notion was that the society was more mobile." McNamee says those themes still exist today. "Look at the Blackberry," he said. "I watch the road warriors pull out their Blackberries when the plane is taxiing in to the gate. Those 40 minutes they save doing emails is a big deal. When people don't have enough time, an extra 40 minutes of sleep is *more* than a big deal."

But McNamee realizes that the breakthrough markets of the past will not necessarily be the ones to do it again in the future. New companies take the lead based on their abilities to fulfill new consumer demands. For one, McNamee believes that business has had its fill of technology for a while. Perhaps technology will lead the way in the next 10 years—for now it is the prime time of the consumer market and products that bring technology *to* individuals. What else may be hot? McNamee thinks that specialty chemicals, semiconductors that drive consumer items, and, in general, consumer services that give people some of their time back will be the drivers of future growth. "A consumer-driven environment will generate fewer big breakout companies," he thinks, "but will produce a small number of Google-like firms."

Balancing a High-Performance Culture

It is important to step back from all the strategic, financial, leadership, and governance issues around Blueprint Companies and consider the company culture implications; consider what these high-performance cultures look like today and what they will need to look like in the next 10 years.

One of the central messages in this book is there can and should be even more Blueprint Companies. But having worked for 20 years as a line executive, I am sensitive to the fact that the culture of such high-performing organizations can be extremely challenging to work in. Terms such as "performance focus," "bottom-line orientation," "accountability," "making the numbers," and "aggressive management style" may have a positive ring in the business sense, but can come at a high human cost: personal and mental health, shortened job tenure, and strains on family life. To be frank, there are a few Blueprint Companies that had reputations for rapidly turning over teams if they failed to meet the numbers. To achieve record growth rates of the four- and six-year trajectory, some Blueprint Companies created a work ethic with nearly endless workdays, and where family life had to be confined to short weekends. One of the CEOs I interviewed, whose company didn't make it to $1 billion revenue, acknowledged that he gave up a degree of performance in return for creating a great place to work.

This is concerning, because most of us need some sense of belief that the place where we work—where we spend the greatest part of our day and most of our energy—is a "good" or "great" place to work. We also want the enterprise to be a success, largely because success is the best form of personal satisfaction and job security. That being said, a successful career in a successful business should benefit not just us who are working there, but our families as well.

Fortunately, we have seen with many Blueprint Companies that the very best corporate cultures are ones with a high-performance focus *and* a nurturing environment. For example, Tractor Supply has managed to maintain the delicate balance between a high-performance focus and a team-promoting environment as it grew to $1 billion revenue and beyond. As Chairman Joe Scarlett told me when we were discussing how a company keeps this balance, "I spend over 50 percent of my time coaching, mentoring, career planning, and training. I am primarily in the stores working with employees and customers." Scarlett consistently strives to ensure *employee* satisfaction because it's the most direct influence on customer satisfaction.

After researching a broad range of companies and conducting an extensive set of interviews for this study, it is my belief that a high-performance focus and a nurturing cultural environment are not mutually exclusive. In fact, when those qualities converge in a company or organization, this culture is not only the most productive, it is the most personally rewarding. One of my personal take-aways from this research is that there are ways of working a lot smarter versus harder, and companies should definitely promote that. For example, encouraging employees to work hard and play hard keeps them more focused and productive, but rest and vacations must be part of that equation, too. So should helping create the almost nuclear fission that comes from excellent, cross-functional teamwork. Ask anyone who has worked at a company what was or is the best part of working there and they will almost invariably say their experience of being part of a high-performing team.

The best leaders of future Blueprint Companies will have to balance these choices in a more difficult world where global competitors will be competing based on the performance ethic—sometimes at all costs. This delicate balance will be one of *the* business conundrums for the next wave of talent and leadership, but one I am convinced must be achieved in order for companies, in general, but also exponential growth, in particular, to be sustainable. If it can't, then a number of these companies will inevitably struggle or even falter.

In order to compete in a global economy, the primary growth challenge will come more from the constraints of recruiting, developing, and retaining the best leadership and talent that a company needs than it will from financial constraints. Another unique challenge the leadership of new Blueprint Companies will face is that business talent will be even more mobile and, given the acceptance of virtual teams, will become even more accessible to employers around the globe. Therefore, companies are compelled more than ever to strike that right balance between employee satisfaction and financial performance. Creating an extremely good and sustainable corporate culture—one that is both professionally nurturing and performance-focused—is about as winning a combination as there is for keeping the people a company will need for growth of any kind, and that companies will especially need for exponential growth.

Talent and Leadership

It is a new fact of life: Business-building leaders cannot rely on importing talent anymore—not in a flat world where people can innovate without having to emigrate. Today, in Silicon Valley, "B to B" and "B to C" stand for "back to Bangalore" and "back to China." This is where a lot of our foreign talent is moving to. Investors and executives have no choice but to consider global sources for human capital if they are going to compete going forward.

In today's flat world, this means recruiting innovative and talented employees not just locally but globally. Rightly so, Blueprint Company CEOs are tremendously concerned about the next generation of leaders for their companies and the development and improvement of business leaders in general. That is why, toward the end of so many of my CEO interviews when we would take a moment for reflection, so many of them would highlight that human capital, the ability to recruit and retain the very best talent a company would need, is both a high priority and constraint—now and in the future. This is not a new thought, but it is a sobering one.

In a book that has been unapologetically about the business-building success rate of American companies, it is essential to say something about the talent that underpins all these achievements. A billion dollars or more is, after all, only the creation of the leaders at every level of the company who, as a team, drive toward financial success. I turn to my former McKinsey colleagues, Ed Michaels, Helen Handfield-Jones, and Beth Axelrod and their book, *The War for Talent*, for insight on what to look for when we look for leaders to power the next generation of business:

> There is no universal definition of an outstanding manager, for what is required varies to some extent from one company to another . . . We can say, however, that managerial talent is some combination of a sharp strategic mind, leadership ability, emotional maturity, communications skills, the ability to attract and inspire other talented people, entrepreneurial instincts, functional skills, and the ability to deliver results.[2]

Your Situation

One big takeaway from this study is that investors and leaders alike cannot continue to win with the paltry probabilities of success experienced in the past. Creating world-class companies with a *much higher probability of one in 400 from taking a small company public to $1 billion revenue* will rely on all necessary resources and talent going forward. It will also absolutely require improving the business building success rate.

As you apply the 7 Essentials to your situation—whether building businesses, investing, or interviewing to join one of these fine companies—you will need to translate and tailor them. To that end, I have developed some tools to get you started. These can be found in the appendixes at the end of this book and at http://www.blueprinttoabillion.com.

A Cool *Billion*

I would like to close by mentioning Nathaniel West's 1934 novel, *A Cool Million*. If you have not heard of this book, it is a rather bitter take on the classic American belief that the good struggle against poverty and temptation leads one to wealth and fame. It is a parody of the optimistic rags-to-riches tale of Horatio Alger.

My book, I hope, is an antidote (and an economic update because a million does not get you very far any more!) to the Depression-era spirit behind West's downbeat novel. I hope you have found *Blueprint to a Billion* to be a clear-eyed, yet unabashedly optimistic book about the success pattern of America's highest-growth companies. And that you have been encouraged about what went *right* with those companies that, since 1980, went from an initial public offering and achieved *a cool billion* in revenue. I hope you have been inspired by stories about what went right when good aims in business combined with very shrewd execution have overcome obstacles and temptations. These lessons apply today and can be applied to your situation.

But remember: Of the 7,454 companies that went public since 1980, 25 percent have failed. Only 5 percent of the companies made it to $1 billion. After having read all the facts and figures explaining how that happened, you may still wonder why America's most successful growth businesses are so few. Is it mostly luck, good or bad, that determines a company's financial success? Do management teams and investors lack strategic focus and the ability to bring great innovation to marketplace? Do both capitalism and American attention spans make room for only a small number of great companies?

No to all of the above. However, if America or any nation is to compete in the new global economy, they must foster the growth of new Blueprint Companies—every year. In the new global economy, we really have to be much better than we were over the past 25 years in terms of germinating Big Ideas and improving the success rate of creating $1 billion businesses. We must not only be leveraging innovation to enable new business growth but, more important, utilizing the business-building success pattern to realize the full potential from these unique innovations.

You can influence this outcome. The companies described in this book started at zero. They started with a Big Idea and a place where each one of us is on equal footing. The difference is that they shaped their ideas into great, economically successful companies. I hope the ideas, frameworks, and interviews in this book can help bring more clarity and vigor into your business, and that they can inspire you to help make a difference in the lives and economic well-being of those around you. Those who work for you, those who work with you, and that you yourself can benefit by the work that you do.

But Can You Really Learn from Best Practices?

As I was finishing this manuscript, my editors and I debated a tough question: "Can you really learn from best practices?" Jim Collins and Tom Peters certainly think so. But can anyone really learn to be a better business leader—or parent, spouse, friend, golf partner—by modeling from the most "successful" behaviors? The answer is yes and no . . . but you have to start somewhere. The human spirit leans toward inspiration like a plant toward sunlight. However, that does not mean that that which inspires is absolutely or even essentially replicable. Perhaps the clearer way to frame the debate about best practices is: What can you do to *influence* the process? What is in your power to observe from the outside and then try to improve from the inside? The intention to influence in a beneficial way may not guarantee success, but you cannot have success, or any kind of distinctive improvement in business or in life, without it.

Whether you are in a large company needing to grow a division, in a stand-alone company, in government, in education, or are a Marquee Customer or an investor, you can take away all or an element of this success pattern and apply it starting today. Starting with Chapter 1, you have already begun the Blueprint Journey.

You can do it. We all can do it. The odds of success are now much better than you may have thought.

Appendix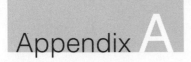

Top 100 Blueprint Companies

Rank	Company Name	Year	Normalized Market-Value ($1 billion revenue)
1	MICROSOFT CORP.	1990	42,490
2	AMGEN INC.	1992	28,306
3	EBAY INC.	2002	28,092
4	VERITAS SOFTWARE CO.	2000	26,079
5	GOOGLE INC.	2003	22,176
6	NOVELL INC.	1993	16,518
7	COMPUTER ASSOCIATES INTL INC.	1988	16,183
8	BOSTON SCIENTIFIC CORP.	1995	15,942
9	SIEBEL SYSTEMS INC.	2000	14,247
10	XILINX INC.	1999	13,932
11	YAHOO INC.	2000	13,099
12	CISCO SYSTEMS INC.	1994	12,596
13	APOLLO GROUP INC. -CL A	2002	11,679
14	TELLABS INC.	1997	11,054
15	CENDANT CORP.	1994	11,038
16	GENENTECH INC.	1997	11,017
17	JUNIPER NETWORKS INC.	2004	10,941
18	COMPUWARE CORP.	1997	10,817
19	CLEAR CHANNEL COMMUNICATIONS	1998	10,545
20	FREEPORT MCMOR COP&GLD -CL B	1994	10,444
21	BROADCOM CORP. -CL A	2000	10,315
22	MAXIM INTEGRATED PRODUCTS	2001	10,268
23	MOODY'S CORP.	2002	9,931
24	UNITEDHEALTH GROUP INC.	1992	9,599

Rank	Company Name	Year	Normalized Market-Value ($1 billion revenue)
25	GENZYME CORP.	2002	9,568
26	CHIRON CORP.	1995	9,347
27	EMC CORP./MA	1994	9,200
28	LIZ CLAIBORNE INC.	1987	8,985
29	AMAZON.COM INC.	1999	8,457
30	AES CORP. (THE)	1997	8,002
31	NVIDIA CORP.	2001	7,741
32	CINCINNATI FINANCIAL CORP.	1990	7,651
33	FIFTH THIRD BANCORP	1994	7,627
34	SUN MICROSYSTEMS INC.	1988	7,362
35	MICRON TECHNOLOGY INC.	1994	7,286
36	LSI LOGIC CORP.	1995	6,907
37	BIOMET INC.	2000	6,829
38	SERVICE CORP. INTERNATIONAL	1994	6,817
39	ALTERA CORP.	2000	6,671
40	BMC SOFTWARE INC.	1998	6,650
41	APPLIED MATERIALS	1993	6,565
42	AUTOZONE INC.	1992	6,498
43	NETWORK APPLIANCE INC.	2000	6,481
44	MEDIMMUNE INC.	2003	6,470
45	MEDCO HEALTH SOLUTIONS INC.	1990	6,454
46	COACH INC.	2004	6,437
47	AMBAC FINANCIAL GP	2003	6,409
48	TOTAL SYSTEM SERVICES INC.	2003	6,316
49	PLUM CREEK TIMBER CO INC.	2002	6,250
50	TIME WARNER INC.	1996	6,243
51	PAYCHEX INC.	1998	6,150
52	SYMANTEC CORP.	2001	6,102
53	MBIA INC.	2000	6,073
54	KING PHARMACEUTICALS INC.	2002	5,975
55	UNIVISION COMMUNICATIONS INC.	2002	5,859
56	SMURFIT-STONE CONTAINER CORP.	1987	5,845
57	ORACLE CORP.	1990	5,787
58	SYNOVUS FINANCIAL CP	1996	5,785
59	AUTONATION INC.	1996	5,751
60	BOWATER INC.	1987	5,737
61	WASTE MANAGEMENT INC.	1996	5,708
62	MANDALAY RESORT GROUP	1994	5,704
63	FRANKLIN RESOURCES INC.	1996	5,691
64	MGIC INVESTMENT CORP./WI	2000	5,687

Rank	Company Name	Year	Normalized Market-Value ($1 billion revenue)
65	REEBOK INTERNATIONAL LTD	1987	5,667
66	INTUIT INC.	2000	5,568
67	NEWELL RUBBERMAID INC.	1989	5,566
68	IVAX CORP.	1994	5,491
69	KLA-TENCOR CORP	1997	5,482
70	BEA SYSTEMS INC.	2003	5,478
71	AUTODESK INC.	2004	5,463
72	CADENCE DESIGN SYSTEMS INC.	1998	5,384
73	RADIAN GROUP INC.	2002	5,297
74	CINTAS CORP.	1997	5,181
75	ATMEL CORP.	1996	5,150
76	GEORGIA GULF CORP.	1988	5,110
77	VALHI INC.	1987	5,099
78	GENERAL GROWTH PPTYS INC.	2002	4,954
79	CALPINE CORP.	2000	4,947
80	SANDISK CORP.	2003	4,897
81	SCHWAB (CHARLES) CORP.	1993	4,778
82	XTO ENERGY INC.	2003	4,765
83	21ST CENTURY INS GROUP	1992	4,701
84	COMMERCE BANCORP INC./NJ	2002	4,688
85	SIMON PROPERTY GROUP INC.	1997	4,625
86	SYNOPSYS INC.	2003	4,545
87	POTLATCH CORP.	1988	4,389
88	ADOBE SYSTEMS INC.	1999	4,347
89	NEW YORK CMNTY BANCORP INC.	2004	4,244
90	HARLEY-DAVIDSON INC.	1992	4,144
91	NIKE INC. -CL B	1985	4,135
92	OFFICE DEPOT INC.	1991	4,114
93	AMERICAN PWR CNVRSION	1998	4,086
94	ALLERGAN INC.	1995	4,063
95	HEALTH MANAGEMENT ASSOC	1998	3,993
96	ENTERPRISE PRODS PRTNER -LP	1997	3,984
97	BELCO CORP. -SER A COM	1997	3,879
98	BED BATH & BEYOND INC.	1997	3,873
99	HOME DEPOT INC.	1986	3,828
100	EOG RESOURCES INC.	2000	3,810

For the complete list of 387 Blueprint Companies, please visit www.blueprinttoabillion.com.

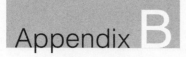

Delivering Breakthrough Benefits Drives Exponential Growth

Blueprint Companies delivered more than a product or service; they delivered breakthrough benefits—the value and meaning a customer attaches to the company's product or service. These make for benefit frameworks that can be used to quantify the relationship and value of functional and emotional benefits. Working with Mark Mitten and Eric Arnson, we show this framework and its benefit categories in a framework we call the Benefits Ladder (see Figure B.1).

Benefits can be distinguished into two categories according to the underlying motivations to which they relate: (1) functional benefits and (2) emotional benefits. Functional benefits address a customer's basic tangible needs. These benefits are often linked to fairly basic motivations. Emotional benefits relate to the intangibles of how one feels to use the product or service.

The Benefits Ladder is based on the principle that connecting a brand to higher-order emotional benefits creates strong and lasting customer loyalty. The higher companies go up the ladder, to uniquely own intangible benefits, the greater the value, the stronger the relationship, and the better the margins.

FIGURE B.1

Benefits Ladder

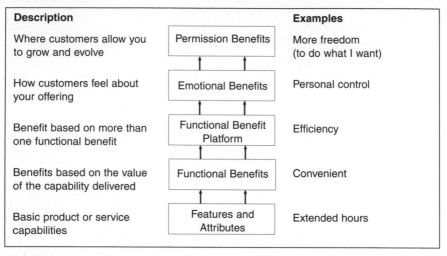

Description		Examples
Where customers allow you to grow and evolve	Permission Benefits	More freedom (to do what I want)
How customers feel about your offering	Emotional Benefits	Personal control
Benefit based on more than one functional benefit	Functional Benefit Platform	Efficiency
Benefits based on the value of the capability delivered	Functional Benefits	Convenient
Basic product or service capabilities	Features and Attributes	Extended hours

Source: © 2005 Mark Mitten and Eric Arnson for Originate Consulting.

Blueprint Company Lessons

Blueprint Companies demonstrated the market and financial impact of delivering higher order emotional benefits. There are three key lessons learned that are important to follow:

1. *Focus on delivering key benefits to attract the most desirable customer segments.* Blueprint Companies gained rich insights from customer segmentation in order to understand the exact nature of the segment needs and then figure out which benefits to deliver.

As Blueprint Companies have discovered, they could not jump immediately to delivering the emotional benefits exclusively. To gain customer permission, they learned that they must start at the bottom of the Benefit Ladder and then connect upward to the next level of benefits after satisfying that level. This is referred to as a *benefit bundles* because companies must deliver the entire bundle, including function and emotional benefits; not a collection of parts.

Many non-Blueprint Companies encountered disappointing trial usage and customer loyalty because their value proposition failed to simultaneously satisfy the most important key buying factors and effectively deliver entry-level functional benefits.

2. *Consistently deliver benefit bundles to create a lasting bond with target customers.* After targeting the appropriate customer segment with the appropriate benefit bundle, the next step is effective delivery. Without it, even the most compelling and distinctive benefit bundle will fail to connect with customers.

Consistent delivery creates strong and lasting relationships. As referenced in Chapter 2, Starbucks builds its strength on superior products for which customers are willing to pay a premium. However, it also extended its brand by placing an equal emphasis on the location and experience benefits (see Figure B.2). Starbucks not only ascended the product ladder, it created competitive advantage and new growth streams by leveraging relevant, complementary benefits. This way Starbucks achieved a lasting bond.

3. *Leverage permission benefits to generate exponential growth.* Trust is achieved by successfully and consistently delivering permission benefits, the highest form of commitment a Blueprint Company can achieve. Trust is earned and only customers grant it. Once a company is in this enviable position, they have created an army of Marquee Customers. Revenue per Marquee Customer transforms from linear to exponential, either through a higher-revenue-per-benefit ladder or broadening the products and services purchased.

For example, once that trusted relationship is established, customers often request additional offerings or underwrite the exploration of emerging needs. Typically the next generation of innovation is right next to the current offering. Google is a classic example of earning trust this way. It lever-

FIGURE B.2

Starbucks, Benefits Ladder

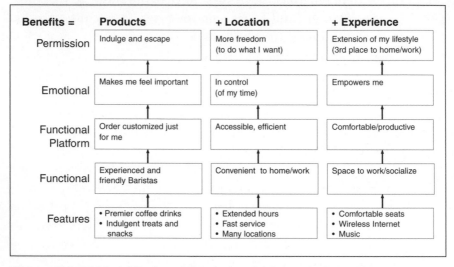

Source: © 2005 Mark Mitten and Eric Arnson for Originate Consulting.

aged the permission benefit of empowerment to a different but related set of services and tools such as e-mail, maps, and ad-blocking. This richer and diverse portfolio offering further strengthens the customer's loyalty and permits an even broader platform for future growth.

A second and equally important advantage of permission benefits is customer endorsement. Marquee Customers either formally recommend or implicitly endorse your company through the informal circles within your category; for example, IBM's endorsement of Microsoft's operating system as an alliance partner.

The Art and Science of Applying Breakthrough Benefits

Applying the concept of benefit ladders, especially in times of rapid change, is a challenging one. Our experience suggests three steps: (1) constructing the ultimate benefit bundle that the company aspires to own, (2) determining the ascension path to deliver the permission benefit and earn customer trust, and (3) envisioning the horizontal extension that drives the next generation of products and services. This is called *managing forward* (also referred to as "feedforward" by Peter Robertson in Appendix C).

The science is depicting the ladder and understanding where your company is on the ladder—through your customers' eyes. The art is determining the adjacent space in order to leverage permission. The final test for leaders is keeping the company, both inside and out, focused on the same benefit bundle and migration strategy.

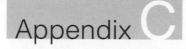

Appendix C

Assessing Management's Focus, Drive, and Ability

The unique work of Peter Robertson of Human Insight, which is discussed in his book *Always Change a Winning Team* (Singapore: Marshall Cavendish, 2005), is highly relevant to understanding the management profile of Blueprint Company management teams. While there are hundreds of team-assessment approaches, I looked for a set of tools that assessed teams along the S curve because Blueprint Company revenue growth was similar to the lower half of the S curve. To this end, Robertson's work served as a lens through which to evaluate teams.

Robertson is a partner of the London-based consulting and research group Human Insight Ltd. Robertson brings a unique background to understanding business management. He studied medicine, was a research fellow at the Mayo Clinic, and specialized in psychiatry and psychotherapy. From 1987 to 1995 he worked at KPMG as an international business consultant in the field of leadership and change management.

Robertson effectively applied the science of comparative behavioral studies, also known as ethology, to business management. This is the only field of psychology that has three Nobel Price winners (Lorenz, von Frisch, and Tinbergen). Robertson's study of ethology for 30 years enabled him to integrate ethology with complexity theory for business management.

Robertson's work applies these concepts to identify the fundamental behavioral dimensions through which we assessed teams. These patterns are:

1. *Focus.* How people form bonds with other people and with tangible ideas such as products, services, and processes.
2. *Drive.* The natural tendency to explore the future or utilize learning from the past to preserve the way people should behave and solve problems.
3. *Ability.* The ability of executives and teams to solve complex problems and manage through situations in which a high degree of skill diversity, teamwork, and multitasking is required.

Robertson has made a direct connection between critical elements of human instinct and business value. This connection is called the *feedforward hierarchy*. In making this connection, he dif-

FIGURE C.1

Feedforward–Feedback Table

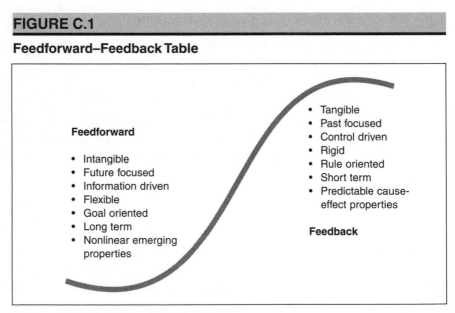

Source: Peter Robertson, Human Insight

ferentiated business impact of feedback from the business impact of feedforward.

Feedforward bases control on information it envisions for the future. Feedback bases control on information that occurred in the past. The feedforward flow is also the underlying dynamic of the classic S curve (see Figure C.1).

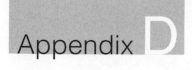

Appendix D

Methodology

Blueprint Company Identification Criteria

Blueprint Companies were selected based on the following criteria:

1. Companies that went public since 1980 with revenues less than $1 billion and that achieved $1 billion revenues and currently have revenues over $1 billion.

2. American companies that have a primary location in the United States and are incorporated as U.S. companies. To be very focused, I excluded American companies with headquarters in foreign locations—even those elsewhere in North America and just offshore, such as Canada and Bermuda.

3. Other kinds of companies that were excluded from the set included:

   a. Companies that became public with revenues greater than $1 billion. This set of 208 companies had no public data below $1 billion from which to analyze. A number of cases existed in which companies were spinouts from larger corporations; they were purposely excluded because they are not considered stand-alone companies at the time of ascent to $1 billion revenue. As a result, their financial growth pattern could not be identified.

   b. Companies that have been acquired or gone out of business. There are a few companies that exceeded $1 billion revenue and that were acquired: U.S. Robotics is one example; General Instruments is another.

  c. Companies that achieved $1 billion but subsequently fell below $1 billion—82 companies in total.

Comparison companies below $1 billion revenue were drawn from companies currently active in the United States today. Companies excluded were companies that have gone out of business or were acquired.

Each company's market valuation at $1 billion revenue was normalized by calculating the market value/revenue ratio in order to determine the market value at $1 billion revenue. The market value was indexed utilizing the ratio of the NASDAQ that year to year-end 2004. This gave a normalized list of companies with normalized market values at $1 billion revenue.

The companies were ranked by normalized market value (market capitalization) to determine the top Blueprint Companies. The top 100 are listed in Appendix A. The entire list is available at www.blueprinttoabillion.com.

Determining the Growth versus Exponential-Growth Methodology

To determine the essentials and financial pattern, I executed a pyramid-structured problem-solving approach (see Figure D.1).

The 7 Essentials were determined by synthesizing over 200 of the 387 Blueprint Company histories into a set of common essentials. The essentials were then defined and refined by studying annual reports, reviewing articles, and conducting in-depth interviews with executives who lead Blueprint Companies.

The financial benchmarks for Blueprint Companies were developed by selecting 264 companies from the 387 companies that had a first revenue period of less than $170 million. They were categorized as being in either one of the four-, six-, or twelve-year trajectories or being *switchers*. Switchers were companies that switched trajectories—either up or down.

FIGURE D.1

Success-Based Methodology

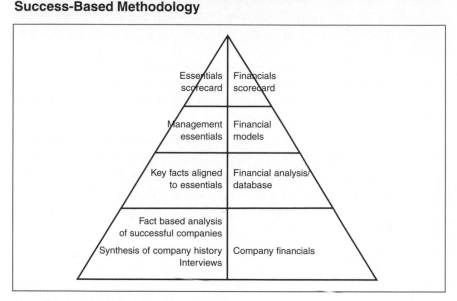

Note: Patent pending. All rights reserved.
Source: Blueprint analysis

Company Comparison Methodology: Growth versus Exponential Growth

The purpose of this methodology is to evaluate two or more companies in "an equivalent market and timeframe" regarding the execution profile of each of the 7 Essentials. The comparison methodology has a simple approach: Identify companies that were founded—or had initial public offerings at similar values—at the same time, were targeting the same markets with similar products or service offerings, and that had equivalent access to capital and resources. Each comparative case study is examined between the founding year and when the selected Blueprint Company achieved $1 billion revenue. The objective of this approach is to comparatively quantify, for each essential, growth companies versus exponential growth companies—the Blueprint Companies.

An Essentials Scorecard was developed based on a summary of comparative case studies. The range of performance for each essential was derived from this collective study. To summarize the Essentials Scorecard approach, each essential is scored on the following criteria:

1. *Create and sustain a Breakthrough Value Proposition.* This criterion frames the Breakthrough Value Proposition as having a set of high-order tangible and intangible benefits that are demonstrably valued by customers. Exponential growth companies tended to interview Marquee Customers prior to product development or worked closely with them in order to develop a highly valued, customer-centric set of benefits. In addition to an industry recognition of these benefits, customers declared their commitment to a value proposition through public statements and/or significant contract awards (as compared to growth companies).

2. *Exploit a high-growth market segment.* Customers in the targeted market have a significant unmet need, the willingness to spend, and a sense of urgency to buy. The targeted market segment exhibits a high growth opportunity either through increased market demand or taking share from competitors. The company's products must address a significant share of the targeted market segment. Finally, the margin structure of the segment represents an attractive business opportunity.

3. *Marquee Customers shape the Revenue Powerhouse.* Marquee Customers are highly visible as measured by sizable commitments to products, publicly articulating a company's value proposition in customer terms, and a significant financial commitment. When companies target small customers, a higher number of Marquee Customers is required as well as higher volume of deals in order to achieve the expected total revenue growth rate.

4. *Leverage Big Brother alliances for breaking into new markets.* Companies that secure Big Brother alliances have a higher probability of breaking into new markets and leveraging

relationships to achieve exponential growth. A hallmark of success is the quality of the alliance partner, as measured by its market position and growth in its markets, combined with the number of complementary Big Brother alliances. Companies that can create a complementary set of high-quality Big Brother alliances are more likely to have high product differentiation and a greater number of sales professionals across the industry recommending/selling their products.

5. *Become the masters of exponential returns.* The financial metrics benchmarked are revenue and revenue growth as compared to the four-, six-, and twelve-year trajectories, gross margins, SG&A, R&D (where applicable), EBITDA, Free Cash Flow, and Return on Investment. Growth companies tend to have lower than the required growth rates, at the inflection point, to achieve one of the three trajectories to $1 billion revenue. They also tend to generate lower revenue for the R&D invested, and have lower returns. Finally, there is a subset that achieves exponential growth early but subsequently falls off trajectory.

6. *The management team: Inside-Outside leadership.* Inside-Outside leadership is highly visible through two measures: the visibility of the CEO (outside-facing) at shaping customer, alliance, and community relationships, the results and operations initiatives led by the COO (inside-facing) and new product innovation and delivery led by the Innovation leader. The effectiveness of the outside-facing executive is measured by highly visible strategic deals that are company shaping. The effectiveness of the COO and Innovation leaders is primarily measured by financial effectiveness and Revenue/R&D effectiveness combined with commitments by (Marquee) Customers to higher-order benefits.

7. *The board: comprised of Essentials Experts.* A board balanced with Essentials Experts is one comprised of a Marquee Customer (or proxy), a Big Brother alliance partner, a com-

munity member (i.e., business consultant, educator), and a Blueprint Company CEO (or proxy who has experienced exponential growth).

We scored each comparison company against each of the seven criteria based on a scale of one to five, with one being the execution of an essential that fails the criteria (or is typical of a company that experiences low growth) and five being the execution of an essential that is typical of a Blueprint Company.

For supplemental information regarding the exhibits in this book, the methodology, or additional information about the 7 Essentials, please visit www.blueprinttoabillion.com.

Endnotes

Chapter 1   The Blueprint Thesis: A Different Approach to Growth

1. The odds that an idea becomes a funded business are based on interviews that asked for the probabilities that a business with Angel investment becomes a funded business. These interviews also included the odds that a venture funded business achieves IPO.
2. Analysis is based on the share of market value and employment at year-end 2004 for all companies that have gone public since 1980 with revenue of less than $1 billion at the time of initial public offering.
3. Harvard Business School Publishing, *Innovation Handbook: A Roadmap to Disruptive Growth* (Cambridge, MA: Harvard Business School, 2005), 2.
4. Janice Revell, "Fortune 2005 500 Largest Companies," *Fortune*, 18 April 2005, F-13.
5. Daniel Southerland, "MedImmune: What Went Wrong?" *Washington Post*, 23 December 1993.
6. "MedImmune, Inc.," *International Directory of Company Histories*, vol. 35 (New York: St. James Press, 2000). Reproduced in *Business & Company Resource Center* (Farmington Hills, MI: Gale Group. 2005). <http://galenet.galegroup.com/servlet/BCRC>.
7. Amy Barrett, Christopher Palmeri, and Stephanie Anderson Forest, "Special Report: Hot Growth Companies," *BusinessWeek*, 7 June 2004, 89.

Chapter 2   The Blueprint Value Proposition

1. "Dell Inc.," *International Directory of Company Histories*, vol. 32 (New York: St. James Press, 2000). Reproduced in *Business & Company Resource Center* (Farmington Hills, MI: Gale Group. 2005). <http://galenet.galegroup.com/servlet/BCRC>.
2. "Genentech, Inc.," *International Directory of Company Histories*, vol. 32 (New York: St. James Press, 2000). Reproduced in *Business & Company Resource Center* (Farmington Hills, MI: Gale Group. 2005). <http://galenet.galegroup.com/servlet /BCRC>.
3. Erik Schonfeld, "Leading the New Chip Revolution, Broadcom's Chips Run High-End Communications Products," *Fortune*, 10 May 1999, 136.
4. "Broadcom Corporation," *International Directory of Company Histories*, vol. 34. (New York: St. James Press, 2000). Reproduced in *Business & Company Resource Center* (Farmington Hills, MI: Gale Group. 2005). <http://galenet.galegroup.com/servlet/BCRC>.

5. Broadcom Corporation, "Broadcom History," *Broadcom.com* 2005. <http://www .broadcom.com/press/history.php> (19 July 2005).

6. Howard Schultz and Dori Yang, *Pour Your Heart Into It* (New York: Hyperion, 1997), 118, 249.

7. Reese, Jennifer, "Starbucks Inside the Coffee Cult: America's Red-Hot Caffeine Peddler Gives New Meaning to 'Addiction,' 'Precision,' and 'Barista.'" *Fortune*, 9 December 1996, 190.

8. Anne Feltus, "Defying the Skeptics," *Petroleum Economist* 72, no.2 (February 2005): 27.

9. Sam Fletcher, "Newfield More Than Doubles Quarterly Profit, Boosts Spending for Aggressive Drilling Plans," *The Oil Daily*, 12 November 1996, 3.

10. "U.S. Firm Newfield Has Made Its First Discovery in the North Sea, with a Well on the Grove Prospect in Southern-Sector Block," *Petroleum Economist*, March 2005, 41.

11. Chris Sherman, "Google Introduces Web Directory Using Netscape's Open Directory Project Data," *Information Today*, May 2000, 14.

12. Dick Kelsey, "Google Is Yahoo's New Default Search Engine," *Newsbytes News Network*, 26 June 2000.

13. Fred Vogelstein, "Search and Destroy: Bill Gates Is on a Mission to Build a Google Killer. What Got Him So Riled? The Darling of Search Is Moving into Software—And That's Microsoft's Turf," *Fortune*, 2 May 2005, 72.

14. Kimberly Vogel, "Google Launches Self-Service Advertising Program; Google's AdWords Program Offers Every Business a Fully Automated, Comprehensive and Quick Way to Start an Online Advertising Campaign," *Business Wire*, 23 October 2000.

15. Mike Angell, "Router Maker Looks Beyond Core Market," *Investor's Business Daily*, 13 October 2004, A5.

16. Robert J. Frank, Jeffrey P. George, and Laxman Narasimhan, "When Your Competitor Drives More for Less," *McKinsey.com: The McKinsey Quarterly*, No. 1 (2004). <http://mckinsey.com>.

17. Ibid.

18. Reed Business Information, "New York Start-Up Strikes Blue Note," *Flight International*, 21 July 1999, 9.

19. Hawn Tully, "Why The Big Boys Won't Come Back for the Nation's Beleaguered Airline Industry, The Tipping Point Is Finally Here: The Discounters Are Winning," *Fortune*, 14 June 2004, 101.

20. James Ellis, "Fast Takeoff," *BusinessWeek*, 6 December 2004, 25.

21. Meredith Cohn, "Jetblue Soars to Top of Airline Fleet in Customer Satisfaction," *Baltimore Sun-Knight Ridder/Tribune Business News*, 15 March 2005.

22. Chuck Hawkins, "Marketing: The Fast-Growing Fix-It Chain is Chewing Up Competitors," *BusinessWeek*, 26 June 1989, 124.

23. Kenneth L. Fisher, "Big Fish in Small Ponds; Doing Business in Tiny Towns on America's Back Roads May Be Unglamorous, But It Can Be Profitable, Safe and Cheap," *Forbes*, 15 December 1997, 278.

24. Ibid.

25. Amy Barrett, Christopher Palmeri, and Stephanie Anderson Forest, "Special Report: Hot Growth Companies," *BusinessWeek*, 7 June 2004, 89.
26. James Detar, "Apple Deal Is Music to SigmaTel's Ears," *Investors.com: Investor's Business Daily*, 22 February 2005. <http://www.investors.com>.
27. Matthew Boyle, Fred Vogelstein, Peter Lewis, et al., "25 Breakout Companies," *Fortune*, 16 May 2005, 155.
28. Ibid.
29. Fred Vogelstein, 72.
30. Peter Lewis, "Living in a Google World Forget Windows. What's It Like to Spend a Day Using Only Google?" *Fortune*, 2 May 2005, 76.

Chapter 3 Exploit a High-Growth Market Segment

1. Based on a sum of revenues from U.S. traded companies as defined in Standard & Poor's Compustat database.
2. Based on a sum of revenues from U.S. traded companies as defined in Standard & Poor's Compustat database.
3. Terence Pare, "Bankers Who Beat The Bust," *Fortune*, 4 November 1991, 159.
4. Based on a sum of revenues from U.S. traded companies as defined in Standard & Poor's Compustat database.
5. Eve Tahmincioglu, "You'll Be Upgrading: Big Retailers Want Tech-Savvy Vendors," *BusinessWeek*, 21 March 2005, 21.

Chapter 4 Marquee Customers Shape the Revenue Powerhouse

1. James Citrin, *Zoom* (New York: Currency Doubleday, 2002), 87. *Note:* An eBay case study.
2. Churchill Club, "Empowering the Business," speech, CIO Agenda, 30 November 2004.
3. Jim Cooper, "DirecTV Taking Flight, Launching Airliner Service," *Mediaweek*, 4 October 1999, 4.
4. R. Karlgaard, "Yin Yang: Big Bang," *Forbes*, 14 March 2005, 33.
5. Performance Food Group, *Performance Food Group Annual Report 2000*.
6. Based on extensive interviews with Marquee Customers.
7. Microsoft Corporation, "Microsoft at 20: Anniversary Edition," *MicroNews*, 1995, 11.
8. Linda Sandler, "Some Wonder if Ciena Will Keep Old Business and Land AT&T after Merger with Tellabs," *Wall Street Journal*, 14 August 1998, C2. *Note:* Ciena is an example of a company that achieved $1 billion revenue and whose revenues are below $1 billion (2004).
9. Microsoft Corporation, *Microsoft 1992 Annual Report*, 10.
10. Microsoft Corporation, "Note to Shareholders," *Microsoft 1989 Annual Report*, 2.

11. Microsoft Corporation, *Microsoft 1989 Annual Report*, 4.

12. "Microsoft Corporation," *International Directory of Company Histories,* vol. 63 (New York: St. James Press, 2004). Reproduced in *Business & Company Resource Center* (Farmington Hills, MI: Gale Group, 2005). <http://galenet .galegroup.com/servlet/BCRC>.

13. Microsoft Corporation, "Note to Shareholders," *Microsoft 1989 Annual Report*, 2.

14. Microsoft Corporation, "Microsoft at 20: Anniversary Edition."

15. Microsoft Corporation, *Microsoft 1992 Annual Report*, 29.

16. "Microsoft Mouse Exceeds 1M Units," *Computer Reseller News*, 27 June 1988, 89.

17. Microsoft Corporation, "Note to Shareholders," *Microsoft 1989 Annual Report*, 4.

18. Ibid.

19. Arthur A. Thompson Jr. and A. J. Strickland III, "Starbucks Corporation," *MHHE.com: Strategic Management, 11th edition by Thompson and Strick-land*, 1999. <www.mhhe.com/business/management/thompson/11e/case /starbucks-2.html>.

20. "Starbucks Corporation," *International Directory of Company Histories,* vol. 34 (New York: St. James Press, 2000). Reproduced in *Business & Company Resource Center* (Farmington Hills, MI: Gale Group. 2005). <http://galenet .galegroup.com/servlet/BCRC>.

21. Howard Schultz and Dori Jones Yang, *Pour Your Heart into It* (New York: Hyperion, 1997), 226.

22. "Toll Brothers Inc.," *International Directory of Company Histories,* vol. 15 (New York: St. James Press, 1996). Reproduced in *Business & Company Resource Center* (Farmington Hills, MI: Gale Group. 2005). <http://galenet.galegroup .com/servlet/BCRC>.

Chapter 5   Leverage Big Brother Alliances for Breaking into New Markets

1. Patterson Technology, "Origins of MS-DOS," *PattersonTech.com.* <http://www .patersontech.com> (23 July 2004).

2. "Microsoft Corporation," *International Directory of Company Histories,* vol. 63 (New York: St. James Press, 2004). Reproduced in *Business & Company Resource Center* (Farmington Hills, MI: Gale Group. 2005). <http://galenet .galegroup.com/servlet/BCRC>.

3. David Ernst and Tammy Halevy, "When to Think Alliance," *McKinsey.com: The McKinsey Quarterly,* No. 4 (2000). <http://mckinsey.com>.

4. Ibid.

5. Eve Tahmincioglu, "You'll Be Upgrading; Big Retailers Want Tech-Savvy Vendors," *BusinessWeek*, 21 March 2005, 21.

6. Broadcom Corp., *Broadcom Corp. Form 10-K Annual Report, 2002.*

7. Chris Sherman, "Google Introduces Web Directory Using Netscape's Open Directory Project Data," *Information Today*, May 2000, 14.
8. "Genentech, Inc.," *International Directory of Company Histories,* vol. 32. (New York: St. James Press, 2000). Reproduced in *Business & Company Resource Center* (Farmington Hills, MI: Gale Group. 2005). <http://galenet.galegroup.com/servlet/BCRC>.
9. Microsoft Corporation, *Microsoft 1989 Annual Report.*
10. "U.S. Cooking Schools Team Up with Le Cordon Bleu," *Nation's Restaurant News*, 20 September 1999, 38.
11. "AOL and eBay Expand Relationship," *Business Wire,* 2 September 1998.
12. Stephen Buel, "AOL Sells Access to Customers to eBay," *Knight Ridder/Tribune Business News*, 25 March 1999.
13. "Cisco Systems, Inc.," *International Directory of Company Histories*, vol. 34. (New York: St. James Press, 2000). Reproduced in *Business & Company Resource Center* (Farmington Hills, MI: Gale Group. 2005). <http://galenet.galegroup.com/servlet/BCRC>.
14. Ron Leuty, "PayPal Hunts for Steady Revenues," *San Francisco Business Times,* 13 July 2001, 28.
15. John Mulqueen, "AT&T, search companies team up," *InternetWeek*, 8 June 1998, S8.
16. Howard Schultz and Dori Jones Yang, *Pour Your Heart into It* (New York: Hyperion, 1997), 221–226.
17. "Siebel Announces Comprehensive Global Alliance Program," *Business Wire*, 22 April 1998.

Chapter 6   Becoming the Masters of Exponential Returns

1. Data provided by Standard & Poor's Compustat.
2. Christina Torode, "MSP Totality Buys Breakaway Assets, More Deals Ahead," *Computer Reseller News*, 24 December 2001, 16.
3. Christina Torode, "Breakaway Breakup: After Two Top Executives Leave, the Company Looks for 'Strategic Alternatives,'" *Computer Reseller News*, 3 September 2001, 71.
4. McKinsey & Company, *Valuation: Measuring and Managing the Value of Companies* (New York: John Wiley & Sons, 2000), 166.
5. T. Koller and R. Dobbs, "Measuring Long Term Performance," *The McKinsey Quarterly*, No. 3 (2005): 19.
6. Ibid., 18.
7. Data provided by Standard & Poor's Compustat.
8. "Fastenal Company," *International Directory of Company Histories*, vol. 42 (New York: St. James Press, 2002). Reproduced in *Business & Company Resource Center* (Farmington Hills, MI: Gale Group. 2005). <http://galenet.galegroup.com/servlet/BCRC>.

Chapter 7   The Management Team: Inside-Outside Leadership

1. Gayle Sato Stodder, "How to Build a Million Dollar Business—Unconventional Thinking: Yahoo!," *Entrepreneur*, September 1997, 106.
2. Randall Stross, "How Yahoo! Won the Search Wars: Once upon a Time, Yahoo! was an Internet Search Site with Mediocre Technology," *Fortune*, 2 March 1998, 148.
3. Jon Swartz, "Yahoo's Other Dynamic Duo," *San Francisco Chronicle*, 6 August 1998, D3.
4. Geoff Baum, Michelle Jeffers, Lee Patterson, and Evantheia Schibsted, "Thirty Who Matter," *Forbes*, 7 October 1996, S82.
5. We found a management assessment tool in Europe with Peter Robertson of Human Insight. We worked with Robertson to perform a feedback assessment of 360 select Blueprint Company management teams to better understand their management characteristics and relationships. This assessment is further described in Appendix C.
6. Mike Angell, "Keeping an Innovative Stride: Leaders and Success," *Investor's Business Daily*, 26 November 2004, A3.
7. Daniel Roth, "Can Nike Still Do It Without Phil Knight?" *Fortune*, 21 March 2005, 58.
8. Jonathan B. Levine, "Microsoft: Recovering from Its Stumble Over 'Windows'—Embarrassed by Problems with the Computer Program, Management Is Reforming," *BusinessWeek*, 22 July 1985, 107.
9. Joshua Greenbaum, "Microsoft Divides Applications Division," *Computer System News*, 6 September 1988, 65.
10. Charles Pelton, "For Bill Gates, Micros Are Personal: Microsoft's Founder Is a Sharp Businessman, But Can He Overcome Slow OS/2 Acceptance and Unix Growth?" *Information Week*, 14 August 1989, 18.
11. Al Siena, "Microsoft Campus Booms under 3 Deans," *Computer Reseller News*, 11 July 1988, 2.
12. "Critical Success Factors: CEO Leadership," presentation, Deloitte & Touche and Silicon Valley Bank CEO Leadership Conference, 27 March 2003.
13. Patricia Sellers, "eBay's Secret: Running the World's Hottest Company Is a Lot Harder than It Looks," *Fortune*, 18 October 2004, 160.
14. Based on data from Microsoft annual reports for the years 1989 to 1992.
15. Don Clark, "Company of the Year: Cisco Systems Soars to Top Spot," *San Francisco Chronicle*, 20 April 1993.

Chapter 9   Linking the 7 Essentials

1. NASA, "3. Trajectories and Orbits: A. Fundamental Types of Trajectories and Orbits," *NASA.gov*. <www.hq.nasa.gov/office/pao/History/conghand/traject.htm> (26 July 2005).

2. Data from Standard & Poor's Compustat.
3. B. P. S. Murthi, "Siebel Systems," *B.P.S. Murthi: Published Papers/Papers Under Review/Working Papers* 7 May 2001. <www.utdallas.edu~murthi/siebel /siebhype .html> (28 July 2005).
4. Clayton Park, "A Discipline Learned at Microsoft," *Puget Sound Business Journal*, 27 June 1997, 35.
5. Jesse Berst, "Customer Centric Firm Creates New Growth Area," *PC Week*, 23 January 1995, 100.
6. "Onyx Software Named the Fastest Growing Technology Company in Deloitte & Touche 'Fast 50' Program: 21,051% Growth Rate Attributed to Focus on Core Values," *Business Wire*, 24 September 1999.
7. Clayton Park, "A Discipline Learned at Microsoft."
8. B. P. S. Murthi, "Siebel Systems."
9. Clayton Park, "A Discipline Learned at Microsoft."
10. Ibid.
11. Ibid.
12. M. Sharon Baker, "Staffing a Challenge for Fast-Growing Onyx," *Puget Sound Business Journal*, 7 February 1997, 12.
13. "ONYX Software Wins Oscar of the Software Industry: Customer Management Software Solution ONYX Customer Center Receives Codie Award for Best Client/Server Application," *Business Wire*, 24 March 1998.
14. John Taschek, "ONYX Makes SFA More Accessible," *PC Week*, 28 September 1998, 1.
15. Tom Siebel, author interview.
16. Peter Coffee, "Labs-Eye View," *PC Week*, 28 September 1998, 20.
17. "Siebel Systems, Inc.," *International Directory of Company Histories*, vol. 38 (New York: St. James Press, 2003). Reproduced in *Business & Company Resource Center* (Farmington Hills, MI: Gale Group, 2005). <http://galenet.galegroup .com/servlet/BCRC>.
18. B. P. S. Murthi, "Siebel Systems."
19. Ibid.
20. Rick Whiting and John Kerr, "The Software 500 Editor's Choice," *Software Magazine*, June 1998, 107.
21. "Siebel Systems, Inc. Announces Production Shipment of Siebel Enterprise Applications Version 3.0: Major Product Release Adds Significant Functionality, Sets Standard for State-of-the-Art Enterprise-Class Client/Server Applications," *Business Wire*, 26 February 1997.
22. "Onyx Expands On Back Of NT Growth," *Computergram International*, 8 February, 1999.
23. *Wall Street Transcript*, "CEO Interview with Brent Frei," *TWST.com* (19 June 2000). <www.twst.com/ceos/onxs.html>.
24. S. Brad Howarth, "Onyx Focuses on Customers," *The Australian*, 21 April 1998, 44.
25. "TechnologyWorks, Inc. Announces Strategic Partnership with Onyx Software," *Business Wire*, 1 April 1999.

26. Hailey Lynne McKeefry, "Late Breaking," *Windows Magazine*, 1 April 1995, 64.
27. Jesse Berst, "Customer Centric Firm."
28. "ONYX Software opens European Headquarters in United Kingdom," *Business Wire*, 30 May 1997.
29. Jesse Berst, "Customer Centric Firm."
30. "Siebel Enters Pharmaceutical Market With $11M Nomadic Buy," *Computergram International* No. 3271 (20 October 1997).
31. "Connext, Siebel Team on Energy Software, Name 1st User" *Newsbytes*, 7 April 1998.
32. "Siebel Buys Scopus As Customer Service Market Consolidates," *Computergram International*, No. 3359 (3 March 1998).
33. "Onyx Software Corporation," *International Directory of Company Histories*, vol. 53 (New York: St. James Press, 2000). Reproduced in *Business & Company Resource Center* (Farmington Hills, MI: Gale Group. 2005). <http://galenet.gale group.com/servlet/BCRC>.
34. "CEO Interview with Brent Frei," *Wall Street Transcript*, 19 June 2000.
35. Geoffrey Brewer, "Siebel is Bulking Up," *Sales and Marketing Management*, September 1998, 56.
36. Kenny MacIver, "On the Front Line," *Computer Business Review*, May 1998, 20.
37. "Motorola Selects Siebel Software to Implement New Sales Support System; Siebel Enterprise Relationship Management System Will Improve Sales and Service Efficiency," *Business Wire*, 4 May 1998.
38. Based on the ratio of revenues and revenue growth to SG&A and SG&A growth.
39. Jesse Berst, "Customer Centric Firm."
40. "TechnologyWorks, Inc. Announces Strategic Partnership with Onyx Software," *Business Wire*, 1 April 1999.
41. "Onyx Software and Arthur Andersen Business Consulting Establish Regional Customer Relationship Management Center of Excellence," *Business Wire*, 28 June 1999.
42. Samia Rauf, "Onyx Teams with Yahoo! UK & Ireland to Deliver Internet Content," *M2 Presswire*, 16 August 1999.
43. "IBM and Siebel Systems Team to Bring Sales, Marketing and Customer Support Solutions to IBM DB2 Universal Database," *Business Wire*, 23 September 1998.
44. "Siebel Systems Announces Comprehensive Global Alliance Program," *Business Wire*, 22 April 1998.
45. Based on data from Standard & Poor's Compustat.
46. Clayton Park, "Onyx Named Fastest Growing Technology Company in Deloitte & Touche 'Fast 50' Program," *Business Wire*, 24 September 1999.
47. Brent Frei, "Taking the Pain out of Growing (The Building and Management of Onyx Software Corp.)," *Nation's Business*, December 1998.

48. Jesse Berst, "Customer Centric Firm."

49. *The Siebel Observer*, "The Biography of Tom Siebel," *SiebelObserver.com*. <http://www.siebelobserver.com/siebel /people/tomsiebel.html>.

50. Jim Evans and Upside Staff, "UPSIDE's 1998 Hot 100 Private Companies," *Upside Magazine*, 1 May 1998.

51. Jennifer Rengold and Ryan Underwood, "Is Built to Last, Built to Last," *Fast Company*, November 2004, 103.

Chapter 10   Blueprint Companies for the Next Decade and Your Part in Them

1. Thomas L. Friedman, "What Me Worry?" *New York Times*, 25 April 2005, 25.

2. Ed Michaels, Helen Handfield-Jones, and Beth Axelrod, *The War for Talent* (Cambridge, MA: Harvard Business School Press, 2001), xii–xiii.

Note: Thomson/Gale is no relation to the author.

Index